HIS ROYAL HIGHNESS THE
DUKE OF CONNAUGHT
AND STRATHEARN

Men in great place are thrice servants: servants of the sovereign or State; servants of fame; and servants of business.

HIS ROYAL HIGHNESS THE
DUKE OF CONNAUGHT AND STRATHEARN

A Life and Intimate Study

BY

MAJOR-GENERAL SIR GEORGE ASTON K.C.B.

WITH THE ASSISTANCE OF
EVELYN GRAHAM

FOREWORD BY
JOHN VAN DER KISTE

A & F Reprints

First published by George G. Harrap 1929
First published by A & F 2020

A & F Publications
South Brent, Devon, England TQ10 9AS

Typeset 11pt Charter

ISBN 9798613777471

Printed by KDP

It is a great privilege to place before the public this life of His Royal Highness the Duke of Connaught and Strathearn.

Grateful thanks are due to Lieutenant-Colonel Sir Malcolm Murray, K.C.V.O., Comptroller of His Royal Highness's Household, for reading and passing the proofs on behalf of the Duke.

CONTENTS

CHAPTER I
BABYHOOD IN A ROYAL NURSERY
(1850-54; FROM BIRTH TO AGE FOUR)

"A very fine boy" — Public Rejoicings at Birth — The Duke of Wellington as Godfather — "Arthur" — A Baby in the Royal Nursery — An Early Voyage — The Royal Christening — The Prince Consort's Chorale — A Seven Dials Poem — The Great Exhibition — The Royal Mother — Little "Arta" — "Godpa" at Apsley House — Child-life at Osborne — Riding and Dancing — 'Dressing up'

CHAPTER II
CHILDHOOD AND BOYHOOD
(1855-65; AGED FIVE TO FIFTEEN)

A Birthday Ball — "Darling little Arthur" — Visit to Balmoral — A Regrettable Incident — A Tour in Wales — "All life and merriment" — Nursery Discipline — Death of the Duchess of Kent — Death of the Prince Consort — The Queen's Grief — A Child Comforter — The Nation's Sorrow — Gloom in Household and Nursery — Prince Arthur's Toys — "Wounded in the execution of my duty!" — Youthful Shyness — Marriages of the Princess Royal and Princess Alice — "Arta's" Opinions — Marriage of the Prince of Wales — London's Welcome to the "Sea-kings' Daughter" — Prince Arthur's Gift — Another Tour in Wales — Steady Studies — A Voyage in the Mediterranean — A Turkish Welcome — Birthday Celebrations at Volo — Return to Balmoral — Early Ardour for Military Service — Queen Victoria's Veto

CHAPTER III
TRAINING AND FIRST APPOINTMENTS
(1866-70; AGED SIXTEEN TO TWENTY)

CHAPTER IV
EARLY MANHOOD
(1871-74; AGED TWENTY-ONE TO TWENTY-THREE)

CHAPTER V
THE YOUNG ROYAL DUKE
(1874-78; AGED TWENTY-FOUR TO TWENTY-EIGHT)

CHAPTER XV
THE PORTSMOUTH AND ALDERSHOT COMMANDS
(1890-98; AGED FORTY TO FORTY-EIGHT)

CHAPTER XVI
ALDERSHOT AND AFTER
(1896-1900; AGED FORTY-SIX TO FORTY-NINE)

CHAPTER XXV
BEREAVEMENT
(1917-20; AGED SIXTY-SEVEN TO SEVENTY)

CHAPTER XXVI
FURTHER BEREAVEMENT AND PUBLIC SERVICE
(1920-21; AGED SEVENTY)

CHAPTER XXVII
A LAST GREAT MISSION TO INDIA
(1921; AGED SEVENTY-ONE)
THE DUKE AS FREEMASON
(1874-1921)

ILLUSTRATIONS

Between pages 176 and 193

FOREWORD

For many years, Sir George Aston's biography of Queen Victoria's third son was the only one available. Prince Arthur was born in May 1850, and created Duke of Connaught in 1874. He survived all but the youngest of his siblings, Princess Beatrice, passing away in January 1942. By coincidence, he and another sister, Princess Louise, Duchess of Argyll, were the joint longest-lived of the nine, both reaching the age of 91 years, eight months and fifteen days precisely.

Aston's book appeared in 1929, thirteen years earlier. Before retiring to pursue a literary career with memoirs, biographies, works on defence and fly fishing to his name, he had served with the Royal Marine Artillery, worked on the Admiralty war staff, lectured at the Royal Naval College, Greenwich, and was an aide-de-camp to King George V. This qualified him well to write the life (so far) of the Victorian prince who had enjoyed a long military career.

According to the inscription on the front of the dust wrapper and an acknowledgement at the front inside, it was an official biography that had been read and passed for publication by the Duke's equerry and comptroller, Sir Malcolm Murray. Noble Frankland, author of the more recent and far more comprehensive *Witness of a Century: The life and times of Prince Arthur, Duke of Connaught* (Shepheard-Walwyn, 1993), calls it 'an inconsequential account', and states that the Duke described it as 'rather a weak production but harmless and evidently well intentioned'. He adds that Murray had not authorised it after all, and dismissed it as 'dreadful trash'.

Aston's cause and possibly his reputation were perhaps not helped by his collaborator, royal biographer Evelyn Graham. The latter was one of several aliases of Netley Lucas, a notorious confidence trickster and self-styled 'aristocrat of crooks', who also published biographies of Princess Mary, Viscountess Lascelles, Albert, King of the Belgians, and King Alfonso XIII of Spain. In 1931 his career came to an ignominious end when he was charged with obtaining money by false pretences, and as a result of exhaustive investigations his numerous aliases came to light. One was Charlotte Cavendish, an army widow and supposedly the author of a published biography of Queen Mary which the subject herself read, marking up her copy with several errors; another was Albert Marriott, Graham's 'literary agent and publisher', Cavendish, Marriott and Lucas being the same person. He was found guilty and spent fifteen months in prison, later became an alcoholic, and died in 1940, aged about thirty-seven. His life was documented by Matt Houlbrook in *Prince of Tricksters: The Incredible True Story of Netley Lucas, Gentleman Crook* (University of Chicago Press, 2016). Aston may have been embarrassed by his association with and tried to distance himself from such a character, and it may be significant that neither his obituary in *The Times* in December 1938, following his death on his 77th birthday, nor his subsequent entry in the *Oxford Dictionary of National Biography*, mention the title.

Such notoriety does it an injustice. The book contains a faithful account of his career at home and abroad, and of his happy marriage, sadly cut short by the Duchess of Connaught's ill-health and early death in 1917, plus added sorrow at the loss of their elder daughter Margaret, Crown Princess of Sweden, after a short illness, three years later. Some might argue that its tone verges on the sycophantic, and there is nothing remotely contentious to be found in its pages. Readers will search in vain for any reference to his relationship with Leonie Leslie, an association fully supported by the Duchess; to the resentment that King Edward VII sometimes had of the younger brother whom Queen Victoria freely admitted was her favourite son; or to the accident in the grounds near Osborne House in 1891 when the Duke joined others in a shooting party at which a careless aim cost his brother-in-law Prince Christian of Schleswig-Holstein an eye. The Duchess's unhappy early home life in Prussia, daughter of a thoroughly unpleasant father, is likewise passed over.

Beyond the scope of this book is the sad fact that he was not only predeceased by his wife and elder daughter, but also by his only son, who died in 1938. The latter's only son, the second Duke of Connaught, died in 1943, and the title thus became extinct.

Notwithstanding its notoriety and Murray's understandably damning verdict, the book remains of abiding interest. It was well received on publication by *The Times,* which commented that 'gratitude should be felt to Sir George Aston for this careful and intimate chronicling of the public service of a Prince who used his rank only as a means to help his country.' It has long found its place on the shelves of many a royal reader, enthusiast and student, and although inevitably superseded by Frankland's more recent work, it will undoubtedly remain so.

I have made minor corrections on pp.36 and 38, relating to the age of the Prince Consort on death and substituting the name Crown Prince Frederick William of Prussia for that of Prince Henry at the Prince of Wales' wedding, removing a reference to a photograph on p.49, and adding a reference source note on p.221. Apart from these, the text – though not the original illustrations – remains unaltered from the original.

John Van der Kiste

INTRODUCTION

The 19th of June, 1928, marked the sixtieth anniversary of the day when His Royal Highness the Duke of Connaught, now the only surviving son of Queen Victoria, joined the British Army as a young subaltern in the Royal Engineers; the 1st of May, 1930, will be the eightieth anniversary of his birth. In the opinion of the authors of this book, the year 1929, coming as it does between the anniversaries of these two events, affords a favourable occasion to place before the public a record of the life of His Royal Highness. The evidence is abundant of his distinguished services to the Army, in which he has served so long with wholehearted and reciprocated affection, to the Empire beyond the seas, especially in India, in the Mediterranean, in the Union of South Africa — where in 1910 he represented the Sovereign at a momentous time in South African history — and above all in the Dominion of Canada. He was destined to be Governor-General in that great realm in time to inaugurate, in 1911, a new era of political development, prosperity, and commercial expansion, and three years later to bear his part in the same great office during a period of intense loyalty and of self-sacrifice to a cause common to the whole Empire.

Upon the Royal House of Windsor has fallen the great mission of maintaining intact the silken threads of sympathy in ethical ideals and community in political and legal procedure, which, woven together by the loom of loyalty to the same Sovereign, form the light cord, stronger than the heaviest of chains, that binds into a single entity the free, vigorous, and independent nations of the British Empire. His Royal Highness the soldier Duke, uncle to His Majesty the King and the oldest male scion of the Royal House, has borne no small measure of that responsibility during a long life devoted to the public service.

No one who meets him in these days of his comparative rest after long years of labour, whether it be in London, near his residence at Clarence House, St James's, or at his country home at Bagshot Park or at his winter retreat in the South of France, can fail to note the marks of the professional soldier in his bearing and upright carriage. Soldiering gives us the keynote to his career. Once a soldier has for him meant soldiering once for all. While upon him rests always the aura of royal dignity and high command, every one with whom former service has brought him into contact can rest assured of recognition and kindly greetings. He shares with other members of the Royal Family the faculty of remembrance not only of faces, but also of the circumstances of previous meetings, even when trivial; and with the officers of the Regular Army, to which he still belongs, he exercises the sympathy and human touch which distinguishes our own form of military discipline from that obtaining in many foreign armies.

His Royal Highness Prince Arthur was born at Buckingham Palace on May 1, 1850. In 1874, a few days after his twenty-fourth birthday, he was created Duke of Connaught and Strathearn and Earl of Sussex. On March 13, 1879, his marriage was celebrated at St George's Chapel, Windsor, to Princess Louise Marguerite, third daughter of Prince Frederick Charles of Prussia. She died in 1917, after just thirty-eight years and one day of happy married life, at the age of fifty-six. One son was born to them — His Royal Highness Prince Arthur of Connaught, a former Governor-General of the Union of South Africa — and two daughters — Her Royal Highness Princess Margaret, who married the Crown Prince of Sweden in June 1905 and died in May 1920, and Her Royal Highness Princess Patricia, who, relinquishing her Royal rank and titles on her marriage in February 1919 with Captain the Hon. Alexander Ramsay, son of the thirteenth Earl of Dalhousie, is now known as Lady Patricia Ramsay.

The Duke of Connaught has been awarded many honours by the Sovereign — the Knighthoods of the Garter (1867), of the Thistle, and of St Patrick (both in 1869), the Grand Cross of the Bath (1901), of which Order he is the Master and First or Principal Knight. He is also a Knight Grand Cross of the Order of the Star of India (1877), of St Michael and St George (1870), of the Indian Empire (1887), of the Royal Victorian Order (1896), and of the Order of the British Empire (on its inauguration in 1917). He also wears the Volunteer Decoration. From May 1871 he has been a member of the Privy Council. He is Grand Prior of the Order of St John of Jerusalem in England, and has the Royal Victorian Chain (1902). The high honours conferred upon him by foreign Sovereigns or Presidents at various periods of his career are too numerous for recital here. In common with other members of his family, he resigned those which were derived from our principal enemies in the Great War during 1917, when the House of Hanover became the House of Windsor.

The Duke's prolonged and varied services in Army appointments, to be noted in due course, and the inclusion among his numerous honours of the war medal and clasp for service (in the Rifle Brigade) in the Fenian Raid in Canada in 1870, and of the war medal and clasp, bronze star, and Order of the Medjidie, 2nd Class, for the Egyptian War of 1882, prove him to be no carpet-knight. In that war he commanded the Brigade of Guards in the action at Mahuta and in the battle of Tel-el-Kebir. For these services he was mentioned three times in dispatches in *The London Gazette*, thanked by the Houses of Parliament, and awarded a Companionship of the Bath.

He was promoted to the rank of Field-Marshal in June 1902. He has been Colonel-in-Chief of the Rifle Brigade since May 1880, of the Highland Light Infantry since September 1901, and Honorary Colonel of the 3rd and 4th Battalions since 1908, Honorary Colonel of the 3rd Battalion Queen's Own Royal West Kent Regiment from 1908, of the 97th (Kent Yeomanry) Royal Field Artillery, and of the 18th London Regiment (London Irish Rifles) (Territorial Army), also from 1908, Colonel of the Royal Army Service Corps since September 1902 and of the Grenadier Guards since May 1904, and Colonel-in-Chief of the Royal Army Medical Corps since February 1919. From June 1883 to April 1904 he was Colonel of the Scots Guards, from June 1897 to November 1922 Colonel-in-Chief of the 6th Dragoons, and from November 1903 to July 1922 Colonel-in-Chief of the Royal Dublin Fusiliers. The Duke has been personal Aide-de-Camp to the Sovereign since May 1876, and has acted in that capacity to three Sovereigns — to his mother, Queen Victoria, to his brother King Edward VII, and to his nephew King George V.

Some idea of his activities and of his service to his fellow-citizens outside the Army can be conveyed by quoting a few of the high offices that he holds or has held in civil life: Honorary President of the Royal Geographical Society, Elder Brother and Master (since 1910) of Trinity House, Grand Master of the United Lodge of Freemasons, Ranger of Epping Forest (1879), Bencher of Gray's Inn, President of Wellington College, St Thomas's Hospital, the Royal Society of Arts, the Kennel Club, and other societies and institutions, Vice-President of the Duke of York's Royal Military School at Chelsea, Chancellor of Cape University (1910); member and President of the General Council of the Royal Patriotic Fund, Vice-Patron of the Royal Colonial Institute (now the Royal Empire Society), and other such organizations. To this long list may be added the Patronage of the Society of Army Historical Research, a comparatively new organization which is performing great service both to the Empire and to the Army by fostering the development of historical research and of closer touch between the nation and its Army. Such are the burdens cheerfully and enthusiastically borne during the 'leisure' time of this and of other members of our Royal Family. With the Duke of Connaught, as with others, intervals between such leisure have been spent in a whole-time occupation — in his case service in the Army. To that service we will now turn.

After a period spent at the Royal Military Academy at Woolwich (familiarly called "the Shop" in the Army), then in its most spartan and strenuous days, Prince Arthur was gazetted to a Lieutenancy in the Royal Engineers, his first commission being dated June 6, 1868. Five months later he was transferred to the Royal Artillery. He completed about fourteen months' service in what were then termed the "scientific corps" before transfer to the Rifle Brigade, in which most of his regimental service was spent and of which he is the revered Colonel-in-Chief, taking a personal interest in its welfare and charged with the duty of initialling every application for appointment thereto. It was in the rank of Lieutenant in the Rifle Brigade that he first saw active service, in Canada in 1870. In May 1871 he became a Captain, and in April 1874 he was transferred in that rank to the 7th Hussars. Six weeks later, on Queen Victoria's birthday (May 24), he was created Duke of Connaught. He was promoted to the rank of Major in the same regiment in August 1875, and in September of the next year he was appointed, as Lieutenant-Colonel, to the command of a battalion in his old corps, the Rifle Brigade.

In the British Army of those Victorian days warfare on land presented fewer complications. Discipline was all-important, but training had not gathered its present-day significance. Regimental duty, especially at out-stations, was monotonous and differed completely from what it is in these more strenuous times, when new weapons, new machines, and new theories of the conduct of land warfare constantly follow the development of rapid progress in scientific invention and research. In Staff work, on the other hand, while there may have been monotony on occasions, there was plenty of varied and important work, which all who aspired to high command did well to master. His Royal Highness bore his full share of such work while he was still a regimental officer. From October 1873 to April 1874 he was an Acting Brigade Major, and from May to July 1875 a Brigade Major, both of these appointments being held at Aldershot, then the chief centre of military thought and progress in the United Kingdom. He also served on the Staff as Assistant Adjutant-General at Gibraltar, so when, in May 1880, he became a Brevet-Colonel in the Army he was well equipped, by experience both of regimental and of Staff work, to fill the higher commands. In the same month his promotion to the rank of Major-General followed, and from September 1880 to September 1883 he commanded a Brigade at Aldershot, with an interval between August and November 1882, when he was on active service in Egypt, performing services and earning honours to which reference has already been made.

After Aldershot his next service was in India, where, among the numerous races and creeds, the Sahib holds sway by long tradition. That tradition the son of the Empress of India fully maintained, both in the rank of Major-General in Bengal between 1883 and 1886 and in the higher rank of Lieutenant-General — in which he was confirmed in April 1889 — in the Bombay Province from December 1886 to March 1890. The tradition of attachment to the King-Emperor, of a high standard of discipline and of military efficiency set by the Duke of Connaught in India, is still kept up in the Indian Army by the denominations conferred upon such units as the 6th Duke of Connaught's Own Lancers (Watson's Horse), the 13th Duke of Connaught's Own Lancers, the 3rd Battalion (Duke of Connaught's Own) of the 7th Rajput Regiment, the 1st Battalion (Duchess of Connaught's Own) of the 10th Baluch Regiment, the 4th Battalion (Duke of Connaught's Own) of the same regiment, the 5th Battalion (Duke of Connaught's Own) of the 11th Sikh Regiment, and the Indian Army Service Corps, of which the Duke is Colonel-in-Chief, as he still is of the 6th and 13th Lancers in the Indian Cavalry.

Home service followed those long years in the East. From August 1890 to October 1893 the Duke was the Lieutenant-General in command of the Southern District, with headquarters at Portsmouth (now the Southern Command-in-Chief, with headquarters at Salisbury). He had been promoted to the rank of full General in April 1893. More attention, in those days, is said to have been paid to fortresses than to field troops, and His Royal Highness was also Lieutenant-Governor of the fortress of Portsmouth. He was thence transferred direct to what has often been called the blue ribbon of the Home Commands, the command of the field troops at Aldershot, the only place in the United Kingdom, at that period of our history, where the combined field training of the three arms of the Service could be performed, except in Ireland. After completing, in 1898, five years in the Aldershot Command he was appointed in January 1900 to the Irish Command, with headquarters in Dublin Castle, where he served until April 1904 in command of the forces, having held the rank of Field-Marshal since June 1902. Due note will doubtless be taken of the point that the Anglo-Boer War (1899-1902) occurred during part of the above period. It was a matter of common knowledge in the Army that the heart of the Royal Duke was with his comrades in the field, whom his exalted rank made it impossible for him to join.

Then, in May 1904, came a call to the Headquarters of the Army in London, where, during a period of complete change in Army organization, he was Inspector-General of the Forces and President of the Selection Board until the end of 1907. The occupation of that office by a Royal Prince, detached by high estate from all suspicion of favouritism or interest other than military efficiency, was a great asset to the Army. In the closing months of 1907 the creation of a new appointment holding military sway over all the British troops distributed in the garrisons in the Mediterranean was being discussed. On the last day of 1907 the Duke was appointed Field-Marshal Commanding-in-Chief and High Commissioner for the Mediterranean, and he moved to Malta, where accommodation was provided in San Antonio Palace, one of the country residences of the Governor. The appointment required not only soldierly qualities and army experience, with which His Royal Highness was well equipped, but also great tact, there being, within the scope of his activities, two soldier representatives of the Sovereign in the military governors of the fortresses of Malta and Gibraltar. That high office he held with distinction, promoting the efficiency of the troops in his wide area of command and inspection, until July 1909, when he returned to England after nearly twenty-nine years of continuous service in important Army appointments, at home and abroad.

His days of comparative inactivity were destined to be short. The year 1909 was momentous in British Empire history. During the summer months an important conference of representatives of the United Kingdom, the self-governing Dominions, the Indian Empire, and the Crown Colonies and Dependencies was held in London to consider the defence problems arising out of the menace to security due to the unexpected acceleration of the German naval building programme. At the same time the necessary legislative measures were being considered in the Houses of Parliament for completing the union, as one British self-governing Dominion, of the four South African colonies — Cape Colony, Natal, the Transvaal, and the Orange River Colony (Free State) — from which delegates of all shades of political and racial opinion, British and Dutch, had assembled in London. The necessary legislation having been passed, the delegates returned to South Africa, the intention being to organize the electoral districts in readiness for a General Election, so that all should be ready for the new Union Parliament to be opened by the Prince of Wales, representing King Edward VII, in November 1910. There occurred, in that year, the death of King Edward in May and the succession of His Majesty King George V to the throne. The responsible task of representing the Crown — the sole link now binding the great nations of the Empire together — fell upon the Duke of Connaught, who, with the Duchess and Princess Patricia, arrived in South Africa in November, just in time for the historic occasion when Boer and Briton combined, under that great Dutch soldier and statesman, the late General Louis Botha, to do honour to the representative of the King.

No one who had the good fortune to be in South Africa in those days can fail to recall the successful performance by the King's deputy of his great mission, in which he was ably supported by the Duchess and by Princess Patricia. There remain in the mind of one of the authors of this volume impressions of royal dignity at public ceremonials and of kindliness and human sympathy on private occasions. After the various assemblies and great functions in the Cape Peninsula their Royal Highnesses visited, in the heat of a South African summer, all the great centres of population in the new Union — Bloemfontein, where a deputation from the great Basuto tribes was received, Johannesburg and Pretoria in the Transvaal, and the leading centres in Natal. Rhodesia was also visited, in spite of the long train journey in the excessive heat. In connexion with the Duke's successful visit to South Africa, it may be noted that he is Colonel-in-Chief of his own Cape Town Highlanders, of the Durban Light Infantry, and of the Rand Light Infantry (Johannesburg).

As already noted, it fell to the lot of the Duke of Connaught to represent the Crown as Governor-General of Canada from 1911 to 19x6. With these years, the climax of his long, continuous public career, we shall naturally deal at length in due course, and it will here suffice to summarize this episode in his public service as it was described in *The Canadian Annual Review* — a weighty historical periodical with no tendency to excess in its statements. We read there that there was no doubt as to the quiet, effective usefulness of the Duke's administration of Canadian affairs during his tenure of over five years. It had been of great importance to have the counsel and experience of His Royal Highness in the organization of Canadian forces during the years of war, and they might perhaps have been utilized to an even greater extent. Then, in the language of The Times, which the editor heartily endorsed, we read, as a final comment, that there had been a "feeble undercurrent of criticism" in Canada when the Duke was originally appointed." There were a few anxious democrats who foresaw a rigid and arbitrary etiquette. "There was talk of 'the trappings of a Court,' whatever these may be, of offensive ceremonialism, and an era of social extravagance at the capital." Not one of these forebodings was realized. There was "greater simplicity at Government House, more gracious hospitality, less social display. In peace 'the Court' was an example of quiet living and unobtrusive service; in war, of inspiration to duty and sacrifice." "Character," as Edmund Burke remarked, "is the school of mankind, and they will learn of no other." Such were the lessons which the Duke and Duchess, ably supported by Princess Patricia, taught to the Canadian nation. The memory of the interest taken by their Royal Highnesses in the Canadian Army is perpetuated in the Royal Canadian Regiment, the 3rd Regiment of Victoria Rifles, and the 6th (Duke of Connaught's Own) Rifles, of which regiments he is Honorary Colonel.

During the following year (1917) the Duke suffered a great bereavement in the death of the Duchess, who for thirty-eight years had supported him in public and in private life. In 1920 he lost his daughter Princess Margaret, Crown Princess of Sweden. These bereavements did not cause him to relax his public activities, and both he and Princess Patricia devoted themselves to many public services both during and after the War years. Then, in 1921, came another call to represent the Sovereign at a great crisis in Empire development, this time in India. What are known as the Montagu-Chelmsford reforms were embodied in an Act of Parliament which was passed in 1919. In January 1921 the Provincial Legislative Councils were opened, and the All-India Legislative Assembly and newly constituted Chamber of Princes (few people in this country realize the extent of the territories of the native princes in relation to British India) were opened early in February. The Duke of Connaught was charged with that important mission, and his nephew the King- Emperor could have had no finer ambassador to the Indian peoples. We read in contemporary reports that His Royal Highness conveyed the greetings of the Sovereign to the Princes of the Indian States and to all his subjects in India on reaching another epoch inaugurated by the Act of 1919 — an Act designed to satisfy the growing desire of his Indian subjects to take a definite step on the road to self-government. He made a personal appeal to them to bury with the dead past the mistakes and misunderstandings of the past and to work together to realize the hopes arising from that occasion. With political questions connected with the reforms we are not here concerned. India at the time was passing through a critical stage, and there was no doubt that the soldier Duke, known and revered by Indians who knew him as he was from his previous years of military service in the country, secured their confident trust in this, his last and not his least, important service to the Sovereign and to the natives and races grouped in that great organization, without precedent in history, the British Empire.

During the past eight years the Duke has contrived to devote much of his time to public activities and service, but these have not brought him to the same extent before the eyes of the nation. He is a member of all the leading Service clubs, of the Travellers', Pall Mall, and of the Marlborough, situated near his London house. Under medical advice, he usually spends the winter months at his house at Saint-Jean, Cap Ferrat, Alpes-Maritimes, where his appearance is welcomed as much as it is at his home at Bagshot, in Surrey, or in the London streets. We have traced, in a very brief summary, the main features of his life as a soldier, as an administrator, and as representative of the Crown in regions beyond the seas, always, as fate has decreed, at critical periods when important developments were proceeding and loyalty to the Sovereign, the sole link of Empire, was of the utmost moment. On all such occasions he has proved himself worthy of the great charge with which he has been entrusted. In the pages which follow it will be our object, with due respect, to lift the curtain which has hitherto screened from the public eye his private life as soldier, husband, and father, and to go into further detail on the subject of his public services.

CHAPTER I

BABYHOOD IN A ROYAL NURSERY
(1850-54; FROM BIRTH TO AGE FOUR)

"A very fine boy" — Public Rejoicings at Birth — The Duke of Wellington as Godfather — "Arthur" — A Baby in the Royal Nursery — An Early Voyage — The Royal Christening — The Prince Consort's Chorale — A Seven Dials Poem — The Great Exhibition —The Royal Mother — Little "Arta" — "Godpa" at Apsley House — Child-life at Osborne — Riding and Dancing — 'Dressing up.'

The morning of the 1st of May, 1850, found the denizens of Buckingham Palace in a state of excited suspense, while the British nation eagerly awaited news of the birth of another child to Queen Victoria, in whose apartments was gathered in waiting the customary assembly of Privy Councillors. These included the famous Duke of Wellington, that Iron Duke whose fondness for and associations with the Royal nursery hardly seem to be in accord with the sobriquet which he had earned as a leader of armies. With Her Majesty were Dr Locock and Mrs Lilly, the specially chosen nurse, and waiting anxiously in the background was the Prince Consort, to whom tradition entrusted the duty of announcing to the waiting Ministers the eagerly anticipated event.

At seventeen minutes past eight the Queen was safely delivered of "a very fine boy" (as the Duke of Wellington described him), and the proud father hastened to acquaint the Councillors that a third son had been born to the Royal House, and, in the time-honoured phrase, that both mother and son were doing well. This they did from the very first, and Prince Arthur, from his earliest moments, displayed that serenity of temper and sweetness of disposition which are greatly promoted by a fine constitution.

The news spread quickly over the country and congratulations began to pour into the Palace even before Sir George Grey had announced to the Commons "the happy event which has taken place to-day" and proposed that there should straightway be dispatched to Her Majesty "an address of congratulation on the birth of another Prince, and to assure Her Majesty that every addition to her domestic happiness affords the most sincere satisfaction to Her Majesty's most faithful subjects."

The immense popularity which the Duke of Connaught has enjoyed throughout the whole of his life would seem to have begun with his birth. For several days succeeding the event the callers at the Palace, all anxious for news concerning the Royal mother and her baby son, numbered from 800 to 1000, and, apart from these callers in person, letters of congratulation arrived from all over the world, from crowned heads and from most of the great ones of the earth. More truly indicative of the place that a Sovereign holds in the heart of the nation were those from humble folk in the lowlier walks of life, from the many who had reason to hold the "first lady in the land" in affectionate esteem.

The date of Prince Arthur's entry into a world where so warm a welcome awaited him was also the Duke of Wellington's eighty-first birthday, and the coincidence, coupled with the respect in which the Duke was held by the nation at large and by Queen Victoria and her Consort, favoured the idea that the Royal baby might bear the Christian name which the Duke had done so much to honour. This feeling was expressed in a letter to *The Times*, which rightly interpreted the views of all ranks of society:

> Allow me through the medium of your journal to invite attention to the fact that the young Prince was born on the birthday of the Duke of Wellington. The name of Arthur, long connected with English history, has derived fresh lustre from being borne by the hero of Waterloo. It would gratify the feelings of the loyal veteran and would, I am certain, please the subjects of Her Majesty if she gave the name of Arthur to the Royal infant.
>
> (Signed) AN ENGLISHMAN

The Queen, however, had already anticipated the suggestion. Before the birth of her third son she had intended, should the expected child prove a boy, to bestow upon him the name of the veteran Duke whose great services to Crown and country had earned him this Royal favour. The coincidence in the dates of birth set seal to the proposal, and the Duke was at once told that it was Her Majesty's intention that her infant son should bear his name and be his godson. This compliment the Duke fully appreciated, and on one occasion is known to have described it as having given him more pleasure than his military decorations.

In the British Royal Family the choice of nurses for the children has always been given careful consideration. These loyal and devoted women have, from generation to generation, figured largely in the early lives of their charges, of whom many have been destined to occupy a throne. The 'Nannas' have been rewarded for their watchful care by lasting affection.

Owing to the country's demands on her own time. Queen Victoria was obliged to engage a foster-mother for her children — a matter which, as the most womanly of women, she never ceased to regret. For this duty Her Majesty chose a young woman, a native of Llannefydd, in the county of Denbigh, the wife of a worthy young railway worker, whose name, like her origin, was a truly Cambrian one — Jane Jones. Her entry into the Queen's service was taken by the Welsh as a compliment to their country, much appreciated in the Principality, If Queen Victoria could not nurse her babies she could and did bath them: the last new baby was always bathed by her own hands, and only very pressing matters were allowed to interfere with this ceremony. Prince Albert, who took his parentage, as he took most things, very seriously, was often present.

All Queen Victoria's children were rocked to sleep in the same cradle — a simple affair of carved wood in which the present Prince of Wales also slept during the first few months of his life. The best gowns worn by the Royal infants, those for State occasions, the christening robe and the veil of real lace, were also handed down from one baby to another, and the christening veil, like Her Majesty's wedding veil, became an interesting and highly valued heirloom, to be worn by fortunate babes having the hereditary right to the honour.

The baby Prince Arthur was soon to have his first experience of the sea-travel that was to play so large a part in his career. The Queen having recovered speedily from her confinement, the Royal Family went for a brief holiday to the Isle of Wight, to which she was deeply attached. The Royal party crossed in the yacht *Fairy*, and they spent the first weeks of June at Osborne. They were obliged to leave on June 18 in order to return to London in time for the Queen's Drawing-rooms and for the infant Prince's christening, and it is in evidence that the Royal baby slept placidly throughout the journey — a fortunate omen, justified by subsequent events. The Duke has had the good fortune to be a 'good sailor' in his many voyages. The Royal christening took place, with much magnificence, on Saturday, June 22, in the chapel within the precincts of Buckingham Palace. The ceremony was attended by eminent guests from all over the world, some of whom had overcome considerable difficulties in order to be present; that this compliment was fully appreciated by the Queen is shown by a letter to her uncle the King of the Belgians, with whom she kept up a full and free correspondence :

> Charles will have told you how kindly and amiably the Prince of Prussia has come here, travelling night and day from St Petersburg, in order to be in time for the christening of our little Arthur.

The Prince of Prussia[1] was one of the sponsors, in association with the Duke of Wellington and the Duchess Ida of Saxe-Weimar, for whom the Duchess of Kent acted as proxy. The chapel presented a brilliant spectacle, overflowing with a galaxy of distinguished guests, and the ceremony in itself was picturesque and impressive. Her Majesty formed a regal figure in her gown of silk brocade, sparkling with diamonds and emeralds and blazing with orders and decorations.

The sponsors were preceded by the Lancaster and Chester Heralds, while all the Heralds and the Garter King-at-Arms were present. The Archbishop of Canterbury officiated, and in due course christened the Royal baby in his arms Arthur William Patrick Albert, afterward handing him back to the Countess of Gainsborough. The name Patrick was bestowed upon the little Prince in commemoration of the Queen's recent visit to Ireland, in August 1849 (after an attempt on her life by a half-demented Irishman), as a direct compliment to her Irish subjects.

It is on record that the baby Prince, who behaved quite well during a ceremony frequently resented by the average infant, wore, besides the hereditary christening robe of Honiton lace over white satin, a cap and mantle to match those worn by his sisters, who took the liveliest interest in every detail of the proceedings. They appeared as fairylike figures in white silk. The Prince of Wales (King Edward VII) and Prince Alfred (the Duke of Edinburgh) wore Highland dress, constantly

1 Afterward William I.

assumed by them under Her Majesty's directions in token of her regard for her Scottish home at Balmoral.

One particularly interesting feature of the ceremony was the performance of a chorale specially written for the occasion by the Prince Consort. Having considerable musical ability, he delighted in employing it to mark such occasions. The chorale ran thus:

In life's gay morn, e'er sprightly youth
By vice and folly is enslaved,
Oh, may thy Maker's glorious name
Be on thy infant mind engraved!
So shall no shades of sorrow cloud
The sunshine of thy early days.
But happiness in endless round
Shall still encompass all thy ways.

In somewhat marked contrast to the dignified simplicity of the Prince's poem, but not without interest in view of the curiously accurate prophecy contained in the second verse, we can quote a doggerel broadsheet, published by E. Hodges, of Seven Dials, and hawked in the London streets on the christening morning. In those days it was a common practice for similar broadsheets to be issued on the occasion of Royal weddings, christenings, and even funerals, and the public, with the best and most loyal motives, bought them as eagerly as the modern crowd buys the picture-postcards and badges that have taken the place of broadsheets to-day. Here is Mr Hodges' masterpiece:

Now early in the morning soon
Old England plays a merry tune;
This 22nd day of June
All at the Royal Christening.

The Prince shall be a soldier tall
And in the field shall never fall.
Old Nosey with his cannon-balls
Ever shall protect Prince Arthur.
The ladies say Prince Arthur sweet
Shall never be a chimney-sweep,[1]

1 A reference, no doubt, to the hero of the ceremony having been born on

But old John Bull his Kid shall keep
All at the Royal Christening.

Here's to the Queen and Albert gay.
And all the children too, huzzay.
May another come the first of May
For another Royal Christening.

As the christening ceremony was a private one in the Palace chapel, a guard of honour of the Coldstream Guards was mounted in the garden of the Palace, and throughout the day sightseers pressed round the railings in the hope of catching a glimpse of that "Prince Arthur sweet" who was destined to be one of the most popular of the Princes born within that Royal home. In the evening there was a State banquet in honour of the day's event, and an object of great interest, especially to the ladies present, was the magnificent christening cake. This was exquisitely decorated, with the top fashioned to represent an octagonal fountain surrounded by small ornamental vases, all filled with the miniature bouquets. This cake was placed on a large gold salver in the centre of the dinner-table.

The memory of the first anniversary of Prince Arthur's birthday has been perpetuated by Franz Winterhalter's charming picture entitled *The First of May, 1851*, and by the opening of the Great Exhibition. Winterhalter's picture, now in the collection at Windsor, represents the aged Duke of Wellington presenting a golden casket to his infant godson, who smiles at him from his mother's arms, while behind the Queen stands Prince Albert, holding in his hand a plan of the Exhibition.

The idea of holding such an exhibition on an international scale had been that of the Prince Consort, who, as President of the Society of Arts, laid his proposals before that society in 1849. After no fewer than 245 designs had been considered that of Mr (afterward Sir) Joseph Paxton was accepted. In less than a year there arose the Crystal Palace, designed, as Prince Albert himself expressed it, " to give us a true test and living picture of the point of development at which the

"Sweeps' Day" (May 1). The writer may have known the story of one of the baby's elder brothers, the Prince of Wales, having announced his intention of being a chimney-sweep when he grew up, after seeing the sweep-boys in the streets.

whole of mankind has arrived, ... a new starting-point from which all nations will be able to direct their further exertions."

Queen Victoria was immensely proud of her husband's part in the Exhibition, and her delight and pride seem somewhat to have overshadowed her celebration of Prince Arthur's birthday. The opening of the Exhibition was a most brilliant ceremony, but the baby Prince was, of course, too young to participate in it. The Queen took her two elder children to it, and the whole day was a triumph for Prince Albert, and through him for the Queen, who wrote:

> God bless my dearest Albert. God bless my dearest country, which has shown itself so great to-day. One felt so grateful to the great God Who seemed to pervade all and bless all.

Writing to the King of the Belgians, she said:

> I wish you *could* have witnessed the *1st May*, 1851, the *greatest* day in our history, the *most beautiful* and *imposing* and *touching* spectacle ever seen, and the triumph of my beloved Albert. ... It was the *happiest, proudest* day in my life, and I can think of nothing else.

Prince Arthur's first attempts at pronouncing his name earned for him the family pet name of "Arta." He developed on the lines of all healthy babyhood, a comely little lad, with the fair skin and fine eyes of all the Royal children, and even as a tiny child he gave signs of that natural courtesy which characterized him in manhood. Lady Augusta Stanley, lady-in-waiting to the Duchess of Kent, with whom the little Prince was a prime favourite, tells a delightful story of him when he was barely six. When out for a walk with his governess he stumbled and fell, but quickly regained his feet, protesting that he was not hurt. His sisters asked him if he had not cut his knee. "Oh, no," came the quick reply, "but I am sorry to have pulled Fraülein's hand so hard!"

As soon as he was of an age to understand what was going on around him the little Prince took the greatest interest in everything affecting the Duke of Wellington ("Arta's godpa"), who to his young mind seemed a figure of martial romance. He would lisp questions about "Godpa" as soon as he could talk, and he delighted in being shown portraits of the veteran warrior in his uniform.

Shortly after his second birthday he was taken to visit the Duke at Apsley House, where his behaviour must have reached a very high standard, since Queen Victoria, a most strict though devoted mother, described him as "so good." The old Duke took his small godson all over the house, and Winterhalter would have had an even more delightful subject for a picture if he could have painted the grizzled old warrior, his spare frame a little bent with the burden of his years, his hook nose giving him that fierce expression, hand in hand with the tiny child who could just talk and was not over-steady on his chubby legs, going from room to room, showing him pictures, pointing out curios that he had collected, and so enchanting the baby heart of his small godson. The date of this incident was June 18, 1852, the thirty-seventh anniversary of Waterloo. The visit to "the Duke of Welliken," as the little Prince called his godfather, must have made a great impression on the child, for when the Duke died in October 1852 he was most anxious to attend the funeral. "Arta does want to go, Arta does want to go," he repeated, and it was not until after many long months that he became reconciled to the sad fact that he would see "little Arta's godpapa" no more. This affectionate admiration for the Iron Duke persisted through his boyhood, and his choice of the profession which he has followed with the utmost keenness was directly influenced by his military hero.

Prince Arthur, like all the Royal children, was brought up very simply, and submitted to a strict routine that was seldom allowed to be altered. The Royal nurseries were under the supervision of Lady Sarah Lyttelton, one of Queen Victoria's ladies-in-waiting, but the Queen herself took an active part in the upbringing of her children. In order that they might always be near her at Windsor, it was arranged that their schoolroom, a large and sunny apartment with spacious views over the Home Park, should be next to her audience-chamber and only one room away from her private sitting-room.

Believing, as she did, that all children — even those destined to fill exalted positions — should have some training in practical matters, Her Majesty made over to her children in 1854 the delightful Swiss cottage which, with its own gardens, is in the grounds of Osborne. Here the girls were taught cooking and housekeeping, not in theory but in practice, and the boys carpentering and gardening. Occasionally the Queen would visit the cottage and be entertained there by the children. The young Princesses made the cakes for the tea-parties and acted as hostesses for the meal, while it was a recognized thing that the boys should present their mother with baskets of garden produce, which Queen Victoria would solemnly bear back to the house. No one was allowed to shirk; even the youngest had his or her little tasks, and they had to be fulfilled. In due course Prince Arthur was given his plot of ground and his little tool-chest, though of the first use he made of this his instructor had a sad tale to tell.

There were riding lessons too, in the Great Park at Windsor. Here Prince Arthur proved an apt pupil and a somewhat precocious one, whose youthful energies and boyish recklessness in the saddle were a source of some anxiety to his guardians. As was usual, he was given a Spanish saddle for his first pony, but that greatly offended his boyish dignity, and he insisted that "Arta" must at once be promoted to a man's saddle, "fit for a proper boy."

Queen Victoria, who was an excellent dancer and very fond of the pastime — it was at a ball that she signified her Royal favour to the Prince who was to become her husband — directed that all her sons and daughters should be thoroughly instructed in the art. The dancing lessons, sometimes resented by the boys when they lasted too long, must have stood them in good stead in afterlife, for all the Royal Family have been noted for the grace and excellence of their carriage and for the ease with which they adapt themselves to new types of dancing. Until the untimely death of the Prince Consort cast a deep shadow over the Royal nursery, private theatricals proved a very popular amusement with the Royal children. They would learn and act short plays suitable to their years, settling the parts among themselves and often providing the scenery and the costumes. The Queen and the Prince Consort would act as audience, and the small performers were required to be word-perfect.

Prince Arthur took great delight in this form of amusement, particularly in the 'dressing up' involved, and if by any chance he could act a military character his joy was complete. In the Queen's private sitting-room at Windsor there hung two portraits of him, taken in fancy dress at the age of three; the first showed him in the full dress uniform of an officer of the Scots Fusiliers, the second as a miniature Bluff King Hal. The military picture is particularly attractive, and in later life the Prince once laughingly remarked that he had never quite recaptured that early splendour, though he had spent the greater part of his life in uniform!

CHAPTER II

CHILDHOOD AND BOYHOOD
(1855-65; AGED FIVE TO FIFTEEN)

A Birthday Ball — "Darling little Arthur" — Visit to Balmoral — A Regrettable Incident — A Tour in Wales — "All life and merriment" — Nursery Discipline — Death of the Duchess of Kent — Death of the Prince Consort — The Queen's Grief — A Child Comforter — The Nation's Sorrow — Gloom in Household and Nursery — Prince Arthur's Toys — "Wounded in the execution of my duty!" — Youthful Shyness — Marriages of the Princess Royal and Princess Alice — "Arta's" Opinions — Marriage of the Prince of Wales — London's Welcome to the **"Sea-kings' Daughter"** — Prince Arthur's Gift — Another Tour in Wales — Steady Studies — A Voyage in the Mediterranean — A Turkish Welcome —Birthday Celebrations at Volo — Return to Balmoral — Early Ardour for Military Service — Queen Victoria's Veto.

Prince Arthur's fifth birthday was celebrated by a great children's ball at Buckingham Palace. At this age "our darling little Arthur," as Queen Victoria described him when writing to the King of the Belgians about the ball, was a most sturdy little lad, well meriting Lady Augusta Stanley's description as "handsomer than ever, so gentle, so dear, so good." After making due allowance for Victorian sentiment we are led to the conclusion by many contemporary accounts that the youthful Prince was specially noted for his charm of manner, and for a spontaneous consideration for other people's feelings which is seldom an attribute of so young a child. He was inclined to be shy, but his brain was very active, and when inspired to talk by loving and sympathetic company his thoughts came so fast that he could hardly find words to clothe them.

The ball was a great success, and Prince Arthur enjoyed it to the full. He wore Highland dress, which is said to have suited him well, while his sisters, the young Princesses, wore light blue tulle over light blue silk, with wreaths of white hyacinths on their hair. They carried

34

bouquets of the same flower, and enthusiasts in such matters reported that their toilettes set off their lovely colouring and bright fair hair most admirably. As quite a small boy the Prince had shown an eye for beauty and fascination by colour; he would stand and admire his sisters in gala attire, patting their dresses and paying them little compliments.

Journeys were a constant feature of Prince Arthur's early childhood, and in September 1855 we find him travelling with the Royal Family to Balmoral. In those days such travel, even when everything possible was done to ease its discomforts, was far from being the rapid and easy matter it is to-day, and this journey to Balmoral proved, even for the period, to be singularly unfortunate.

The axles of the railway coach were faulty, and it was feared that the wheels might take fire. So serious was the danger that the train had frequently to be stopped. One of these delays occurred at Darlington, and here a great crowd which had assembled to sec the Royal train pass behaved rather badly. They climbed up and peered into the windows, their faces within a foot of the inmates, somewhat to the annoyance of the elders but greatly to the amusement of the children. Little Prince Arthur took the matter philosophically. He asked why the people were behaving like that, and when he was told that it was because they wanted to see his parents and their family, he considered the matter for a few moments, then gravely remarked, "It is kind of the engine-driver to stop where they could see us best!" This point of view his Royal mother did not share. A little later a really serious accident occurred. One of the 'greasers,' while attending to the wheels, fell under the train and was killed. This mishap greatly disturbed the Queen and the Prince Consort, and cast a note of gloom over the remainder of the journey, for which the Royal party was conducted to another carriage.

Four years later Prince Arthur was taken for a tour in Wales. There he stayed at Penrhyn Castle, and was shown some of the beauty spots of the neighbourhood. These he fully appreciated. Destined to be a world-wide traveller, he was extremely fond from his earliest years of all kinds of travel, by almost any method of conveyance. When any expedition was afoot "Arta" would beg so persistently to be allowed to join in it that, if it had been decided that he could not go, his guardians used to conspire together to keep the journey a secret from him. Activity, both of mind and body, was one of the little Prince's outstanding qualities. He was "all life and merriment," whether playing with his brothers with the toy wagons in which they delighted or looking after his animals. He had a special pen of fowls of his own which were great favourites, and his own pony to ride. He was always the essence of childish vigour and boyish vitality, and animation was the chief characteristic that impressed itself upon those who were in charge of him. This may not always have conduced to their satisfaction, for, however sweet and amenable to recognized authority his disposition may have been, he was anything but a 'milksop,' and his high spirits not infrequently led him into good, healthy mischief.

The Royal children led a simple, happy life, with plenty of lessons and strict nursery discipline, for Queen Victoria trained all her family to implicit obedience, and she was a believer in the old-fashioned maxim about the young being visible rather than audible, a humorous doctrine to many modem children. They were given plenty of healthy exercise, and they were surrounded always by the care and deep affection both of the Queen and of the Prince Consort, who took the greatest interest in the education of his children and himself often drew up the time-table of their studies.

When Prince Arthur was ten years old Queen Victoria suffered a sad loss in the death of her mother, the Duchess of Kent, a bereavement which naturally had an effect on the Royal nursery. The Duchess died on March 16, 1861, and her funeral took place on March 25. Her Majesty and her daughters did not attend, fearing that the strain of the occasion would be too much for them; but Prince Albert was present, and, as the Queen announced in a letter to her uncle Leopold, "poor little Arthur went too." The boy's sympathetic disposition caused any occasion of grief or sorrow to weigh heavily on him, and he was touchingly anxious to do his childish best to comfort those who were left to mourn, considering their grief in a hundred little ways possible only to a naturally sensitive and keenly perceptive nature. His own childish griefs and ailments he bore well, and when, together with his brothers and sisters, he developed measles — the children called it 'weazles' — he proved a good patient, joking with his fellow-sufferers and only giving trouble in the difficulty that was encountered in making him prolong his convalescence to the necessary limits.

Toward the close of the year in which the Duchess of Kent had died the Royal Family and the whole British nation suffered a severe loss which cast a deep shadow over the childhood of the Royal children and from which Queen Victoria never wholly recovered. At the end of

November the Prince Consort fell ill. At first it was not considered anything very serious, and on December 1 he was well enough to write a memorandum, relating to the affair of the mail steamer *Trent*, to Lord John Russell, but that was the last matter of State in which he was able to take any interest. Within a few days he had developed gastric fever. The Queen, assisted by her daughters, nursed him day and night, but, despite all that medical skill combined with unceasing care could do, the Prince's condition did not improve. Congestion of the lungs set in, and, at the early age of forty-two, he died at midnight on Saturday, December 14. Toward the end he was not wholly conscious, and though his children came in to him one by one he did not always recognize them. The Prince of Wales, Princess Alice, and Princess Louise approached the bedside and pressed their father's hand; but when it came to Prince Arthur's turn he lifted his father's hand to his lips and kissed it, but, as the Queen herself pathetically records in her journal, "he was dizzy and did not perceive it."

The Queen's grief was tragic in its intensity. She and her husband had been most devotedly attached to each other, and for a time it seemed as if life had ceased to hold any interest for her; only in the affection of her children did she find any solace. The Prince Consort had been an ideal father. His high character and wide culture had enabled him to exercise great and most beneficent influence over all his children, between whom and himself there had existed the deepest affection, and their grief at their loss almost equalled that of the Queen herself.

Prince Arthur took his full share in trying to comfort his mother. He made touching little efforts to make her forget, even for a moment, her desolation. He would offer her little bunches of flowers, slide his hand into hers and press it in silence, and spend much time in trying to think of some means by which he might help to lighten her sorrow. Her Majesty herself made special reference to his efforts, and though it seemed that during those first grief-stricken months no shaft of light could pierce the black cloud of bereavement, there is no doubt that the Queen, more perhaps than she herself realized, was consoled and supported by the affection of her sons and daughters.

The nation sincerely mourned for the Prince, and sympathized with the Queen in her widowhood. As the husband of a constitutional sovereign, his position during the first years of their marriage had not been altogether an easy one, and though his wisdom and his supreme integrity had never for a moment been questioned, he had not been encouraged to take a very active part in matters of State, but his interest in art and education, and his enthusiasm for social and industrial reform, so greatly increased his popularity that, at the time of his death, the nation had come to hold him in the high esteem which his character so fully merited.

When grieving for the dead it is sometimes a little difficult to remember our duty to the living. In losing her husband Queen Victoria lost not only a dearly loved consort, but a helpmeet who was an unfailing strength to her in all matters connected with her sovereignty, one who shared in the responsibilities attached to the throne as well as to her domestic life. In her great sorrow she let the shadow of their mutual loss fall very darkly upon the lives of her children. As she grieved, she took it for granted that they must grieve, and the death of their father made a vast change in the life of the Royal Family. The spirits of youth being happily elastic, it was natural that, after the first poignancy of sincere and natural grief had passed away, the younger members of the family should indulge in some of the pastimes natural to their age, but most amusements were forbidden them. Many years passed after the death of the Prince Consort before even the most harmless of private theatricals in which they had once indulged were again to be sanctioned. Queen Victoria's attitude, quite understandable though subjected to criticism, can best be illustrated by an extract from a letter which she wrote to General Bruce, the Prince of Wales's tutor, just before the Prince's return home from a tour abroad. In this the Queen bids the General warn her son against indulging, in her presence, in "worldly, frivolous, gossiping kind of conversation. . . . The Prince must be prepared to face in a proper spirit the cureless melancholy of his poor home."

Apart from the great change which was wrought by the death of the Prince Consort in the whole regime of the Royal household, including the nursery, it also affected the children's education. The Prince had from their infancy concerned himself directly with every detail of their training, particularly with that of his sons. He had not only endeavoured to fit them for the positions which they were to hold, but also, largely by that most powerful agent the force of personal example, had striven to bring them up in the paths of rectitude, to imbue them with courage, honour, and self-discipline. These were the traditional qualities attached to Prince Arthur's chosen career, in which the death of his father made no difference. From the first he had been destined for the Army, and the whole of his education was directed toward that end. Reference has already been made to the influence which had been exercised over his childish imagination by the military record and achievements of his godfather, the Duke of Wellington, and even in his boyhood the Prince displayed more than the usual boyish interest in 'playing at soldiers.' Far better than any manoeuvres with his fine collection of wooden and leaden warriors he enjoyed drilling his brothers, or even his sisters when the latter would permit, and in the Home Park at Windsor or in the grounds at Buckingham Palace great battles were planned and fought, strategy was devised, and every phase of mimic warfare was executed.

Nothing pleased Prince Arthur better as a gift than a gun, a sword, or some other item of a soldier's equipment, and he prepared himself for his military duties long before his actual training for such work began. How seriously he had taken his prospective career is shown by a little incident that took place when he was quite a small boy. He owned a small terrier, to which he was much attached, and one morning, while the Prince was taking the animal for a run in the grounds, they encountered one of the stable cats, which attacked the dog and threatened to maul him badly. Prince Arthur succeeded in rescuing his pet, getting severely scratched in the process. Then, when he was carrying the dog back to the house, he met his governess, who was much dismayed by his condition. "What have you done?" she cried. "How is it you are hurt?" "Wounded," was the proud and dignified reply, "wounded in the execution of my duty!"

The fact that his two elder brothers were his seniors by several years caused them to figure more largely in the public eye, and the nation really heard very little during his boyhood of the Prince who, in later life, was to be so universal a favourite. The fact that the Prince of Wales was heir to the throne naturally gave him greater prominence, and both he and Prince Alfred, the Duke of Edinburgh, had taken part in many public functions and had figured to a large extent in public life while Prince Arthur was still in the nursery or schoolroom.

When he became of an age to consider it at all this gave the Prince considerable satisfaction, for, as we have noticed, he was inclined to be shy. Though of a friendly disposition, he would have been glad to have escaped the publicity inevitably attached to those of his high social rank, and the idea of being 'on show' worried him. His military training, which, as we shall see, involved mixing freely on equal terms with the cadets at the Royal Military Academy, did much to cure him of his diffidence, and in later years he played his part in the many public functions which it was his duty to attend with ease and composure. During the years of his boyhood, however, he was, as the third son, more than well content to remain in the background, and here we can take note of the point that a shy dread in early years, while in some countries a handicap to those born to high estate, has in Britain added to the popularity of scions of the Royal House. Among other examples can be quoted those of the Duke's niece, the Duchess of Fife (once dubbed "her Royal Shyness"), and the Prince of Wales, whose Army experiences, like his great-uncle's, may have contributed to the self-possession now apparent at public occasions and ceremonials.

After the death of his father the next event of importance in the life of Prince Arthur was the marriage of his sister, Princess Alice, to Prince Louis of Hesse on July 1, 1862. His eldest sister, the Princess Royal, had married, in January 1858, the Crown Prince of Prussia, and these gaps in the home circler grieved the small brother, whose family affections were deep, and who, throughout his whole life, has maintained the most cordial relations with all who are in any way bound to him by ties of blood. Prince Arthur took a great interest in his sister's wedding (particularly in the magnificent wedding cakes, which were a special attraction to him); but he strongly disapproved of the bridegrooms' taking the Princesses so far away from him. His elder sisters, being his seniors by several years, had spoiled and petted their small brother, "Arta," so he felt their leaving the family party; and he shed not a few tears when the Princess Royal journeyed away to her German home. When Princess Alice married he had grown too old to shed tears, but he felt the pang of parting with a beloved sister and most willing playmate all the more keenly since, being a 'man,' he was deprived of the usual safety-valve for childish emotions.

Princess Alice was married in the drawing-room at Osborne. Queen Victoria attended as a sombre figure in her widow's weeds. The parents and brother of the bridegroom were also present, but, owing to the recent death of the Prince Consort, the wedding lacked the magnificence of other similar ceremonies.

After the young couple had left on their bridal trip Prince Arthur voiced his sentiments feelingly. "When I marry," he announced, "I shall bring my wife home to live with us all, and we shall eat our own cake."

During the next year Prince Arthur attended the wedding of his eldest brother, the Prince of Wales, an event which exceeded in importance the previous two weddings in which he had been an interested spectator. His eldest brother had been something of a hero to him, and it was in compliance with his own special and oft-repeated requests that he was allowed to be present at the ceremony, at which, in common with the nation at large, he promptly fell in love with the "Sea-kings' daughter from over the sea."

England had been pleased with the news that the heir to the throne was betrothed to Alexandra, eldest daughter of Prince Christian, heir to the throne of Denmark, but when England saw the girl who was destined to be its future Queen her beauty, great personal charm, and elegance aroused the most remarkable enthusiasm. Princess Alexandra received one of the most cordial welcomes that have ever been given to a foreign princess in Great Britain.

The London streets blazed with scarlet and white, the Danish national colours, which everywhere waved side by side with the Union Jack. Princess Alexandra had many gifts, not a few of them worth the traditional king's random, but it is doubtful whether anything pleased her more than the little nosegay of red and white flowers that Prince Arthur timidly offered to her, as his own personal tribute to her charms, an hour after he first met her.

The marriage took place on March 10, 1863, in St George's Chapel, Windsor, the ceremony being conducted by the Archbishop of Canterbury and Dean Wellesley. It was a brilliant scene which Queen Victoria, still in her widow's garb but wearing the Order of the Garter, witnessed from the Royal Gallery. The Prince of Wales was attended by the Duke of Saxe-Coburg and by Crown Prince Frederick William of Prussia, while for her bridesmaids the Princess had the Ladies Victoria Scott, Diana Beauclerk, Elena Bruce, Victoria Howard, Emily Villiers, Agneta Yorke, Feodora Wellesley, and Emily Hare.

Prince Arthur was in Highland costume, which he wore when the family wedding group was taken later on. This group was posed by the special wish of the Queen. It was quite apart from the conventional portraits of the actual wedding group, and Her Majesty's arrangement of the picture is plainly shown by the fact that in the centre there is a bust of the Prince Consort. Prince Arthur sits at his mother's feet, looking, as is his sister, at a book which the Queen holds; he has himself admitted since that it was only by a supreme effort that he could keep his eyes fixed on the volume, for the great attraction was his eldest brother, who, with his bride on his arm, was standing behind his mother.

During a tour in North Wales in the summer of 1863 the young Prince, accompanied by Major Elphinstone, visited various beauty spots and places of interest, especially those near Dolgelly, Bala, and Festiniog. The Cambrian and Clogan gold-mines were inspected, and specimens of gold in quartz presented to the Royal visitor. The High Sheriff of Merioneth, Mr H. Morgan, paid an official call, attended by a "splendid retinue of javelin-men," and the Cader Idris Rifle Volunteers paraded for inspection by His Royal Highness. A day was spent in climbing the celebrated Cader Idris, from which a glorious view was obtained.

For the next three years the whole of Prince Arthur's attention was concentrated on his studies. Fortunately, he had been allowed to follow his inclinations in the choice of a career, for Queen Victoria expected much from her sons, and their instructors were expressly directed to make them work and to permit of no 'slacking' or no evasion of tasks. She always pointed to the life of the Prince Consort as an example; but Prince Arthur needed no spurring to fit himself for the military life upon which his heart was set. He accordingly delighted his tutors by the steadiness of his application and by the thoroughness with which he applied himself to his tasks.

An interesting tour in the Near East widened the scope of his education. The Prince, travelling *incognito* with his tutor and Major Elphinstone, spent the spring of 1865 in the Admiralty yacht *Enchantress*, visiting places of interest on the coast of the Mediterranean. At Tunis he was given an ovation "greater than could have been offered to anyone short of the Padishah himself," and he received from the Bey the exceptional compliment of the Nicham-ed-Deru, or Decoration of Blood, never before given to anyone not a member of His Highness's family. Of the greatest interest to the young student of military history in ancient times were visits to various places in Turkish territory such as Kavalla, the ruins of Philippi, the mouth of the river Stryma, whence a visit was paid to the ruins of Amphipolis near the spot where Xerxes offered human sacrifices to the success of his cause, then to Athos, where the traces of Xerxes' canal were inspected, and to Salonica. An expedition was thence made by sea to the mouth of the Peneus, and a visit paid to the historic Vale of Tempe, escorted by a squadron of Turkish lancers, whose regimental band caused the surrounding hills to resound with the strains of the British

National Anthem. "To the amazement of the Turkish onlookers," the young Prince took off his shoes and stockings to wade in the River Peneus on returning to his tent.

On the last evening in April the Enchantress dropped anchor in Volo Bay, causing great excitement in the small town, which had never before been visited by a Royalty of any nation. At daybreak next morning — the Prince's fifteenth birthday — the whole town, the harbour, and the vessels in the bay were dressed with flags, and the small boats were decked with flowers and boughs in honour of the occasion. Salutes were fired from men-of-war and shore batteries. The Prince, who was received by a guard of honour at the Consulate, spent the day in arranging an expedition to Mount Pelion.

Travelling Venice, and thence by land across Europe, the Royal party joined the Royal Family at Balmoral before the end of the month.

At about this time the young Prince began his collection of books upon the life of the Iron Duke and of souvenirs of his career. He has made a singularly complete collection which has afforded him the greatest interest. In his earlier youth it was a constant source of inspiration to him during his military training. He was impatient to begin that training in real earnest, and he wanted to enter the Royal Military Academy before he was allowed to do so. The Queen, however, seldom allowed her arrangements to be altered, so Prince Arthur had to wait, not very patiently, as he would be the first to admit, until he was sixteen before he could realize the first of his ambitions and become a 'gentleman cadet' at Woolwich.

CHAPTER III

TRAINING AND FIRST APPOINTMENTS
(1866-70; AGED SIXTEEN TO TWENTY)

Woolwich Cadet, 1866 — Fluency in Languages — Life at "the Shop" — The Applewoman and the Prince — The Order of the Garter — Visit to Lord Derby — Visit to Liverpool — Visit to Ireland — "Sure, he's a fine boy" — Gazetted Lieutenant in the Royal Engineers — Walking Tour in the Swiss Mountains — Transferred to the Rifle Brigade — Visit to Canada — First Active Service — The Fenian Rising — The Prince and Small Friends.

Prince Arthur became a Woolwich cadet in July 1866, the year of the battles of Custozza and Königgrätz and other important military events in Europe, but he did not join the Royal Military Academy until February 11, 1867, when within three months of his seventeenth birthday. Queen Victoria gave particular instructions to all the officers in command that he was to be treated in exactly the same way as any other cadet. This course was naturally in accordance with the Prince's own wishes, which were emphasized by the manner in which he mixed freely with the other cadets, sharing both their studies and their amusements. Throughout the whole routine his unaffected manners and genial charm gained for him a high measure of popularity.

Like all the Royal children, Prince Arthur spoke French and German fluently, and, owing to this linguistic ability, he did not attend the modern language classes. His drills and exercises were undertaken with the fourth and fifth classes for his first term, but in August he joined the second class, and in due course passed for a commission in the Royal Engineers.

The authorities were much impressed by his keenness, by the ease with which he mastered his studies, and by the extreme smartness of his turn-out. He showed in himself, from the very first, the attribute of correctness in every detail of uniform and equipment — a mark of the keen soldier which he is well known to have enjoined upon others throughout his military career. "The Shop" certainly never enrolled a more apt pupil than the Royal 'gentleman cadet,' who, whether studying with the other embryo officers, taking his turn with the other cadets in the charge of classrooms, or performing his drill, always had his heart in his work. From infancy he had been a 'born soldier.' For private study the Prince was given a room in the centre building, part of which was allotted to his orderly officer. Lieutenant Pickard, V.C., R.H.A. While he was a cadet at Woolwich Prince Arthur lived at the Ranger's House, Greenwich Park, from whence he rode or drove over to his studies, taking his meals in hall, being mustered in the roll-call, and being, as were the other cadets, in every way subject to the Commandant, Major-General Sandham, R.E. The Crimean War having occurred so recently, fortification was a subject that loomed largely in military instruction during the sixties, and some miniature forts, of which the vestiges remained for many years in the Ranger's House, were attributed by tradition to the young Prince's activities.

During the examinations, the papers of which were afterward bound for Queen Victoria, the Prince of Wales came to visit his brother, much to the delight of the cadets, as they were granted an extra week's vacation in honour of the event. At a later date Princess Louise executed a bust of the Prince, which Queen Victoria presented to the cadets.

One feature of his daily ride from the Ranger's House to Woolwich along Shooter's Hill Road or through Charlton caused him some embarrassment. He had to pass on the way some of the ladies' boarding schools in which the neighbourhood abounded. A comely young Prince being naturally an object of great interest to the girls, the number of curtseys that were dropped as he passed caused him some disquietude. He preferred that his rides should not coincide with the appearance of processions of schoolgirls — familiarly called 'crocodiles' — during their daily walks.

He was a great favourite with all classes in the neighbourhood. An amusing incident is recorded of an old Irish applewoman, whose stall Prince Arthur often passed when visiting the house of Miss Hillyard, former governess to his sisters. Kitty, as the applewoman was called, judging by his dress, thought that the Prince was a private soldier at Woolwich, and she pitied his lot. "For he's that gentlemanly looking and with such a handsome face on him I'm sure he comes of dacent people. I do be wondering why his people don't buy him out!" When later on she was told of the Prince's rank her surprise can be imagined.

"Sure, I knew he was by way of being a swell," she explained, "but me thoughts didn't go quite so high."

Throughout his life the Duke has retained kindly memories of "the Shop." On December 8, 1899, he revisited the scene of his early studies to unveil four memorial windows in the dining-hall. Each window contained two portraits: the Queen and the Prince of Wales, the Duke of Connaught himself and the Duke of Cambridge, Lord Roberts and Sir Lintorn Simmons, and Sir John Burgoyne and Sir Richard Dacres, the last two having commanded the units of the Royal Engineers and of the Royal Artillery engaged in the Crimean War. After the unveiling the Duke, who was accompanied by the Duchess, lunched at the Commandant's house, and when they left the cadets turned out *en masse* and gave them unofficially a most enthusiastic send-off.

Soon after his seventeenth birthday Prince Arthur received the Order of the Garter. The Queen bestowed it upon him on the occasion of her birthday, at the time when she gave the Order of the Thistle to his eldest brother, the Prince of Wales.

Prince Arthur at this period always took a full share in the Christmas and similar festivals that were celebrated at the Royal residences. When, as sometimes happened, Queen Victoria spent the New Year at Osborne he helped in decorating the Christmas-trees and in distributing the gifts which Her Majesty always presented to the servants. He also helped to choose them — a task to which he took naturally and one to which he gave much care and consideration, suiting the gift to the exact needs of the recipient, and thereby showing characteristics for which he has been noted throughout his whole life.

In January 1868 Prince Arthur, accompanied by Prince and Princess Christian and his tutor, Colonel Elphinstone, who had recently been promoted, paid a week's visit to Lord Derby at Knowsley. This visit was the first of its kind that the Prince had paid, and the Queen, showing that care with which she arranged all details of her children's lives, was careful to give full instructions about the visit. She wrote to her son's host:

> The Queen, yesterday evening, consulted Major Elphinstone about Prince Arthur going with his brother and sister [Prince and Princess Christian] to Knowsley, and he sees no objection to it, so that the Queen gladly accepts for him Lord Derby's very kind invitation,

knowing that he could not go to a better house. The Queen would ask Lord Derby to consult Major Elphinstone about all that Prince Arthur should do, and also has asked him to explain to Lord and Lady Derby her wishes about the shooting.

Prince Arthur thoroughly enjoyed this visit, and particularly the shooting, of which there was a great deal. He was naturally a good shot, killing his birds clean, but his opportunities for indulging in the sport had up to that time been limited, and the shoots at Knowsley were on a big scale, involving much quick and continuous shooting — rather a trial for a novice. The experience is thus described in a letter from Lord Derby:

> Prince Arthur ... is all that could be wished — very lively, good-humoured and easily pleased. He seems to enjoy his shooting, as does Prince Christian; and though, from not being used to so much of it, he made his shoulder black and blue on Tuesday, he is gone out again to-day, after a day's *relâche* at Liverpool, where, I am happy to say, the Royal Party were very well received.

His bruised shoulder apparently did not handicap him badly, as on one day he was credited with sixty-seven birds as his personal bag.

The visit to Liverpool, where the Prince inspected the municipal buildings, was not of a public nature, but the large crowds which gathered to cheer the Royal visitors gave the young Prince a most cordial reception, which he acknowledged by repeated salutes and pleased smiles. A magnificent ball was given at the Liverpool Town Hall, to which three thousand guests were invited. This the Royal party attended, and the usual pleased comments were made upon the young Prince's charm of manner and modest bearing. As we have seen, the late hours had little effect upon successful participation in the next day's sport.

Later in the same year Prince Arthur paid his first visit to Ireland. He was accompanied on his tour by Colonel Elphinstone and Captain Pickard, and though the populace are said to have been a little disappointed at the absence of ostentation and military display which an Irish crowd loves, they gave him a hearty welcome. His soldierly bearing and sincere interest in all that he saw and in every one with whom he spoke made a good impression in a portion of the United Kingdom which at that time was so unaccustomed to Royal visitors that, as *The Times* reported, "the people had almost forgotten how to cheer." During this visit the Prince gave early indications of the tact for which he has always been famed. In many similar unrecorded ways this attribute has helped him to serve his country in various missions and in many countries within and without the Empire.

Unfortunately, the weather was decidedly unfavourable on this occasion. When the Prince visited Punchestown Races it poured the whole of the time, but he did not allow the elements to interfere with his very strenuous programme. His itinerary included a visit to Maynooth and to the Royal Hibernian School, where he was much interested in the miniature military display given by the boys. Wherever he went he made evident a real concern for the people's welfare and a most sympathetic interest in all that he was shown. There was no doubting the sincerity in his reply to the address of welcome which was presented to him at Dublin:

> I do hope that opportunities will frequently occur of my repeating these visits, as I have the deepest interest in all that concerns the welfare of Ireland.

In later life he was given such opportunities.

One old Irishwoman summed up Ireland's opinion of the Prince when she said: " Sure, he's a fine boy. Indeed, ye might think he'd been born in Oireland from the look on him! " And no doubt she felt that she could give no higher praise.

The fact that Patrick was one of the Prince's names greatly pleased the Irish people. In the address that was presented to him at Maynooth reference was made to the fact, and Prince Arthur replied:

> I thank you in particular for the reference to my name, and I can well believe that Irishmen will accord a national welcome to one who unites in himself the names of their patron saint and that of the most illustrious of their countrymen.[1]

This was the first occasion on which the Prince had set foot on Irish soil, and he then laid the foundations of his popularity with the Irish people, which has been increased by every subsequent visit.

1 A reference to the Duke of Wellington.

In June of that same year the Prince was gazetted as a Lieutenant in the Royal Engineers, and he went to the School of Military Engineering at Chatham, then under the command of Sir Lintorn Simmons. He took up his residence, accompanied by Colonel Elphinstone, in the Admiral-Superintendent's house in the Dockyard. When at Chatham Prince Arthur went through a field-works course with a squad of officers under Colonel Lennox, and learned bridge-building, entrenching, and something of the general technical work, such as sapping and mining, with which the Royal Engineers are charged. The Prince took his practical training as seriously as he had his theoretical studies; his capacity for spadework became a standing joke among his companions, who used to chaff him for digging as if he really enjoyed the experience.

The Prince left Chatham in August, after a review given to mark the occasion, and he went for a walking tour in the Swiss mountains. There, accompanied by Colonel Elphinstone and General Harrison, he did some hard climbing, including the Rosenlaui, the Gauli, the Lauteraar, the Oberaar, and the Fiescher. The party travelled as simple tourists, sleeping in the mountain huts often on trusses of hay and cooking their own meals. Prince Arthur took his turn with the rest, enjoying the freedom and the hard exercise. Some of it proved almost too strenuous, for the Fiescher Glacier was in very bad condition. They had to climb up the rocks at the mountain-side, and at one place to be let down over a torrent by ropes. Queen Victoria was staying at the time at a *château* near Schweizerhof, and the Prince spent a day or two with Her Majesty. At the end of the tour the Prince and his companions walked over the Simplon Pass into Italy, and there spent a few days among the beautiful Italian lakes until the Prince was due to join the Queen at Braemar.

In November Prince Arthur was transferred to the Royal Artillery, and served with B Battery of the 4th Brigade, Royal Horse Artillery, Woolwich, in the days when breech-loading guns were generally in vogue and the art of the gunner comprised more rigid drill than practical gunnery. This battery was equipped with breech-loaders of the Armstrong type. A photograph showing the Prince in the centre of a group of officers posed round one of these guns has been preserved. If by no other test he can easily be distinguished by the smartness of his turn-out and the superior fit of his stable-jacket.

On August 8, 1869, Prince Arthur was transferred to the Rifle Brigade, a unit which may be considered pre-eminently his own regiment, and shortly afterward he set out for his first visit to Canada, with which country he was in after-years to be so long and so intimately associated. There was a political motive connected with this tour, as at that time Canada was in a somewhat troubled condition, owing to Fenian riots, and it was felt that a visit from one of the Royal Princes might have a calming effect and create a good impression.

The 1st Battalion of the Rifle Brigade was already in Canada, and the Prince joined it in Montreal after the first part of his tour was over. When he arrived at Montreal no formal reception was arranged, but great crowds had assembled, and the Prince's first landing on Canadian soil was greeted with enthusiastic cheering. Montreal was to be the Prince's headquarters, to which fact he alluded in his reply to the address which was presented to him on his arrival:

> Most anxious am I to consider for the time being Montreal as my home, and to lose no opportunity of becoming fully acquainted with its institutions, its people, and its commerce. The selection of Montreal as my residence is a sufficient proof of the confidence Her Majesty places in the devotion of the city to her throne.

The confidence was not misplaced. Prince Arthur's visit, his personality, the ease and freedom with which he mixed with all classes, the unmistakable excellence of his intentions, and the sincerity of his personal interest created the most favourable impression. They did very much to revitalize loyalty to the Throne, to create a new devotion to the Mother Country, and to awake, for the Prince himself, a lasting affection which in later years enabled him to wield a beneficent influence upon Canadian affairs.

From Montreal the Prince journeyed to Ottawa, where he met with an equally enthusiastic reception. There he paid a visit to the lumber mills, and, to the huge delight of the workers, 'ran a slide' in a 'crib,' or, in words more readily understood by the average reader, he took a trip on a log raft down the narrow channels through which the logs are sent. From one of these rafts the lumbermen sent to the Prince and his party some plates of the pea-soup off which they were dining, and, much to their amused gratification, the young Prince demolished his plateful with obvious enjoyment.

At Ottawa the school-children, who had assembled to the number of 1500, hit upon an ingenious plan to gratify their ambition and have a good long stare at Prince Arthur. As the Royal party approached they struck up the National Anthem, and they sang it through from beginning to end. The Prince naturally stood uncovered until the end of the last line, when the youngsters cheered with delight and the Prince, much amused, went smiling on his way.

On October 13 he left for a trip up the Ottawa river, and this formed one of the most interesting and certainly the most picturesque features of his tour. All through the backwoods the men turned out to greet him and to offer him a hearty welcome. All places that the Prince visited were en fete for the occasion, but there was no monotony in the decorations. At one stopping-place during this Ottawa tour the inhabitants had enlisted the aid of nature with a novel and pleasing effect. An archway of growing pine-trees was enlaced for the Prince to walk under, the gracefully bent trees being here and there surmounted with crowns made of entwined palm branches.

Apart from his public duties, which he fulfilled to the letter, allowing neither fatigue, the discomforts of travel, nor the inclemency of the weather to interfere with his itinerary, Prince Arthur enjoyed participating in the sports which the season of his visit offered. In the cold season there was good skating, sleighing, tobogganing, and every form of winter sport, at which he quickly became an adept, while at other times, there was cricket, racquets, fishing, shooting, and other pastimes much to the Prince's taste. In his regiment he was popular both with the officers and with the men, for whose welfare he has always showed the greatest consideration.

Prince Arthur was in Canada in time to take a part in dealing with the Fenian Raid — his first experience of active service. In common with others who took part in these skirmishes, he received the medal and clasp for the operations. A rifleman in his battalion won the Victoria Cross for one of the bravest deeds for which that coveted decoration has been awarded. Timothy O'Hea was mounted on guard over a railway-van, loaded with 2000 lb. of ammunition. At Danville Station the van caught fire, and amid a scene of panic it was detached and passed down the line. Frightened spectators fled hurriedly, while the occupants of the neighbouring houses rushed out of them and joined in the stampede. O'Hea chased and mounted the van, wrenched open the door, tore the covering from the ammunition, and succeeded in quenching the flames, thus averting the expected catastrophe.

Prince Arthur returned from Canada in July 1870, and was met at the South Pier, Cowes, by the Queen, who, as her journal shows, was much gratified by the effect of the Prince's tour and by the personal impression he had made upon the Canadian people. This impression was widespread. It extended to widely different people, and we find Mr Gladstone, who was not given to flattery, writing to the Queen to tell her:

Mr Gladstone had the honour on Wednesday of receiving a visit from Prince Arthur. He only echoes the general opinion in saying that the Prince's frank, intelligent, and engaging manners adorn the high station which he holds.

At the end of that year a Royal refugee arrived in England in the person of the Empress Eugenie, who had been offered the hospitality of Windsor Castle on escaping from the horrors of the Franco-Prussian War. Prince Arthur was with the Queen at this time. He helped her to receive the tragic Empress, and devoted much of his time to entertaining the young Prince Imperial, showing him round the Castle, taking him for walks in the Park, always at pains to make him feel at home in the country of his exile. He made the Prince Imperial his special charge, doing his best with his usual tactful consideration for others to keep him away from his mother, the Empress, at moments when his questionings might have deepened her grief.

As Prince Arthur approached his majority he took a greater share in public life. He soon developed a useful gift for public speaking and an aptitude for happy impromptus which added both point and attractiveness to his speeches. Early military training developed his personality to a marked degree. The *régime* under which Queen Victoria ordained that her children should live did not have the repressive effect on Prince Arthur that it might have had on a weaker character; even before he attained his majority he was singularly independent. In private life he was thoroughly human, and he was a great favourite with the children of the men of his regiment. He would often stop to chat with them, discussing military matters quite seriously with his small friends. Once he asked a small mite of a boy whether he was going to be a soldier. "Yes," was the reply; "I'm going to be an officer!" "I see, like I am," came the rejoinder, with a smile. "Oh, no, not like you. You're only a captain, I'm going to be a general!"

CHAPTER IV

EARLY MANHOOD
(1871-74; AGED TWENTY-ONE TO TWENTY-THREE)

Coming of Age — His Mother's Affection — Grant of an Annuity by Parliament — A Second Visit to Ireland — "Prince Patrick" — Marriage of the Princess Louise — Illness of the Prince of Wales — A Nation's Thanksgiving — Attempts on the Queen's Life — Prince Arthur's Action — Acting Brigade Major at Aldershot — Transfer to the 7th Hussars — Varied Military Experience — His Work for the Soldier — A Mission to Russia — Prince Alfred's Wedding — Russian Diplomacy — A Royal Memory — An Eye for a Bulging Tunic.

Prince Arthur came of age in 1871. He spent his twenty-first birthday at Osborne, and the occasion was marked by an extraordinary number of gifts and letters of congratulation. These reached him from all classes of persons and from numerous countries. They included tributes from his Canadian friends and from many people with whom lie had become acquainted on his various tours, as well as from his brother officers. Both the Prince and Queen Victoria were specially pleased at the many congratulations which arrived from Ireland in memory of his visit to that country.

At twenty-one the Prince was a stalwart figure, looking well in his uniform and combining the qualities of a hard-working enthusiast in military affairs with the charm and polished courtesy of a scion of a Royal House destined to fill a high position in the public life of his time. He was very popular — a fact that never caused a trace of self-consciousness. He was a great favourite with the fair sex, but until the advent of the Princess by whom he was so attracted at first sight Prince Arthur was a follower of Mars rather than of Venus. He was one of the few popular Princes for whom rumour did not contract engagements before the actual event.

The day of the Prince's majority provided a real May Morning, and as a prelude to the festivities of the day he was serenaded by a regimental band — a tribute which he much appreciated. After this ceremony he went to the Queen to receive her congratulations, and Her Majesty wrote in her journal:

OSBORNE
1st May

Dear Arthur's twenty-first birthday. . . . My thoughts were with my dearest Albert, who had been so delighted at the birth of our little third boy on the dear old Duke of Wellington's birthday. And my warmest prayers were offered up that this dear good boy might continue as good, pure, unspoilt, and amiable, now that he [is] his own master, as he has been hitherto. How I trust and hope he may realize all these wishes for him! Gave dear Arthur a nosegay of lilies of the valley and took him into his father's room, where his presents were spread out.

It was Queen Victoria's unvarying custom, throughout the whole of her life, to do all in her power to keep the memory of the Prince Consort before his children, and most particularly before Iris sons. There is no doubt that their father's high standards and his personal character and example did much to influence the early lives of the young Princes. As a young man Prince Arthur was inclined to resemble his father, and this fact tended to increase the deep affection felt for him by the Queen. On attaining his majority the Prince was granted by Parliament an annuity of £15,000, of which sum he devoted a large proportion to many good causes in which he has always taken the keenest interest.

Later in the year Prince Arthur paid his second visit to Ireland, the conditions there differing considerably from those which he experienced on the first occasion. Ireland was in a very disturbed state. In some parts of the country the Fenians were causing great trouble, and it was doubted in some quarters whether at that moment it was a safe place for a Royal visit, but the outcome was a happy one, the people proving then, as on other occasions in Ireland and elsewhere, that words must not always be taken as an indication of deeds. Lord Spencer had been specially anxious that the Prince of Wales should accompany him on a visit to Dublin in August, believing that such a visit would test the strength of Irish loyalty and also that it would prove to the Irish nation that their interests had not been overlooked. Queen Victoria was rather doubtful about the wisdom of the visit and its possible results. She would have preferred that it should not take place at that critical time, but she was persuaded to give her consent.

The Prince of Wales arrived in Dublin on August 3, when the great annual horse-show was in full swing and the capital was filled to overflowing. As Prince Arthur had achieved so much popularity on his previous visit to Ireland, it had been arranged that he should accompany his elder brother, and later they were joined by the Marquis of Lorne and Princess Louise. Their reception was, on the whole, very much better than had been expected. The agitators contrived to arrange for a certain amount of hissing, but most of the people were anxious to show their loyalty, so the cheering far outweighed the hissing. With the cheering there mingled constant shouts for "Prince Patrick," or sometimes just for "Pathrick," for the Irish people had adopted Prince Arthur as their special Prince and lost no opportunity of showing it. The Prince's contempt of danger particularly endeared him to them as a cognate spirit. It was his express desire that no special precautions should be taken to protect him, and he moved freely about among the people, trusting to their sense of fairness to realize that their wrongs, both real and imaginary (and they had plenty of both), were not his fault but his genuine concern.

Prince Arthur has always cherished a warm liking for the Irish people who took him so speedily to their hearts, and in later years, during the time of his career in Canada, he took a special interest in the welfare of the Irish-Canadians, many of whom had good cause to be glad of their native country's reception of "Prince Pat."

Writing to the Queen from the Viceregal Lodge, Dublin, the Marquis of Lorne gave an interesting account of the impression made by the Prince:

> Louise has to-day gone to a picnic with the Prince of Wales, Arthur, . . . and a number of people from Dublin. . . .
>
> All who speak to me about the visit say that such opportunities thus given for the expression of the feeling of the people in Dublin are of the greatest service, and are most anxious that yearly visits should be paid, if it be not possible for any of the family to live permanently in the country.
>
> The cheers for "Prince Pat" are incessant, and wherever he has been he has received ovations. He quite deserves all the popularity he can get, and seems so anxious to do all that is good and right.

In that last sentence lies the clue to the popularity the Prince has enjoyed throughout the whole of his life. He has always been anxious to "do all that is good and right," to maintain the very best traditions of the Throne which he has represented. On the last occasion when the Prince appeared before his departure the crowd cheered him again and again, shouting to him to "Come back soon!" while one ardent loyalist cried, " Come and live with us. Prince Pat, and we'll make you a king!"

By this time the Royal family circle had been further depleted by the marriage of Princess Louise, who on March 21, 1871, was married to the Marquis of Lorne in St George's Chapel, Windsor. The Marquis of Lorne had been supported on the occasion by Earl Percy and Lord Ronald Gower, while our present Sovereign, His Majesty King George, was present as a small boy in a kilt. With his parents and his brother he figures prominently in the picture of the wedding, which was painted by Sydney P. Hall for the Royal collection; excellent portraits of Gladstone and Disraeli are included in the same picture.

Toward the end of that same year the Royal Family and the nation at large passed through a period of most critical anxiety caused by the serious illness of the Prince of Wales, from which it was feared he might not recover. The illness was in many respects similar to that which had caused the death of the Prince Consort ten years previously. The Prince of Wales was taken ill very shortly after his thirtieth birthday, in November. During the early part of December it seemed impossible that he could recover, and urgent prayers for his recovery were offered in all the churches throughout the land. On two occasions Queen Victoria and other members of the Royal Family were summoned hastily to Sandringham, where he was being nursed devotedly by the Princess of Wales and Princess Alice of Hesse. As may be readily understood, it was a period of the most acute suspense for all the members of the Royal Family, including Prince Arthur, who was sincerely attached to his eldest brother. He was a great support to his mother during the critical period.

By December 11 the fever was at its height, and though the relatives still hoped against hope, the physicians in attendance had practically given up all hope of saving their Royal patient's life. Then, on the 14th of the month, a change took place for the better. The fact that the hour of the improvement was the tenth anniversary of the Prince Consort's death seemed to Queen Victoria little short of a miracle; the coincidence was indeed remarkable, for from that time the Prince's condition improved until, to the intense joy and relief of the Royal Family and the great satisfaction of the nation, he was pronounced out of danger.

In February a great thanksgiving service was held at St Paul's Cathedral, and dense crowds lined the routes to cheer the Royal procession. London was profusely decorated with flags as an expression of the nation's joy that the life of its future King had been saved. Every window along the streets through which the procession was to pass was filled with cheering spectators, many of whom tossed flowers down upon the Royal carriages as they drove slowly on their way. N. Chevalier painted for the Royal collection a picture of the procession passing through Ludgate Circus which gives an excellent idea of the city's enthusiasm.

Three times during the early years of her reign Queen Victoria was forced to undergo the ordeal of having a pistol thrust in her face by half-witted would-be assassins. The first attempt upon her life occurred in the year 1840, soon after her marriage to Prince Albert. As she was driving up Constitution Hill with the Prince a crazy potboy discharged a pistol at her, but, fortunately, neither the Queen nor anyone else was hurt. The next attempt took place nine years later, and Constitution Hill was again the scene of the outrage. This time the would-be murderer was a deranged Irishman; his pistol was rusty, and it was suspected that the charge was not very dangerous, but the incident naturally alarmed the Queen, who was driving with three of her children. Despite her fears, she paid the Irish the compliment of visiting their country very shortly afterward, believing that the event had no political significance.

The third attempt took place in February 1872. Prince Arthur was present, and he took a personal part in securing the assailant. The occasion is best described in the words which the Queen herself used in her journal:

At half-past four drove in the open landau and four with Arthur, Leopold[1] and Jane C., the equerries riding. We drove round Hyde and Regent's Parks, returning by Constitution Hill, and when at the Garden Entrance a dreadful thing happened, which God in His mercy averted having any evil consequences. It is difficult for me to describe, as my

1 The Duke of Albany.

impression was a great fright, and all was over in a minute. How it all happened I knew nothing of. The equerries had dismounted, Brown had got down to let down the steps, and Jane C. was just getting out when suddenly some one appeared at my side, which I at first imagined was a footman, going to lift off the wrapper. Then I perceived that it was some one unknown, peering above the carriage door, with an uplifted hand and a strange voice, at the same time the boys calling out and moving forward. Involuntarily, in a terrible fright, I threw myself over Jane C. calling out, "Save me" and heard a scuffle and voices! I soon recovered myself sufficiently to stand up and turn round, when I saw Brown holding a young man tightly, who was struggling, Arthur, the equerries, etc., also near him. They laid the man on the ground and Brown kept hold of him until several of the police came in. All turned and asked if I was hurt, and I said "Not at all." Then Lord Charles [FitzRoy], General Hardinge, and Arthur came up, saying they thought the man had dropped some- thing. We looked, but could find nothing, when Cannon, the postilion, called out "There it is," and looking down I then did see shining on the ground a small pistol! This filled us with horror. All were as white as sheets, Jane C. almost crying, and Leopold looked as if he were going to faint.

It is to good Brown and to his wonderful presence of mind that I greatly owe my safety, for he alone saw the boy rush round and followed him! When I was standing in the hall General Hardinge came in, bringing an extraordinary document which this boy had intended making me sign! It was in connection with the Fenian prisoners. . . . Then the boy was taken by the police and made no attempt to escape. . . .

Arthur soon came in, who, as well as Leopold, did all they could. Arthur said he had jumped over the side of the carriage, but that Brown had been too quick for him to catch the boy. He had tried to push his hand aside, for both Arthur and Leopold had seen the pistol pointed at me, close to my face, which neither I nor anyone else did. The pistol had not been loaded, but it easily might have been!

I sent Arthur off at once to Bertie,[1] so that he should not hear an exaggerated account.

The name of the boy who had presented the pistol at Her Majesty was Arthur O'Connor. He was afterward proved to be insane, but it is doubtful whether even in his madness he really intended to injure the

1 The Prince of Wales was unwell at the time.

Queen. In his crazy brain had probably hatched some plot whereby he hoped that she might be induced to do as he wished.

On October 16, 1873, Prince Arthur was appointed Acting Brigade Major at Aldershot — a post that he held until April 1874, when he was transferred as a Captain to the 7th Hussars. Thus he served in all branches of the service — Engineers, Artillery, infantry, cavalry, and Staff — and he was distinguished for keenness and efficiency in them all. The personal knowledge of the actual life of a soldier, at home and abroad, in peace and in war, has enabled him to do much to ameliorate the lot of the man in the ranks, and he has availed himself of every opportunity to help the men who have done so much to uphold the interests of the British Empire in critical situations which have occurred during his lifetime. When he first joined the Army the lot of private soldiers was often hard, and the treatment meted out to them harsh. They were expected to be able to fight, to endure, to perform feats of valour, and in return to be content with very little reward. The Duke has done great service to the cause of raising the status of the ordinary soldier and of abolishing the harshness of his lot. He realized that the "Tommy Atkins" of history was a man before he was a soldier, and if treated as a man, and not looked upon merely as a fighting machine, would yield even better results in the future.

When opportunity offered the Prince pointed out that the methods of many gymnastic instructors of the day were over-harsh. They imposed far too great a strain on young recruits, who were not built up by the system but broken down, their health often being seriously impaired. By drawing attention to the evil he caused it to be remedied to a very large extent, but many years passed before the old Army gymnastic system gave place to the wiser methods which obtain in the present day.

The health of his men and everything that affected it has always been the Duke's primary concern during the years of his military service. As an illustration of this we can here quote an incident that occurred when he held the Southern Command in later years. It is typical of his methods in dealing with those who served under him. A troopship, arriving at Portsmouth, was met by the Duke and his staff. The ship came into harbour in the forenoon, and the day was so stiflingly hot that the Duke delayed the order for disembarkation until the cool of the evening, when the men could disembark without discomfort and be paraded for the necessary inspection. "It is easier," wrote Nelson, "for an officer to keep his men healthy than for a doctor to heal them," and the Duke showed equal wisdom. Instances such as these could be multiplied, and there is no regiment in which the Duke has served in which tales are not told of his unfailing care for the physical and moral welfare of the men in the ranks.

To resume our narrative. A journey which Prince Arthur found very interesting and which promised many novel features was one he undertook to Russia in January 1874 with the Prince and Princess of Wales. He went to St Petersburg for the wedding of his brother. Prince Alfred (the Duke of Edinburgh), to the Grand Duchess Marie, daughter of the Tsar. An interesting picture of this ceremony, in which Prince Arthur figures, was painted by N. Chevalier for the Royal collection. As the bride and bridegroom were of different nationalities and different religions, there had to be two marriage ceremonies. The first, which was celebrated with all the rites of the Greek Church, to which the bride belonged, took place at the Winter Palace. It was followed by the Anglican service, conducted by Dean Stanley.

Much was made of the two Princes during this visit to Russia, but Queen Victoria had doubts about the sincerity of the welcome, and these doubts were shared by the Prince of Wales. The Russians were suspected of having their own reasons for the warmth with which they greeted the Prince of Wales and Prince Arthur, and for the magnificence of the festivities that were arranged for their entertainment. In consequence there was a certain restraint in the atmosphere, even at the banquets and similar ceremonies given in honour of the English Royal visitors. The Queen wrote to Lord Granville about the visit, and expressed her opinion that the flattery with which the young Princes were being received was for the purpose of "throwing dust in our eyes." This seems to have been the general opinion in England at the time, and even the visit of the Tsar to England later in that same year did little to relieve the tension; but, in spite of the political difficulties. Prince Arthur enjoyed the novelty of his visit, particularly a wonderful boar-hunt which was organized near St Petersburg, in which nearly eighty boars were killed. This was a new experience to the young Prince, as were many of the scenes in which he took part. He also visited Moscow and its historic buildings, and saw something of the life of the ill-fated country from which his brother had chosen his bride. He had the Royal memory for faces, which sometimes startled those who were given proof of its excellence.

When the Duke of Edinburgh brought his bride to England later one of the Duchess's suite was presented to Prince Arthur, who observed that they had met before, adding, "You do not remember it, I see. You were going into the Kremlin as I was coming out. We passed on the steps."

Powers of observation, combined with an unusually retentive memory, have done much to establish his popularity. He was always observant, and he would notice evidence of any grief or sorrow in those around him. Having noticed, he would make it his concern to find out the reason and to do anything in his power to help, and, even years after the event had occurred, he would remember to inquire about any occurrence that had affected his friends. An amusing story which bears upon this faculty of observation and remembrance is told about one of the Prince's soldier servants. The man was understood to be 'walking out' with a pretty parlourmaid, and the Prince asked a brother officer on whose estate the man had been employed before he had joined the Army whether the engagement had been broken off. "Why should you think so?" was the reply. "Well," said the Prince, "I notice that the photograph-case that has bulged his tunic pocket for the last three months is missing!" Incidentally, that story also illustrates his eye for the fit of a uniform tunic.

CHAPTER V

THE YOUNG ROYAL DUKE
(1874-78; AGED TWENTY-FOUR TO TWENTY-EIGHT)

Influence of Aldershot — Duke of Connaught and Strathearn and Earl of Sussex — Brigade Major of Cavalry at Aldershot — Assistant Adjutant-General at Gibraltar — A Soldier's Life on the Rock — Visit of the Prince of Wales — "God save your dear Ma" — The Duke's "gimlet eyes" — Promotion to Lieutenant-Colonel — Command of the Rifle Brigade in Ireland — Warm Hearts for "Prince Pat" — Interest in his Regiment — The Unpopular Helmet — The Queen-Empress — " V.R. and I." — The Star of India — Interest in Canada — Death of Princess Alice — Correspondence with Princess Louise — A Visit to Berlin — Royal Marriages — A Fateful Meeting.

In writing of the Duke of Connaught's military career one tends naturally to revert constantly to his experiences at Aldershot. The famous camp was then a collection of huts in the heather, resembling but slightly the array of well-built quarters and broad avenues of the present day. It was, nevertheless, the military centre which set the pace in the organization and peacetime activities of the British Army. Queen Victoria and the Prince Consort had taken a great interest in the camp, and many social and recreative schemes had sprung up as a result of their concern for the welfare of the soldiers. These schemes the Duke did his best to further. He was particularly interested in the large military library for the use of the soldiers which the Queen maintained out of the resources of her private purse. This was known as Queen Victoria's Soldiers' Library. A substantial brick building, situated close to the Royal Pavilion, was built by the Prince Consort as a gift to the officers of the Army. He equipped it at his own expense with all the best military books of the day. These volumes the Duke of Connaught augmented, often sending abroad for any book he thought likely to prove useful, and encouraging students of the military profession by every means in his power to make use of the facilities for improvement which the library offered.

On the more human side, he did not believe in enforced celibacy for the soldier, and he did his utmost to better the position in this respect, which in those days by no means favoured the wives and children. He took a personal part in inaugurating several schemes for the improvement of the married quarters. It was also largely owing to his efforts that flogging was abolished in the Army. The plea for abolition was a strong one. Flogging undoubtedly tended to brutalize the men and to render them indifferent to any further result of their misbehaviour.

In later years Queen Victoria visited the Duke and stayed at the Royal Pavilion, of which both she and the Prince Consort had been very fond. Indeed, from the time of the fall of Sebastopol there had been so many military reviews and similar ceremonies that the Royal Family were often at Aldershot, and Court news was dated on such occasions from the Royal Pavilion. By her express wish the Royal Pavilion was a very plain affair, and the Duke took great pains to see that everything was kept for the Queen as it had been in the lifetime of his father. Everything connected with it had some military significance. Portraits of famous military commanders adorned the walls, and the ceiling of the dining-room was covered with a billowy kind of drapery to give the impression that the party was dining under canvas. Here the Duke and the senior officers would dine with Her Majesty during her visits.

The Queen always took a great interest in the Duke's military career, and when she was at the camp she would sit at her window, from which she could command a view of the Long Valley stretching away from Gesar's Camp, on which the special manoeuvres took place, and watch her son inspecting the troops and taking part in his military duties.

Her Majesty was specially attached to the Royal Scots, the regiment of her father, the Duke of Kent, the only one of the sons of George III who received the thanks of Parliament for service in the field. At a later date (September 1876) she presented new colours to the regiment when the Duke of Connaught was at Balmoral, he accompanying the Queen when she made the presentation. In the course of her speech she said:

> My dear father was proud of his profession, and I was always brought up to regard myself as a soldier's child. I rejoice in having a

son who has devoted his life to the Army, and who I am confident will ever prove worthy the name of a British soldier.

The most cursory knowledge of the Duke's career will serve to show that the Queen's confidence was not misplaced. To that career we will now revert.

On May 24, 1874, Prince Arthur was created Duke of Connaught and Strathearn and Earl of Sussex. Strathearn had been one of the titles of his grandfather, the Duke of Kent, but it is as the Duke of Connaught that the British nation has known him and it is that title that he has done so much to honour. The arms allotted by the Heralds' College were:

> The Royal Arms differenced by a label of three points argent, the centre point charged with the St George's Cross, and each of the other points with a fleur-de-lis azur. *Crest:* on a coronet composed of crosses-patée, and fleur-de-lis, a lion statant guardant or, crowned with the like coronet, and differenced with a label of three points argent, charged as in the arms. *Supporters:* The royal supporters, differenced with the like coronet and label.

In August of the next year the Duke was promoted Major in the 7th Hussars, and led the ordinary regimental life, varied occasionally by dudes at Court, and spending some of his time at Balmoral, where it is on record that the band of his regiment on one occasion played at dinner. As Queen Victoria lived much in retirement at that time, he was occasionally called upon to take her place at levees when this office could not be performed by the Prince of Wales. When he was in Scotland deer-stalking was a favourite pursuit, and the Duke spent much time in the company of Prince Leopold, his delicate younger brother. He was appointed Brigade Major of the Cavalry Brigade at Aldershot on May 1, 1875, which post he held until July 1, when he went to Gibraltar as Assistant Adjutant-General.

The Duke spent six months at Gibraltar, where he added greatly to his experience as a soldier. He gained a thorough knowledge of the fortress and took part in the social life, sharing in many festivities that were arranged in his honour. His military keenness increased. Nearly all the important work of the Army Staff came in those days under the purview of the Adjutant-General's department, and after a long period of peace garrison life had developed into a matter of routine, and even overseas fortresses had assumed the nature of 'sleepy hollows.' Keen soldiering on the part of the most influential branch of the Staff may have come as a surprise in military quarters where it had been hoped to find in a Royal Assistant Adjutant-General a 'show' soldier who, beyond an occasional appearance on the parade ground and at the mess dinners, would take little active interest in regimental affairs. In this they were greatly mistaken.

When the Duke of Wellington was once asked to what he attributed his military success he answered, "I attribute it entirely to the application of good sense to the circumstances of the moment," and the Duke of Connaught has often quoted this remark of his famous godfather. His own success in the various posts which he has filled can largely be attributed to his own application of the same principle.

At Gibraltar, as elsewhere, he was constantly in the limelight. Much was expected from him, and, representing as he did the Royal House, his sayings and doings were sure to be watched and discussed with the freedom and readiness of criticism for which those of high estate are unfailing targets, but his tact, his sincere desire to perform his duties to the very best of his ability, his unvarying courtesy, and his consideration for the welfare of all those around him disarmed all such criticism and gained him the esteem and regard of all with whom he was associated.

While the Duke was at Gibraltar the Prince of Wales, who was returning from his Indian tour in the *Serapis*, stopped there and stayed for a short time with his brother. Gibraltar did its best to *fête* the Prince, so both he and the Duke of Connaught attended a long series of banquets, balls, and other ceremonies that were given in their honour.

The Duke, who has a keen sense of humour, tells a good story of his eldest brother's encounter at one of these ceremonies with an old woman who in her younger days had been employed at Osborne and still cherished a deep reverence for Queen Victoria. The Prince recognized her, and, much to her satisfaction, inquired after her welfare. The woman dropped him a gratified curtsey, and told him she was getting on well, as she was doing some of the soldiers' washing and on occasion had actually been the washerwoman to the Duke. "Ah, your Highness," she said solemnly, "you don't know what a difference your noble brother makes to me being here!"

"Indeed," said the Prince gravely.

"Yes," she went on, "for everywhere he goes the band plays 'God save your dear ma'!"

The Duke always says that this is one of the best left-handed compliments that he has ever received.

Those who served under him had full occasion to discover that he was not deceived by outward appearances. He had a way of quietly but persistently getting to the root of the matter that sometimes proved disconcerting to those who were unprepared for his thoroughness. An officer who served under him at Aldershot describes an incident which fully illustrates the Duke's determination not to be taken in by any amount of 'eyewash.' Manoeuvres were in progress, and certain battalions which had marched in from out-stations to take part in them were paraded under service conditions for the Duke's inspection. The troops, drawn up in line of quarter columns, presented a very smart appearance. Their buttons were well polished, their uniforms spotless, their valises packed in regulation perfection, and the whole turn-out the last word in soldierly smartness. The inspection began, and the officers in command were congratulating themselves on the fine appearance of their men when suddenly the Duke came to a halt and announced that he wanted to see the entire kits of No. 1 Company in each battalion. If the inside of the platter had been as good as the outside that order would certainly not have caused the secret consternation that it did. There was no help for it, the order could not be evaded; and when the valises were unpacked and the kit paraded it was shown that appearances had been deceptive. Nearly every valise was empty, although the men were parading under service conditions. One battalion's contribution to the prescribed service kit consisted of one solitary polishing brush.

From that time forward when it was known that any regiment was to be paraded before the Duke care was taken that the equipment should be complete to the last detail. His passion for detail soon became a byword among those whom he commanded, and an amusing story is told about the impression he made upon two privates who, having been dismissed from parade, were discussing the next inspection.

"I've come to my last sixpence," one announced gloomily, "and now that'll have to go on extra polish."

"Extra polish!" echoed his companion. "Why, the C.O. has just passed the lot of us!"

"Oh, 'im!" was the scornful reply. "He's only got eyes — the Dook's got gimlets!"

Keenness and military thoroughness did not prevent the Duke from taking a sincere interest in the lighter side of Army life. He was an enthusiastic supporter of regimental sports, which he always attended whenever possible, frequently presenting the prizes. He was particularly anxious to encourage young recruits to take part in every sort of healthy pastime, believing as he did that the comradeship, the spirit of friendly competition, and the interest aroused did much to add to the moral of the men.

It was a great pleasure to Queen Victoria when by her special wish the Duke was, in May 1876, appointed personal Aide-de-Camp to the Sovereign — an appointment that he has now held for over fifty-three years. Later in the same year he was again transferred to the Rifle Brigade, in which regiment he had already served for four years as Lieutenant and as Captain. He now, as a Lieutenant-Colonel, took command of the 1st Battalion at the Royal Barracks in Dublin, where he renewed his acquaintance with the Irish people and further increased his popularity both in the regiment and with the populace. Though he was now Duke of Connaught to the majority of the public, he remained to the Irish the "Prince Pat" whom they had welcomed as a lad. They still looked upon him as their own special Prince, and they were delighted that, even if only for a short time, he had returned to take up his residence among them. The Duke had always advocated Royal visits to Ireland as a means of fostering the people's loyalty and showing them that their interests were not overlooked, as many at that time may have believed. If it could have been so arranged he would willingly have taken up his residence in the country, and it is permissible to speculate whether, had such a proposal materialized, the history of Ireland during the last half-century might not have been differently written. During his stay in Dublin the Duke made many excursions in the 'outside cars' of the country, and on one of these an old blind fiddler was presented to him. The man had walked many miles that he might 'see' the Duke, and he immediately struck up St Patrick's Day. Some one gently suggested to him that he should substitute God save the Queen. "No, no," protested the old man. "'Tis Prince Pat himself that I want to be saved."

So anxious were the Irish people to see the Duke that the wish provoked many examples of national impulsiveness. Once, when he was driving in a formal procession, an Irish girl on a smart little pony galloped up to the carriage, looked eagerly at him, gave a deep sigh, and exclaimed, "Now I can go home happy." The Duke, much amused but somewhat taken aback, replied with a military salute.

While he was in Dublin he was frequently reminded of the time when his eldest brother, the Prince of Wales, had received his military training at the Curragh Camp, Kildare. The Prince had occupied a hut which Queen Victoria described as "very comfortable, nice little sitting-room, bedroom, drawing-room and good-sized dining-room." Her Majesty also thanked Colonel Percy for "treating Bertie just like any other officer, and keeping him up to his work."

On the soldiering side, the Duke's battalion found that he always "kept to his work." When he returned to England both they and the Irish people said good-bye to him with sincere regret. Many expressions of loyal regard were displayed in the streets, including the old one which reads, "Better lo'ed ye canna be; wull ye no come back again?" whereby we are reminded of the visit of the Queen and the Prince Consort to Ireland in 1849, when they took with them their four elder children. During that visit an old Irishwoman had voiced prophetically Ireland's sentiments regarding a future "Prince Patrick." "Oh, Queen dear," she cried, "make one of them dear children Prince Patrick, and all Ireland will die for you." When Prince Arthur was born in the following year the Queen recalled the wish when the name was bestowed on the Royal baby.

The Duke's interest in his regiment embraced every side of Army life. All ranks knew that their wishes would receive the most sympathetic attention, and this they certainly did in the matter of headdress. The brassbound cloth helmet was introduced officially for all the infantry in 1877, and it has endured, much to their chagrin, until the present day. From the first the helmet was very unpopular in the Rifle Brigade, and the opinion among the men was so strong that the Duke himself took the matter up. He made personal representations to Queen Victoria on the subject, and persuaded her to take steps to bring about the substitution of the smart Rifleman's cap of astrakhan.

In 1877, momentous year for the Queen and the Empire, the Prince of Wales visited India, and the Prime Minister asked the House of Commons to vote £142,000 to defray the expenses of the tour. This sum was far in excess of any hitherto devoted to the purposes of Royal travel. It was accounted for by the ceremonies considered necessary in the visits to Eastern potentates and by the costly presents the Prince would be required to exchange with them. It was on the Prince's return that we find mention of the Duke of Connaught in Queen Victoria's writings, when it was announced that hereafter she would, in addition to her other titles, style herself Empress of India. We read in her journal that it was in January 1877 that she first signed herself in that manner:

1st Jan., 1877

I have for the first time to-day signed myself as V.R. & I.

[At dinner] I wore the Star of India, which I conferred on Arthur this morning, and some of the beautiful gifts brought back by Bertie. At dessert Arthur gave out my health as "Queen and Empress of India."

On the 12th of the month Her Majesty wrote to Lord Lytton, the Viceroy, telling him that she had conferred the Star of India upon Prince Arthur — a significant decoration, in view of his later associations with the country.

The next public event of outstanding importance to the Royal Family was the appointment of the Marquis of Lorne to the Governor-Generalship of Canada in 1878. The Duke took much interest in his brother-in-law's new post, and he had a lengthy and most interesting correspondence with his sister, the Princess Louise, during her stay in the country to which he himself was to be appointed in later years.

Soon after the Marquis of Lorne and Princess Louise had taken up their residence at Rideau Hall, the official residence at Ottawa, the Royal Family suffered a great bereavement in the death of Princess Alice. The Duke of Connaught felt this keenly. His elder sister's gentle nature and the sweetness of her disposition had made her a great favourite with the younger members of the family, whose *confidente* she had always been and whose childish amusements and joys and sorrows of adolescence she had always shared.

Princess Louise sketched well, and while she was in Canada she sent to the Duke many specimens of her work, including some most amusing little thumbnail portraits selected from the members of deputations which greeted the viceregal party at their halts at Indian stations where paint and feathers constituted a full Court dress. Many lifelike sketches of Canadian notabilities who had been presented to her were also forwarded.

While the Princess was so employed the Marquis wrote of life in Canada, and the Duke was one of the first to receive a copy of his book

Canadian Pictures, which gave a most interesting account of Canada and its government.

Residence at Rideau Hall and recording his experiences inspired the Marquis also in the production of his later books, *Memories of Canada and Scotland, Imperial Federation,* and *The United States after the War.*

The Duke's own tour in Canada when he first joined the Rifle Brigade naturally deepened his interest in his sister's experience in that country. He wrote jestingly to tell her that he envied his brother-in-law and wished himself in his position as Governor-General. Princess Louise's reply was strangely prophetic. She wrote:

> I think it possible you may come here, one day. Canada is so loyal, so interesting, and with such a marvellous future that it really seems as if the Governor-Generalship should always be filled by a member of our family.

Princess Louise was a keen angler, and while she was in Canada she hooked a salmon of such lordly proportions that it was frozen and sent home to Windsor to be mounted. In due course it was hung in the Queen's dining-room, much to the amusement of the Duke, who said that when next he went to Canada he must catch one twice as big to hang opposite.

The Duke having now reached the age of twenty-eight, the gossips, from whom it is the usual fate of Royal bachelors to suffer, began to discuss the question of when he would take unto himself a wife. The names of several highly eligible Princesses were mentioned, but the Duke so far was heart-whole, and, as he had firmly resolved to enter into no attachment that was not founded on sincere mutual affection, his engagement seemed as remote as ever.

Although his own wedding was not yet to take place, it was often his lot to attend the weddings of relatives and friends. In February 1878 he accompanied the Prince of Wales in a journey to Berlin for a wedding ceremony of special family interest. One of the brides was their niece Princess Charlotte, the eldest child of the Princess Royal (Crown Princess of Prussia) and the first grandchild of Queen Victoria to be married. By the special wish of the old Emperor William I, it was to be a double wedding. The eldest daughter of his nephew, Prince Frederick Charles (the "Red Prince" who had won distinction in the Franco-Prussian War), was to marry Frederick Augustus, heir to the

Grand Duke of Oldenburg, while Princess Charlotte was to marry the Hereditary Duke of Saxe-Meiningen.

The wedding took place on February 18, and it was a most imposing affair, celebrated with great pomp and magnificence. Six hours passed before the final formalities were concluded. The German people, as well as the German Court, gave the two English Princes a most cordial reception, as the Prince of Wales reported in his letter to his mother describing the wedding:

> We have been most cordially and, I may say, affectionately received by all the family, and it is evident the very great pleasure it has given them all that we came for the two marriages.

After the wedding Lord Odo Russell, a friend of the Prince of Wales, gave a banquet which was attended by both the newly married couples and by the German Emperor and Empress. Both of them paid marked attention to the Prince of Wales and to the Duke of Connaught, and these attentions were extended throughout their stay in Berlin.

The wedding ceremony being over, the Duke stayed for some little time with his sister, the Crown Princess, and while he was there he made an excellent impression upon a people so strongly imbued with the military spirit. They appreciated the soldierly smartness of his bearing when he attended the banquets, balls, and dinners that were given in his honour. He was introduced to his sister's most intimate friends, and also those of the daughter whose wedding he had just attended, and it was in this family and matrimonial atmosphere that the Duke of Connaught met the girl with whom he was destined to spend a lifetime of married happiness.

CHAPTER VI

COURTSHIP
(1878-79; AGED TWENTY-EIGHT)

Princess Louise Marguerite — Parentage and Early Life — Adolescence and Friendships — First Meeting with the Duke of Connaught — Queen Victoria's Reluctant Consent — Her Dislike for Prussians — A Prussian Dowry and Wedding-presents — The Meeting at Queenborough — England's Welcome to the Princess — Wedding-presents — Ireland's Gift — "Louischen a dear, sweet girl" — *The Times* on the Wedding — A Popular Pair — The 13th of March — Mascots as Gifts — King George at the Age of Thirteen — A Royal Love-match.

Princess Louise Marguerite of Prussia was the third daughter of Prince Frederick Charles — the famous general in the Prussian Army who was given the sobriquet of "the Red Prince" by his men because his bright red uniform was always to the fore — and of his wife, the Princess Marie Anne, daughter of the Duke of Anhalt. The Princess was born on July 25, 1860, at the Palace of Potsdam, and she spent most of her girlhood in Berlin.

It was fitting that the Duke, himself so keen a soldier, should choose for his bride the daughter of a high commander of armies. She was brought up in a soldier's home, so she knew in her childhood what it was to have a father on active service, as in later years she was destined to face the suspense of having a husband engaged in similar duties.

As a small child the Princess was delicate, and the care with which she had to be brought up largely accounted for the shyness which characterized her throughout the whole of her lifetime. Her two elder sisters, Marie and Elizabeth, were her seniors by some years, and her only brother, Leopold, was five years younger, so the Princess was inclined to be rather lonely as a small girl. Despite her shyness, she possessed a gaiety of spirit which helped her to join in the amusements of her elder sisters. In the possession of the Princess's family there is a portrait of her known as "The Little Beggar Girl," about which a good story is told. The two elder Princesses had been to a ball, which Princess Louise herself was too young to attend. They went in fancy dress, one in Russian and one in Spanish attire, and on the next day they were photographed in their costumes. Princess Louise watched the proceedings, and was sorely disappointed that she had no fancy dress of her own for the occasion. "Mimi," as she was called in the nursery, was not to be outdone. Seizing a long wrap lying near, she threw it round her small person and demanded to know whom she represented. "A little beggar girl!" exclaimed her sisters in amusement, and so delightful did the little Princess appear that she was at once photographed in her impromptu costume.

Princess Louise was trained with the thoroughness which is characteristic of German methods of educating girls. She was surrounded by the punctilious etiquette common to all branches of the Hohenzollerns, but from her childhood she was linked with England by her English governess and by the deep affection she bore for the Crown Princess of Prussia, who was Queen Victoria's eldest daughter and the mother of the ex-Emperor William II. She was, moreover, the playmate and inseparable companion of the Crown Princess's eldest daughter, the Princess Charlotte.

Their homes were not very far apart, and the two little girls read together, studied together, and played together. Princess Louise spent almost as much time with her friend as she did under her own roof, so great was her attachment to the Crown Princess, who exercised a great influence over her in her early girlhood. Throughout their lives there remained an affectionate bond between them.

When the Duke first met his future bride she was just eighteen, ten years younger than himself, a most attractive girl beneath whose quiet exterior there lurked a keen sense of humour which occasionally revealed itself in the caricatures which she drew of sundry pompous personages attached to the German Court. Like her future husband, she had great charm of manner, and she was a general favourite in the circles in which she moved. When in congenial society she was a good conversationalist, possessing, too, great tact and sympathy, and in their life together this quality was of considerable service to the Duke in his dealings with the people with whom he came into contact.

Though from the first it was evident that the strong attraction between the young people was mutual, the Duke did not declare himself at that time. He returned to England to consult the Queen regarding the match, but his last act on leaving Berlin was to present the Princess with a bouquet of her favourite flowers. The Princess doubtless knew how to interpret this souvenir.

Queen Victoria tells in her journal of the Duke's conversation on his purposed engagement:

Dear Arthur arrived and stopped with us while we were taking tea. Afterwards remained talking with me a little while, and told me that he had taken a great liking to young Louise of Prussia, Fritz Carl's youngest daughter, who was brought up by an English governess. The latter is now gone to Alice's girls. He said he did not wish to marry yet, and no one had breathed a word about it, but he liked her better and better, and meant, if I had no objection, to ask to see her this summer again. I could not help saying that I dislike the Prussians, and told him he should see others first, but he said it would make no difference. What could I then say, but that of course his happiness was the first thing? He assured me he liked her better than anyone he had seen, but that he would not do anything without my consent, and looked so sad and earnest, yet so dear and gentle, that, having heard nothing but good of the girl, I could not object.

The Crown Princess of Prussia wrote to Queen Victoria giving her opinion of Princess Louise and expressing her entire approval of the match, which she considered highly suitable for both young people. She said:

I could not choose for a sister-in-law anyone I like better than Louise. She will make Arthur a most delightful wife. Each is the complement of the other, and I foresee that each will make the other supremely happy.

In due course Queen Victoria gave her full consent, and at a great Court banquet given in Berlin there was announced a double betrothal, that of Princess Louise to the Duke of Connaught and that of her elder sister, Princess Marie, to Prince Henry of the Netherlands. Owing to the death of Princess Alice of Hesse, the engagement lasted for the unusual period of a year, but the Duke's deep attachment caused him to pay numerous visits to Berlin, where the young people met and made their plans for the future in the manner common to lovers the wide world over. Then at last, much to the Duke's satisfaction, it was arranged in March 1879 that his bride-elect should come to England.

At the Berlin Court there was a formal leave-taking of the Princess and a presentation of some of the many gifts that had come to her from all parts of the German Empire. Among presents costly and rare there were none that pleased and charmed the Princess more than one which came from her old nurse. This was a pair of her baby shoes, the first pair that she had ever worn, and these arrived mounted on a cushion in the centre of a wreath of myrtle and orange-blossom.

Prussia gave the Princess the usual dowry of £30,000, half of which she spent on her trousseau and on the usual contributions to her new home, including a magnificent assortment of the very finest linen, some of which, after the custom of German girls, she had herself embroidered with her monogram. The trousseau, which, as may be imagined, contained some exquisite specimens of needlework, was exhibited at the Palace at Berlin, and it became at once the envy and despair of every girl who enjoyed the privilege of inspection.

Princess Louise set out for England under the escort of her mother and father and of her brother. Prince Leopold. The Royal party paid two visits, one of congratulation and one of condolence. The first was to Princess Elizabeth of Oldenburg, who had just become the mother of a son. The second was to Princess Marie of the Netherlands, who had suffered a sad bereavement in the loss of her husband only a few months after their marriage. The Royal yacht went to Flushing to fetch the Princess. Lord Torrington and Colonel M'Neill, V.C., were on board, and they journeyed with her and her parents back to Queenborough, where the town was gaily decorated for the occasion. A triumphal arch on the pier on which stood out the words "Welcome to Louise" was a prominent feature of the decorations. Queenborough has historic associations with Queen Philippa of Hainault, who interceded for the burgesses of Calais, but Royal visitors were rare in modern times, and the townsfolk, determined to make the most of the occasion, turned out *en masse* to cheer the Royal couple. When the *Victoria and Albert* appeared, flying the Prussian standard at the main, H.M.S. *Duncan* greeted her with a salute of twenty-one guns. The rest of the fleet anchored off Queenborough at about nine in the morning. It was regarded as a happy omen that the day was bright and sunny and the sea smooth. 'Queen's weather' greeted the young Princess who was to make her home in what was to her a new and strange country.

The Duke of Connaught journeyed to Queenborough in a special train, arriving at about eleven, and as his train steamed up to the pier the Victoria and Albert began to move toward the shore — 'good staff work' for which the Royal Navy and the railway authorities shared the credit. The Duke, who was in morning dress with a buttonhole of violets, the Princess's favourite flower, eagerly awaited her arrival on the landing-stage. At the moment when the yacht came alongside he sprang on board carrying a bouquet of lilies and violets for the Princess and one of roses for her mother. He met his betrothed in private. After a few minutes they appeared on deck, and the Princess appeared so modest and so charming that the crowd took her to their hearts at once. There was a burst of spontaneous and heartfelt cheers, which increased in volume as the Royal party stepped on shore. The Princess was naturally dressed in the height of the fashion of the day, but, in the light of women's dress of the present time, it seems quaint to recall that this attractive girl of nineteen made her first public appearance in England attired in a long velvet jacket trimmed with black sable, a black bonnet decked with grey feathers, and a grey silk gown. In spite of this somewhat sombre splendour, she presented a charmingly girlish appearance as, leaning on the arm of the Duke, she shyly acknowledged the people's welcome. It is a pity that so attractive a theme did not inspire any contemporary painter.

After they had landed they were presented with an address by the Mayor, who, accompanied by the jurats and bailiffs of the ancient municipal corporation of Queenborough, had come to congratulate the Royal pair and to wish them happiness. Every station through which the Royal train passed on its way to Windsor was packed with people, all anxious to cheer the Duke and his Princess. Many, and sometimes amusing, were the greetings that were called out to them as they passed. The Duke was obviously touched and delighted by the warmth of the welcome extended to his future wife, and he acknowledged the cheering on every possible occasion.

The wedding-presents were magnificent, and among the costly offerings there were many humble gifts from those who had received kindnesses from the Duke himself or from other members of the Royal Family, from a few soldiers' wives who were aware of the Duke's efforts to raise their status, from men who had served under him and had reason to be grateful for many unrecorded acts of consideration, and from many others in similar circumstances.

The Irish recognized the Duke's efforts to serve their "distressful country" by sending a deputation with an address and a magnificent piece of plate — a table centre-piece which could be used alternatively either as a dessert-stand or as a candelabrum for twenty-one lights. The stand was five feet high, and it was fashioned to represent the four seasons, the four elements, and the four quarters of the globe. A horse stood for Europe, a camel for Asia, a giraffe for Africa, and a bison for America, while the star and badge of the Order of St Patrick, encircled with shamrocks, were exquisitely engraved.

The deputation, which was headed by the Duke of Leinster, recognized in its address the good which had been done by the Duke's stay in Ireland, and continued:

> During the several periods of your Royal Highness's sojourn in Ireland you have gained the affections of all who have had the good fortune to approach you, and have won universal popularity.

The Royal Engineers subscribed for a dessert service of plate, and the Rifle Brigade presented a series of massive silver bowls, graduated in size and arranged on silver pedestals, "as a witness of the high esteem and respect in which he is held by his fellow-officers."

The Royal Artillery gave an interesting centre-piece representing a squad of artillery serving a sixteen-pounder gun. The whole was modelled from life, and the figures were actual portraits of men known to the Duke.

The inhabitants of Windsor subscribed for a diamond bracelet for the Princess, to whom the Queen gave some magnificent jewellery, including a diamond tiara, a pearl and diamond pendant, the jewel of the Royal Order of Victoria and Albert (a medallion showing the Queen and the Prince Consort), and the jewel of the Imperial Order of the Crown of India. The Crown Princess of Germany presented an oil-painting of fruit and flowers which she herself had painted specially for the occasion. The Prince of Wales gave a great mixing-bowl.

Whatever doubts Queen Victoria may have harboured as to the wisdom of the match on account of her dislike of the Prussians, these were speedily dispelled by the charm and sweetness of her prospective daughter-in-law. She soon conceived a deep affection for her, and afterward she spoke and wrote of her by the pet name of "Louischen."

She wrote to the Crown Princess:

Had I seen Louischen before Arthur spoke to me of his feelings for her, I should not have grieved him by hesitating for a moment in giving my consent to their union. She is a dear, sweet girl of the most amiable and charming character, and whatever nationality she was, I feel sure dear Arthur could not have chosen more wisely.

In commenting on the prospective marriage *The Times* said:

Of the Royal bridegroom nothing but good has ever been heard. Had he not been born in the purple he would have made a place for himself. . . . He has used his rank as a means of preparing himself for opportunities and been willing to leave it to circumstances whether they came or not. . . . He has a character which has made itself felt. . . . Princely rank promises to be used by him, not as itself a profession and an excuse for lethargy, but as a title to serve his country.

For over half a century since these words were written their purport has been abundantly justified.

Owing to the Duke's personal popularity great satisfaction was felt at the fact that his was a love-match into which no political or national considerations entered. He and his bride had considered nothing but their attachment, and their future happiness was thus secured. Everywhere the Princess went during the brief interval between her arrival in England and the wedding ceremony she was feted and made much of, and the impression which she made upon every one who came into contact with her gave rise to the feeling that the Duke was indeed to be congratulated on his fortunate choice. Though the wedding was to be a State ceremony, it was felt that it indeed represented a union of hearts. *The Times* summed up when commenting on the marriage:

Although a certain formal state is necessary to be observed on this occasion, the distinction between the marriage of Her Majesty's third son and that of, for instance, the Prince of Wales will not fail to be remembered in this respect. The wedding of the Heir to the Throne was a public act, the arrangements for which were made by the Government of the day, whilst the Duke of Connaught's marriage is a family solemnity carried out by direction of the Queen.

No one who saw the Duke in the days before his wedding could have any doubt as to his happiness. His pride and delight in the charming girl whom he was to marry were pleasant to watch, and a mere glimpse of the young couple turned formal congratulations into a heartfelt desire for a happy married life for them. This desire was fully to be gratified.

The Princess had hitherto been called Louise Marguerite, but on the occasion of her marriage her official title became Princess Louise Margaret, the latter name having a more familiar sound to English ears.

The wedding had been fixed for March 13, 1879, and as the day approached preparations were apparent everywhere. In all the regiments in which the Duke had served it was arranged that the day should be kept right royally. The Duke's battalion, the 1st Rifle Brigade, which was then stationed at Woolwich, spent the day at Cambridge Barracks, where there was much rejoicing, enhanced by the generous supply of plum pudding and by the quart of ale per man which the Duke had provided.

The officers of the battalion were all invited to the wedding, and a detachment, with Captain Burnell in command, was to form a guard of honour. To Mr Miller, who had been Bandmaster of the 1st Battalion for forty years, the Duke gave a handsome sword with a pearl and ivory handle, while to his personal servant, Edward Brown, he gave as a souvenir of the occasion a scarf-pin, with the Royal monogram and a crown in jewels.

Some slight surprise was caused by the fact that the thirteenth day of the month had been chosen for the Royal wedding-day, but neither the Duke nor his bride was superstitious, and when some one raised the point with him he replied, "No day that gave me my wife could possibly be anything but lucky." Here and there throughout the country were sprinkled a few cautious souls who thought that the day was ill-chosen and sent to the Duke, or more often to the Princess, various mascots to avert misfortune. These varied from a wishbone to a crooked sixpence. From Ireland came a four-leaved clover, delicately mounted in gold, which the Duchess prized for many years.

The children of the Prince of Wales soon took a great liking to their new aunt, and our present King, then a lad of thirteen, decidedly approved of his Uncle Arthur's choice.

"I think," he declared thoughtfully, "that before I choose my wife I shall have a look through Germany myself" — an announcement concerning which the Duke is credited with having twitted him in after-years.

Though the marriage was a genuine love-match, it was hoped in certain quarters that it would form yet another link to draw two great nations together. An English Princess was to be Germany's future Empress, a Prussian Princess was one of Queen Victoria's daughters-in-law, and it was felt that this would surely draw the German and the British Empires together. Perhaps for a time it did, until the son of the Empress who had had such a deep affection for the little Princess as she watched her growing up bore his part in bringing about a world war which threw so dark a shadow over the closing years of the life of the Duke of Connaught's beloved consort.

CHAPTER VII

MARRIAGE AND HOME LIFE
(1879; AGED TWENTY-NINE)

The Wedding — The Guests — Queen Victoria attends in State — A Gorgeous and Brilliant Ceremonial — Honeymoon at Claremont — Return to Windsor — "Madame, it is worthy of you!" — The Bride on Kilts — A Tour in the Mediterranean — A Veteran in Hospital — Bagshot — The Young Bride's Home Life — The Duke's Love of Music — "I'm the Connaught Rangers, sorr!" — The Duchess and the Bagpipes — An Annuity voted by Parliament — "Aunt Louischen" — The Duke still the Keenest of Soldiers.

The marriage of the Duke of Connaught and Princess Louise Margaret was celebrated with great pomp at St George's Chapel, Windsor, and it proved to be the most magnificent religious ceremony that had taken place there since the wedding of the Princess Royal twenty-one years previously. The wedding of the Prince of Wales had been comparatively quiet, for the Queen was still in mourning, but the Duke of Connaught led his bride to the altar amid surroundings of gorgeous ceremonial. The Chapel was brilliant with uniforms and ablaze with jewels. Everywhere the glitter of diamonds, the flash of emeralds, and the red glow of rubies caught the eye, while the gems worn by the Eastern potentates literally dazzled the onlookers. The exalted company included the King and Queen of the Belgians, the Crown Prince and Princess of Germany, Prince William of Prussia (now the ex-Kaiser), and the Maharajah and Maharanee Duleep Singh, but to English eyes the most interesting group was formed by the Princess of Wales and her daughters, the Princesses Louise, Victoria, and Maud, wearing picturesque costumes matching those of their mother, who looked regal in pearl brocade and amethyst velvet, with lace and sable trimmings.

Prince George (the present King) was also with his mother, while his elder brother. Prince Albert Victor, who was then a lad of fourteen, accompanied Queen Victoria.

The only shadow over the day was the absence of the Princess's brother, Prince Leopold. It had been arranged that he should be one of the supporters of the Duke, but unfortunately he had injured his knee at Darmstadt, where he had had to remain, and his place was taken by the Duke of Edinburgh, who, with the Prince of Wales, attended the bridegroom at the altar. The enforced absence of her brother was a great disappointment to the Princess, who, if circumstances had permitted, had hoped to have all the members of her family present, but the general happiness of the day was not marred by this slight trouble, and when at length the bride appeared her radiant expression gave good measure of her feelings.

Queen Victoria attended, in full state, but even the happy occasion did not cause her to cast aside the heavy mourning which she had worn continuously since the death of the Prince Consort. She was clad wholly in black, her sombre garb being relieved by some magnificent jewellery, which included the famous Koh-i-noor diamond, to be seen to-day in the Tower of London. This she wore mounted as a brooch, and it outshone even the jewels of the Indian visitors.

The Duke and his brother, the Prince of Wales, both wore the dark uniform of the Rifle Brigade, the bridegroom's tunic being ablaze with Orders, both British and Prussian. He made a gallant figure as he stood at the head of the aisle awaiting his bride, motionless and with his eyes fixed on the spot where she would first appear.

Of all the brides who have entered that famous Royal Chapel none walked up the nave with more magnificent escorts than did Princess Louise. On her right was her father, the Red Prince, in his general's uniform of scarlet with the black sash of the Prussian Eagle across his tunic; on her left was the Crown Prince Frederick, a kingly figure in his white uniform crossed by the vivid blue of the Order of the Garter.

Although the ceremony must have been of a somewhat trying character for a young girl, the Princess Louise was too happy to be self-conscious. She walked erect, timid yet radiant, bowing repeatedly to the assembled company as she passed up the aisle.

Her gown was of the richest white satin trimmed with lace, and she wore the myrtle leaves which are as much a part of the bride's wedding array in Germany as the orange-blossom is in England. Diamonds glittered in her hair, and a diamond necklace round her slender throat, while from her bridal wreath was suspended a lace veil of *point d'Alençon*.

She was attended by eight bridesmaids in white satin gowns embroidered with wild roses, and with the rose, the thistle, the shamrock, and the emblematic flowers of Germany. The gift of the bridesmaids to the bride was a bracelet of diamonds and pearls, representing myrtle and marguerites, the latter in reference to her second name.

The bride and groom both spoke their responses in firm, clear tones that could be heard all over the Chapel, and as the bride walked out of the church on the arm of the Duke it was agreed that no more radiant couple had ever passed through that historic porch.

At the private luncheon which followed the newly made Duchess cut the cake with her husband's sword, according to time-honoured tradition, the Duke smiling as he watched the operation. Pieces of the cake were, according to custom, distributed to friends and relatives in due course, but the young Duchess cut one special fragment herself and dispatched it to her old nurse in Berlin.

Shortly before four the bride changed into her travelling costume of white, and they set off for the honeymoon in a carriage drawn by four grey horses and escorted by a detachment of the Royal Horse Guards, but before they drove away they had to submit to the usual bombardment of old slippers, in which the Duke's young nephews took their part with much zest. The Duke deftly fielded one of them as it was about to hit the carriage and tossed it back to Prince George, with the laughing remark that he hoped that he batted better than he bowled, and so, through cheering crowds, the young couple left Windsor, the scene of the bridegroom's childhood and youth, to enter the married estate.

They drove straight to Claremont, which had been the residence of the King of the Belgians and once the English home of the deposed Royal House of France (Louis Philippe died there). There the first week of the honeymoon was spent in the quiet privacy to which even Royalties are entitled when newly wed. After that they returned to Windsor, and during the few days which they spent there the Duke was able to show his bride the Castle and some of the beauty spots of the neighbourhood. His young Duchess was enchanted with the grand old building. She and the Duke would wander all over it, the Duchess often with a guide-book in her hand, from which she would turn to her husband with eager questions about the history and legends of the Castle. The Duke has always been very much attached to Windsor. He knows its history from the time of its founding by William the

Conqueror to the present day, and as he and his young bride roamed about the grounds or paced the stately terraces he would tell her of the times when William the Norman rode out through its massive gateways to hunt the deer in Windsor Forest, of the State visits paid there by the monarchs of past centuries, and of the courtly compliment which had been paid to his mother by the Tsar Nicholas. On seeing the Castle for the first time the Tsar had exclaimed, "Madame, it is worthy of you!"

The Duchess was particularly interested in the pictures by Winterhalter of the Queen's nine children when they were young, and in one, already mentioned, in which the Duke figures as a child in fancy dress. The portraits of the little Princes in kilts — a garment unknown in Germany — gave rise to a good story. These portraits attracted her greatly, and in later years the Duke used often to repeat with amusement his young bride's remark when she first saw likenesses of him as a boy in Highland costume.

"You look very nice," she said, "but in my country we do not keep the boys so long in petticoats!"

In later years her own son (Prince Arthur) was destined to look "very nice" in the same dress, and the Duchess herself was sometimes photographed in family groups in Highland attire.

Although the people of Windsor respected the fact that the Duke and Duchess were on their honeymoon, yet sometimes, when they were out driving through the narrow streets of the old town over which the Castle broods or walking in the Great Park, there would be much raising of hats and dropping of curtseys, supplemented by the fluttering of handkerchiefs by ladies who wanted to win an answering smile from the pretty young bride whom their popular Duke had brought to his old home.

The Duchess was very fond of animals. The kennels at Windsor provided a great variety, especially of collies — at that time Queen Victoria's favourite breed. These were a great attraction to her, and if she chanced to be missing the Duke would usually find her in the Queen's special room at the kennels, where the walls were covered with portraits of old favourites. These portraits were often supplemented by locks of the deceased animals' hair.

Once the Duke, on returning to the Castle, sought immediately for the Duchess, as was his wont. Knowing that she was somewhere in the grounds, he turned rather sharply to a gardener's boy and asked the lad if he had seen the Duchess pass that way. The boy, rather frightened at being addressed for the first time in his life by the Duke, nodded his head and stammered, "Please, your Royal 'Ighness, Her Royal 'Ighness has gone to the dawgs!"

Both the Duke and Duchess were very fond of the sea, and after they left Windsor the Duke took his bride for a cruise in the Mediterranean. They called in at Gibraltar, where, remembering the fact that the Duke had served in the garrison, the Duchess made many tours of exploration. She also visited the soldiers in hospital, and several of them recounted to her their memories of service under the Duke.

"A fine soldier he was, miss — ma'am. Beg pardon, your Highness," one old sergeant said to her as she sat by his bedside. "Keen as mustard, in fact." Then, in a burst of confidence, "He couldn't have been better if I'd had the drilling of him meself."

The Duke on hearing this said that it was one of the finest compliments that he had ever been paid!

All this time Bagshot Park was being prepared for the reception of the Royal couple, and when it was ready the Duke and Duchess returned to England to take up their residence.

Bagshot, which is about twelve miles from Windsor, is surrounded by beautiful country. The village itself had in those days rather an old-world look, with its long village street beginning at a picturesque bridge over a small stream and ending at a country inn, the Hero of Inkerman, once, according to local tradition, an old coaching inn. Even at the time when the Duke took up his residence in the adjacent park all that remained of the original hostelry was a half-ruined white building which had long been tenantless.

The Duke's home is built of red brick in the Gothic style and faced with white Portland stone. It is of moderate size, and stands on a slight eminence not far removed from the site of old Bagshot House, once the home of the Duke and Duchess of Gloucester of the beginning of the nineteenth century. The surrounding park is of exceptional beauty. It is well timbered with various trees, including some fine old cedars. The carriage-drive leading through the park is nearly a mile long. It runs between broad avenues, and on either side woods and open country extend to Windsor in one direction and to the heather-clad Surrey hills in the other. The grounds are charming. The Duchess made the rose-garden her special care. It is in a secluded part of the grounds, and in the summer there are roses everywhere — round the fence by which it is enclosed, over the trellis-work, and distributed in beds and borders. It was always a favourite resort of the Duchess, and here, strolling amid the fragrant beauty of the roses or sitting in the summer-house, she spent many hours during the early part of her married life. There is also a fine shrubbery of rhododendrons blooming in profusion and in every variety of colour. The soil being particularly favourable, the rhododendrons and azaleas of Bagshot are famed throughout the kingdom.

Though the house is of moderate dimensions, the rooms are large, and some of them are decorated with fine examples of Indian carving. There are many pictures and one of the most highly prized among them depicts the Palace in Potsdam, where the Duchess was born; it was painted by the Empress Frederick. A path leads through the grounds to Bagshot Church, where the Duke and Duchess often attended divine worship while they were at Bagshot.

When they finally took up their residence there they quickly settled down to a country life, varied only by the Duke's absences on his military duties, and soon they took an intimate part in the life of the neighbourhood. They entertained their friends, paid the usual visits, and were often to be met with strolling through the lovely grounds of Bagshot Park or driving in the neighbourhood.

The Duchess took a great personal interest in the villagers, and though the strict Hohenzollern etiquette in which she had been brought up prevented her at first from following the example of our English Princesses and personally visiting the cottagers in the neighbourhood, she took a practical part in furthering all the philanthropic schemes of the village, often suggesting some plan whereby the lot of the sick and the needy might be alleviated. She was an excellent horsewoman and whip, and she was soon to be seen driving a pair of spirited ponies about the Surrey lanes. Once these ponies took fright and bolted, but the Duchess kept her head, and after rather an alarming drive she succeeded in getting her charges under control, though damage to the carriage compelled her to walk home through Bagshot Park, where she reported the accident herself, not having thought it worth while to procure a messenger.

The Duchess spent the first year of her married life much as any other English lady of rank would have spent it. She supervised her household, and her thorough domestic training made all homecraft easy. She took an enthusiastic interest in the gardens, in which she introduced several distinct improvements. She read a great deal, for she had a decided taste for literature and a wide knowledge of the authors of both her own and her husband's country, and she worked quantities of exquisite embroidery, for which she was noted in the family circle.

In the evenings there would sometimes be music, of which the Duke has always been fond. He always took a great interest in Army music, and he did much to improve it, besides being responsible for several innovations. In his own Brigade at Aldershot he introduced an improvement in the regimental quicksteps to which the men marched past at reviews and on parade. Each regiment played its own regimental call on brass instruments before the military march itself, and the change was acknowledged to be both effective and arresting.[1]

A good story is told of the Duke's visit to the school at Kneller Hall where so many military musicians have been trained. When he arrived all the students were drawn up ready to receive him, and before his inspection the Quartermaster passed up and down the ranks telling the lads that if, by any chance, the Duke should address them they were to be sure to call him "your Royal Highness" in reply. The boys listened with great attention, but they were unused to talking to Royalty, and it so happened that the very first boy to whom the Duke spoke was an Irish lad, who promptly forgot the Quartermaster's warning. The Duke asked the boy to what regiment he was attached, and what instrument he was learning. "I'm the Connaught Rangers, son, and I'm larnin' the cornet, sorr."

The Duke has always had a *penchant* for the bagpipes, and this the Duchess, not having been used to them, did not at first share. "You know," the Duke once explained to her, "to appreciate the bagpipes you ought to hear them coming towards you over the hills in the Highlands."

"No doubt," replied the Duchess, with a touch of humour, "but I appreciate them best when they are going away from me!"

The Duke had not been long in residence at Bagshot Park before he was known to every man, woman, and child in the village. He had a cheery word or a nod and a smile for every one, and he became as popular there as he had been at Woolwich, at Dublin, and at Gibraltar. His military duties naturally kept him much away from his home, but if possible he always returned to Bagshot for the week-end, much to the satisfaction of the Duchess, who often strolled down to the lodge

1 *Fifty Years of Army Music*, by Lieutenant-Colonel J. Mackenzie-Horan, C.V.O. (Methuen).

gates in order to be the first to see him enter the park.

Upon the occasion of his marriage Parliament had voted the Duke an additional £10,000 a year, but both he and his Duchess had simple tastes, and though the *régime* at Bagshot Park was consistent with the rank of the Royal residents, there was no trace of ostentation or of unnecessary expenditure either in the house itself or in the entertainments.

The Duchess speedily became a prime favourite with the Royal Family. The younger members openly adored "Aunt Louischen," as they called her, and there was always eager competition when it was known that a visit to Bagshot Park was proposed.

Happy though the married life of the Duke was, and greatly as he appreciated his home, it did not diminish his zeal for his military duties. He continued to pursue his professional career with the thoroughness which characterized him from the day on which he entered the Royal Military Academy to that upon which, as a Field-Marshal, he vacated his final appointment.

CHAPTER VIII

EACE SOLDIERING AT ALDERSHOT
FATHERHOOD
(1879-82; AGED TWENTY-NINE TO THIRTY-TWO)

A Visit to Balmoral — A Highland Welcome — The Wedding Cairn — Promotion to Brevet-Colonel and Major-General — Colonel-in-Chief of the Rifle Brigade — Brigade-Commander at Aldershot — "We didn't turn out to you, but to the Duchess!" — Dislike of Publicity — Politics — "Dear Arthur is so just" — A Review at Holyrood — The Queen's Account — The Duke's Spoiled Uniform — Birth of Princess Margaret ("Daisy") — Mother and Child — Fatherhood — A War-cloud on the Horizon.

In the autumn of the year of their marriage the Duke and Duchess of Connaught went to Scotland to stay with Queen Victoria at Balmoral. The Duchess was charmed with her husband's Highland home, where she took long walks with him over the hills, visiting the various little 'sheils,' or shelters, which the Queen had had built in the most picturesque parts of the estate.

Apart from its natural beauty and its associations with the Duke, Balmoral had an additional attraction for the Duchess because the Crown Prince Frederick had wooed his bride there, and the Crown Princess had shown her a little faded bunch of heather which had been gathered for her by her husband on a visit to Balmoral. He had climbed Craignaban, and on his return he laid the heather on the Princess's knee, saying, "I gathered this for you at the very top." The Empress Frederick treasured that bunch of heather until the day of her death.

The Highlanders gave the Duke and Duchess an enthusiastic welcome when they arrived at Balmoral, and as they drove up to the Castle many bouquets of flowers were tossed into the carriage. Some were of heather, and there was one, of the lucky white variety, of such dimensions that it must have taken many hours of patient searching to gather. One was of marguerites, in special compliment to the Duchess.

The Duke from his early boyhood had been a great favourite with the tenants on the estate, and he delighted many of the old retainers who had retired from service by paying a long round of calls, taking his bride with him, at the trim cottages with which the Queen had replaced the peat huts of former days.

"Prince Arthur" — the Duke was always Prince Arthur to them — "came to see me the day he brought his bonnie young leddie with him. I'd been wondering a lot aboot her, but noo I'm weel satisfied," was the sentiment confided by one old crone to another, and from a Scotswoman it was high praise.

It was Queen Victoria's custom to raise cairns, or little pyramids of stones, in different parts of the grounds in memory of the various members of the family or of family events. As far back as 1852 the Queen had raised her own cairn, the Prince Consort adding the final stone, and as the years went by the estate became dotted with these memorials, including one for each of her children. In her book *More Leaves from the Journal of a Life in the Highlands* Her Majesty described a visit to the Duke's cairn when he first brought his bride to Balmoral:

> Breakfasted with Beatrice, Arthur, and Louischen in the garden cottage, and at eleven we started for Arthur's Cairn. . . . When we had got to the top and had our glasses filled, and were standing close to the cairn, Dr Profeit, with a few appropriate words complimentary to Arthur, and with many good wishes for both, proposed their health, which was drunk with three times three. Then Arthur, with great readiness, returned thanks in a little speech. . . . We all placed a stone on the cairn, on which was inscribed:

ARTHUR DUKE OF CONNAUGHT AND STRATHEARNE,
Married to Princess Louise-Margaret of Prussia,
March 13, 1879

On May 9 in the year following his marriage the Duke was made a Brevet-Colonel, and on May 29 he was promoted to the rank of Major-General and appointed Colonel-in-Chief of the Rifle Brigade, in succession to the Prince of Wales. On September 30 he assumed the command of an Infantry Brigade at Aldershot, an appointment which he held until September 1883.

During the period of this command at Aldershot the Duchess used sometimes to stay at the Royal Pavilion, in order to be near her husband, and while they were there the Duke and Duchess used to attend the service at St George's Church. When the Duke relinquished his command they presented to the church a cross and candlesticks for the High Altar.

The Duke's dislike of all ostentation, and his desire to be treated, during his soldiering, in accordance with his military and not with his Royal rank, can be well illustrated by a story told by one who served with him at Aldershot.

While he was there he let it be understood that it was his direct wish that the honours and salutes offered to him should be given in accordance only with his military standing, and not with his position as a Royal Prince. He wished the soldiers to treat him as an officer who was in no way different from all the other officers. As a rule this was faithfully observed, but on one occasion, as he was driving with the Duchess past the lines of one of the regiments, the guard turned out, presented arms, and gave the Royal salute. The Duke stopped the carriage, and leaning out beckoned to the Irish sergeant in command of the guard. "Weren't you told," he asked, "that I was only to receive the salute as a general officer?"

"Yes, sorr," said the sergeant, with a twinkle in his eye, "but we didn't turn out to you, but to the Duchess!"

The Duke drove on with never a word.

So far did the Duke carry his dislike of any undue prominence being given to actions which he considered to be only part of his ordinary career that the public learned little of the many ways in which he served his country or of the real force and vigour of his views. Though his military work naturally and rightly absorbed most of his time, he took a keen interest in politics. The Queen often discussed matters of State with him, and she sometimes displayed to him the rather strong antipathies against some public servants for which Her Majesty was noted. The Duke was essentially a just man, and though he was a staunch Conservative he was in no sense a bigot. Among his most intimate friends he numbered men of varying political views.

"Dear Arthur is so just," the Queen once remarked to the Prince of Wales. "He seems to see the point of view of others, however widely their views may differ. In this he follows his dear father, and I love him most dearly for it."

The Duke, though by no means a bookworm, has been throughout the whole of his life a great reader, but he has not confined his reading to any particular lines of study, deeming it more essential for a man in his position to know something of everything rather than everything of something. So wide have been his excursions into literature that there is no topic of the day, no new movement, and nothing in any way touching the life of his country upon which he is not well informed.

During the early years of his marriage he held several levees, and he was also present at most of the reviews and military ceremonies that took place in various parts of the country.

He was present at a review which Queen Victoria held at Holyrood on August 25, 1881. As it was a wet day Her Majesty was much concerned (considerably more so than the Duke himself) about the rain, lest the Order that he was wearing should have a disastrous effect on his new uniform.

The Queen describes in her journal how she went to the review

in the open landau and four. . . . Affie, Arthur, George C. and his staff, and my gentlemen, all in uniform, riding with us. . . .

At 6 we got back . . . everyone soaked. . . . I had to change many undergarments. After with great difficulty getting a fire lit, I ran down to look after Beatrice and Marie. ... I went also to see after Arthur, who had been quite wet through, and his nice new General's uniform quite spoilt by the green of the ribbon of the Thistle coming off on to his tunic.

The Duke was much amused at the incident, and also at his mother's womanly concern over his spoiled clothes. "Doubtless," he remarked, "the ribbon was taking part in the agitation for Home Rule!"

Toward the end of 1881 it became generally known that there was to be a happy event at Bagshot Park, and Queen Victoria was much pleased by the prospect of again becoming a grandmother. She took the greatest interest in the arrival of the little stranger, and herself helped "Louischen" to make some of the small garments which the Duchess prepared for the layette. The Duke was much pleased at the prospect of fatherhood. He had always been fond of children, and he was a great favourite with the many small nieces and nephews who looked to "Uncle Arthur" for soldier stories and for gifts dear to the heart of warlike youth.

On January 15, 1882, a little daughter was born to the Duke and Duchess. In due course the baby was christened Margaret, after her mother. As she grew older she was known to her friends as "Princess Daisy."

From the first the baby led a normal life, sleeping, weeping, chuckling, and taking nourishment after the manner of babyhood. She was the delight of her young mother's heart, while the Duke, who had wished for a daughter, was delighted with her, and spent as much time as his many duties permitted in the nursery. The little Princess was inclined in her early childhood to resemble her mother, and this gave additional pleasure to the Duke, though the Duchess professed to find in her first-born a distinct resemblance to her husband.

After the birth of the Princess Margaret the Duke continued to divide his time between Aldershot and his home at Bagshot. To his Surrey home he became increasingly attached, constantly making some improvement and sometimes planning little surprises for the Duchess, whose affection for her English home deepened as the years went by.

The Duke had always taken a great interest in the foreign policy of the country, and for twelve months he watched the progress of events in Egypt with much anxiety. During the disturbances which took place in Alexandria early in 1881 he prophesied that there might be serious trouble within the next year or so, but he has never at any time been a scaremonger, so he only mentioned his fears to a few intimate friends.

Determined as he always had been to lose no opportunity of serving his country in the field, the Duke made up his mind that, should the occasion arise, he would by some means or other join any force to be sent overseas, and, when the Egyptian War broke out in 1882, he saw his opportunity. In those days, long before the late Lord Haldane, "the greatest War Minister of his generation," had reformed the Army, it was the practice to take battalions promiscuously, to form them into brigades under selected commanders, who might have had nothing to do with their peace training, and to send those extemporized brigades to the seat of war; so even an Aldershot brigade-commander had no certainty that he would be selected for a similar command when on active service.

Decisions in such matters rested with the Horse Guards, where His Royal Highness the Duke of Cambridge was commanding, subject to the approval of the Queen, so upon them the issue must depend before the Duke's desire could be fulfilled.

CHAPTER IX

ACTIVE SERVICE IN EGYPT
(1882; AGED THIRTY-TWO)

The Egyptian War — The Prince of Wales volunteers for Service — The Duke recommended for the Command of the Brigade of Guards — The Queen's Distress and Consent — Family Letters — A Brave Duchess — "My beloved little wife" — Interest in the Duke's Outfit — Farewells and Departure — Alexandria and Ramleh — March on Tel-el-Mahuta — Care for the Men in the Ranks — Tel-el-Kebir — Anxiety and Joy at Balmoral — Correspondence between Sir Garnet Wolseley and the Queen — "Mentioned in Dispatches" — "Cool courage under fire" — A Rumour without Foundation — "He took his chance like anyone else" — "No better Brigadier."

For some time affairs in Egypt had been causing serious anxiety. Ahmed Arabi Bey had formed a party which, though it called itself national, was really military and insurrectionary in its aims; it had as its slogan for raising disturbances "Egypt for the Egyptians." By May 1882 matters had come to such a pass that both the English and French fleets were ordered to anchor off Alexandria. The Khedive committed the rather serious error in judgment of making Arabi War Minister, a position which was used for the purpose of strengthening the fortifications of Alexandria and gathering troops in the town itself. In June there were serious disturbances at that place, with loss of life and danger to foreign residents. In July Sir Beauchamp Seymour, the Admiral in command of the British Fleet, warned Arabi to discontinue his warlike tactics, threatening to fire on the city unless he complied.

Arabi disregarded the warning, and after ships had been provided for the safety of the European inhabitants Great Britain sent an ultimatum demanding that the works of defence should be at once yielded to British custody. Arabi remained truculent, and eight British ironclads and five other vessels cleared for action and on July 11 began to bombard the forts. The French fleet weighed anchor and proceeded to Port Said before the bombardment, the French

Government being unwilling to act in concert with the British. Arabi's guns replied, and the firing continued until late in the afternoon.

On the next day the British bombardment was resumed until the white flag of surrender was hoisted on shore, but when British landing parties entered the city it was found that Arabi had withdrawn his troops and abandoned the town to the mob.

A terrible massacre followed. The dregs of the populace ran amok, pillaging, looting, and burning shops and houses in a wild frenzy and massacring nearly 2000 Europeans who had remained in the city.

Great Britain undertook the task of dealing with the situation, and at the appeal of Mr Gladstone the House of Commons passed a vote of credit for £2,300,000. At the end of August an army of about 23,000, reinforced later by about 11,000, arrived off Alexandria, and many troops landed there.

Sir Garnet (afterward Viscount) Wolseley was in command from first to last. He strongly resembled the Duke of Wellington in his dislike of exaggerated praise and of anything even approaching enthusiasm either in speech or in writing. He could appreciate good military qualities, but his dispatches were always couched in cold, almost bald language. Thus, when he did praise it might be taken for granted that there was excellent cause.

Directly it was known that an army was to leave England for active service in Egypt the Prince of Wales went to the Commander-in-Chief of the expedition and begged to be allowed to accompany the troops. He was most insistent, and Sir Garnet, whose opinion naturally carried much weight, did not at first refuse definitely, although he was opposed to any Royal Prince going to the seat of war unattached. The Prince went from Wolseley to the Queen, who at once vetoed the idea, much to the Prince's chagrin.

The Duke of Connaught, holding as he did the active command of an Aldershot brigade, saw his chance. He knew, in view of Her Majesty's recent decision, that it would not be expedient to apply direct to the Queen, and after the Prince of Wales's experience he had little hope of obtaining his desire through Sir Garnet Wolseley. He was determined, by some means, to accompany the field force to Egypt. He therefore approached the Duke of Cambridge, and persuaded him to mention the matter to the Queen. This, with much diplomacy, the Duke did. In his letter he wrote:

Finding that Arthur is medically fit to go, it has occurred to me as most advisable that he should have the command of the Brigade of Guards, which I think would be considered as a high compliment by those distinguished and admirable troops.

Even then the Queen could not at once be persuaded, and it required the earnest personal entreaty of the Duke himself before, with many anxious tears, she gave her consent.

She wrote in her journal at this time:

OSBORNE
20th July, 1882

When I read that my darling, precious Arthur was really to go, I quite broke down. It was like a dreadful dream. . . . Still, I would not on any account have him shirk his duty. Went with a heavy heart to bed.

Three days later she made another entry, in which she refers to a letter from the Duke:

I had such an affectionate letter from dear Arthur on the 22nd, in which he says, besides many loving words: "The parting from you and my beloved little wife is a thing I dread to think of, and I try to keep it out of my head as much as possible. . . . For me, who hate partings as much as any of my family, the idea of my leaving my home, wife, and child indefinitely is very sad, but duty comes before everything and my duty to my Sovereign and my country must ever come first." What a wrench, what an anxiety. He does not yet know when he will have to leave.

The Duchess, as may easily be imagined, was as much distressed as the Queen at the thought of losing her husband, but as a soldier's daughter it never occurred to her to try to dissuade him from what he considered to be his duty. She took a deep and practical interest in all matters connected with his equipment, and she contrived to hide her anxiety and grief with fortitude.

The day of leave-taking was one of mingled pride and sorrow for the Duke's family. The Duke, accompanied by the Duchess, visited the Queen to say good-bye on the evening of July 28, and the Queen has left on record a moving account of the farewell:

A little after 5 dear Arthur and Louischen arrived, come for the terrible leave-taking. We took tea all together, and sat talking for some time. Arthur told us of all his preparations, that he took only one horse, and was selling the others, what his dress would be, serge, quite loose, flannel shirt, high boots over breeches, and white helmet with a pugaree. His canteen and spy glass I gave him, and Louischen his *tente d'abri*. Felt very low. We four dined together. Arthur and Louischen both looked sad, but we tried to talk as cheerily as we could of all the preparations.

The Duke and his staff sailed in the Orient, and in August the Brigade of Guards (consisting of the 2nd Battalion of the Grenadier Guards, the 2nd Battalion of the Coldstream Guards, and the 1st Battalion of the Scots Guards) assembled at Ramleh, near Alexandria, under the Duke's command, with Captain Ivor Herbert as his Brigade Major and Major R. Lane, of the Rifle Brigade, as his A.D.C.

As the Guards marched through the streets of Alexandria and Ramleh their appearance and fine physique caused something like a panic among some of the onlookers, who, seeing these reinforcements, feared the final overthrow of Islam.

Sir Garnet Wolseley never had any doubt about the success of his campaign, but he expected that it would cost somewhere about 1200 casualties. He had made up his mind, rightly as events proved, that Arabi would make his great stand at Tel-el-Kebir, on the Cairo road, thirty miles from Ismailia, on the Suez Canal. For this reason he was anxious to muster his forces there secretly, believing that if he could deliver a sudden and really crushing blow from that direction the campaign would be over.

He had already cleared the Suez Canal, near which the enemy had placed dams to cut off the fresh-water supply and on August 26 General Graham advanced to seize Kassassin Lock, which controlled the flow. Here he was attacked by a superior force, but contrived to hold his own until reinforcements arrived under the command of Sir Baker Russell. Their combined force soon routed the enemy, with a total British loss of only eleven killed and sixty-eight wounded.

The transports which were carrying the Guards arrived at Ismailia on August 21, and they remained there until Wolseley discovered that Arabi was mustering his forces at Tel-el-Mahuta, on the Sweet Water Canal. He then directed that the Guards and a brigade of infantry should push on at once. In this campaign it was usually arranged that troops should march at dawn and again after the intense heat of the sun had passed away in the late hours, but the necessity of the occasion demanded that this particular march should be undertaken in the full heat and across soft sand that blistered the feet of the men, who had to plod through it ankle-deep. There were some cases of sunstroke and collapse, but the Duke kept his men well in hand during their trying five-hour march under a desert sun, and the powers of endurance they displayed under his leadership elicited strong praise from Sir Garnet, who, in his own words, "had every reason to be satisfied with the exertions they have made."

The Duke hurried the Guards up at once to the support of the troops already engaged, and under heavy shell-fire they occupied a line of outposts. This was the beginning of the Duke's first experience of active service since taking part as a regimental officer in the skirmishes in Canada, which had not been of such serious import. According to contemporary reports, he exhibited the coolness and resource of an old campaigner and a good leader, doing all that was possible for his men's welfare, and himself showing an example of indifference to personal danger.

In the morning they advanced on Tel-el-Mahuta, but, as this position had been abandoned by the enemy, the cavalry was sent on to Kassassin. The Guards remained at Tel-el-Mahuta, as Wolseley wished to concentrate his force before the battle of Tel-el-Kebir.

The Duke was anxious to push on with the cavalry, so that his Guards might be in the front line, and the idea of delay was irksome, but Wolseley's plans were well laid, and the Guards had to remain at Mahuta until September 30. They were not left in idleness. The clearing of the Canal had to be completed, railway lines required repair, and defences in the form of redoubts had to be undertaken. The Duke worked in person with his men, doing his utmost to cheer them and making every effort to get up supplies when they ran short. The same applied to equipment, and some sort of shelter, for lack of which the men had suffered greatly, had to be constructed. The heat, the dust and dirt, and the great difficulty of obtaining enough fresh water, all added to the burden under which the men laboured. The Duke shared all discomfort with those under him. In wax, as in previous years in peace, he insisted upon being given no preferential treatment, so his troops had the encouragement and the satisfaction of knowing that they served under a leader who not only appreciated their hardships, but was himself willing to endure them without complaint. It is rather times of such monotonous hard work and endurance of discomfort that test discipline than periods of spectacular effort, when all do equally well.

That the work of his Brigade was well done was proved by Colonel Drake, commanding the Royal Engineers of the First Division, who reported:

> I wish to bring to the notice of the Lieutenant-General Commanding the excellent work which has been done by the Brigade of Guards on the important work of opening the communications of the railway and canal. Engineering work, always fatiguing to the troops employed on military duties, has been especially harassing in this climate, but in consequence of the great interest shown in this work by the Guards officers in charge of parties, it has been executed by the men cheerfully and well, and it is my opinion that, had this spirit not been shown by officers and men, the progress of the army must have been for several days delayed.

On August 28 Arabi tried to recapture Kassassin, and the Guards were hurried forward from the reserve, returning to Mahuta at midnight. On September 9 he attempted a reconnaissance with over 8000 men and twenty-four guns; he was driven back with the loss of some of his guns. On the evening of September 12 Sir Garnet Wolseley had collected the whole of the British forces at Kassassin, only eight miles from Tel-el-Kebir, which was defended by about four miles of earth- works, with redoubts containing guns at intervals.

There followed a night march, no easy undertaking with men carrying full equipment and the need for complete silence in order to achieve surprise. The operation was entirely successful, and by dawn 2000 cavalry, 11,000 infantry, and sixty guns were massed secretly within a quarter of a mile of the enemy's lines. General Graham's Brigade was on the right, and Sir Archibald Alison's Highland Brigade on the left of the front line. This arrangement greatly disappointed the Duke, who had confidently hoped and expected to be in front of the advance. He expressed this hope to Sir Garnet Wolseley, who, however, decided otherwise. It was Sir Garnet's intention to keep the Guards in reserve. He expected a stout resistance, and he wished to use these fine troops as reinforcements, so the Duke had no course but to obey.

The attack had been planned so well that the enemy did not detect the approach of the British troops until they were within a few yards. Then the first shot rang out. A Highlander fell, and the battle began in earnest. Along part of the line the enemy offered a furious resistance at first and kept up so heavy a fire that at one time it seemed as if the assault would be held up. The second line came up and pressed forward with a will, carrying the position with the bayonet, much of the fighting being at close quarters. The British losses were small. Eleven officers and forty-three men were killed; twenty-two officers and 323 men were wounded. The enemy lost heavily. Their dead numbered nearly a thousand, and three thousand were taken prisoners, with sixty guns.

When Arabi's army realized that the battle was lost they took to flight, and the British cavalry pursued until it was seen that the enemy was entirely disorganized and that all that the men wanted was to get away and make for their homes.

On the next day, September 14, Arabi himself surrendered, and, the fighting being over, the British pushed on and occupied Cairo. Sir Garnet Wolseley, with the Duke and a company of the Scots Guards as escort, went by train to the capital. The Guards Brigade followed, and was soon called upon to render further proof of its discipline in dealing with an explosion which occurred at Cairo railway station. Its prompt appearance under the command of the Duke did much to prevent panic in an excitable populace.

The Duke's coolness under fire and his conduct in action had attracted the attention of Sir Garnet Wolseley, who reported promptly to the Queen. Her Majesty and the Duchess had naturally been waiting with intense anxiety reports of the battle of Tel-el-Kebir, in which they knew that the Duke was to be engaged. The Queen records in her journal her feelings when at last the news arrived:

BALMORAL
13th Sept.

Had a telegram saying that . . . fighting was going on and that the enemy had been routed with heavy loss at Tel-el-Kebir. Much agitated. On coming in got a telegram from Sir J. McNeill: "A great victory, Duke safe and well." The excitement very great. Felt unbounded joy and gratitude for God's great goodness and mercy.

The same news came later from ... Sir G. Wolseley, which most welcome and gratifying telegram I annex. [After giving an account of the battle the telegram ended with the words, "Duke of Connaught is well, and behaved admirably, leading his Brigade to the attack."] Showed it at once to Louischen, who was quite overcome with joy at knowing dear Arthur safe and so much praised. In all our joy, it is grievous, though, to think of our losses.

Later the Queen wrote to Sir Garnet Wolseley in reply to his announcements:

BALMORAL CASTLE
13th Sept.

The Queen begins her letter to Sir Garnet Wolseley, by congratulating him again on the very brilliant victory of her brave troops, which he may well be proud of having commanded. The praise of her beloved son and his safety are subjects of deep thankfulness and rejoicing. The last few weeks have been most trying to her daughter-in-law the Duchess of Connaught and herself, and the last few days before the victory of Tel-el-Kebir were almost unbearable, from the suspense and uncertainty.

Of his personal impressions of the Duke Sir Garnet wrote to Her Majesty:

TEL-EL-KEBIR
Sept. 14*th*

On all sides I hear loud praises of the cool courage displayed yesterday when under extremely heavy fire by His Royal Highness the Duke of Connaught.

I need scarcely say what a relief to my mind it was to find him unhurt and so cheery and happy when I met him at the enemy's works. He is a first-rate Brigadier-General, and takes more care of his men and is more active in the discharge of his duties than any of the Generals now with me.

He has this moment rode up to my tent. I never saw him looking better or in better spirits.

To this letter the Queen replied:

Sept. 30*th*

. . . She need not say how immensely gratified and proud she is to hear his high praise of her darling son Arthur. This dear soldier son has never given her a day's sorrow or anxiety except on the score of his health occasionally, and she cannot deny that she suffered terrible anxiety during those four weeks of this exceptionally trying campaign.

. . .

The Queen would wish to thank Sir Garnet very particularly for what he has said in that letter about Arthur. He has proved himself worthy of his own dear father who she wishes could have lived to see his child distinguish himself as he has done, and of the name he bears, and of his great godfather. The Duchess of Connaught is equally proud naturally of her dear husband.

The Duke was twice mentioned in dispatches, *The London Gazette* of October 31 recording:

Major-General H.R.H. the Duke of Connaught, commanding the First Brigade, has evinced on all occasions throughout this war the utmost zeal for his profession. No one could have taken a greater care of his men than he has done, providing for their wants and comforts and setting them an example of cool courage under the very heavy musketry fire by which they were assailed on the 13th September.

In a dispatch dated October 6 there appeared this tribute:

The Brigade of Guards took part in the night march when the column was guided by the stars before Tel-el-Kebir. . . .

The Second Brigade was well supported by the Brigade of Guards under H.R.H. the Duke of Connaught. . . .

I cannot close this dispatch without placing on record how much I am indebted to the following officers who took part in the battle of Tel-el-Kebir and by their zeal and ability contributed so largely to its success.

Among the names there figured that of the Duke.

The Queen was staying at Balmoral during the battle of Tel-el-Kebir, and the Duchess also was staying there, glad of Her Majesty's support during this most anxious time. When at last the news of the decisive victory came through there were, as may be imagined, great rejoicings in the Duke's Highland home. In *More Leaves from the Journal of a Life in the Highlands* Her Majesty gives an interesting account of the proceedings:

I asked Leopold[1] to propose "The Victorious Army in Egypt," with darling Arthur's health, which was heartily responded to, and poor Louischen was quite upset. After this. Dr Profeit proposed "The Duchess of Connaught" and at Brown's suggestion he also proposed "The little Princess." The sweet little one had watched the procession in Chapman's (her nurse) arms with her other attendants, and was only a little way off when her health was drunk.

... Louischen had received a very long and most interesting letter from Arthur about that dreadful march on the 25th.

That night a bonfire blazed on Craig Gowan to celebrate the victory and the news that the Duke was safe.

The Duke of Connaught, on his part, felt deeply the British losses and the discomforts and sickness which followed among the men. In volunteering for active service he had felt that his training for the high Army commands which he was destined to fill would not be complete without that experience. He learned a great deal in his Egyptian campaign, and this experience stood him in good stead in later days. It helped him to understand the needs of troops on active service, and it inspired many of his later efforts to improve their lot and in many ways to promote their welfare. Of these we can here quote one example. Knowing the Duke's influence in high quarters, Wolseley was able, through his aid, to point out the great superiority in such campaigns of the khaki clothing of the Indian contingent over the red and blue in which British troops had for the last time taken the field. Although the boon to the British Army has been inestimable, many years were to pass before the lead was followed by foreign armies.

The Duke of Connaught was destined, years after the event, to suffer from unfounded rumours of the type which cause distress but must be borne in dignified silence by those in high places, who can look for no redress. In March 1893 Lord Wolseley found it necessary to write the following letter:

The story printed in *The Manchester Guardian* that I received a communication when in Egypt from one in high authority to take care of the Duke of Connaught and keep him in the rear and out of danger is absolutely and entirely untrue. No one suggested that I should in any way deal with H.R.H. differently from the other Generals in command of brigades, nor did I do so.

1 The Duke of Albany.

He took his chance like anyone else, and, as I reported to you at the time, I had no better Brigadier in the force then under my command.

I am glad to have this opportunity of explicitly denying this absurd story, as ungenerous as it is untrue.

This letter explains the nature of the rumours.

If, as is probable, the rumour reached His Royal Highness's ears during the ten years that intervened before it was so decisively laid to rest and buried, it must have caused much pain to one who had always resented being treated as a Prince when doing his duty as a soldier, and on this occasion "took his chance like anyone else."

CHAPTER X

AFTER THE WAR— RETURN TO ENGLAND
(1882-83; AGED THIRTY-TWO)

The Aftermath — The Queen and Sir Garnet Wolseley — Enteric Fever — The Duke's Influence — His Care for the Patients — His Study of the People of Egypt — His Views on the Situation — Official Visits — The Queen and the Guards — The Sacred Carpet — Home again — The Queen presents War Medals at Windsor — Pictures of Tel-el-Kebir — The Duke's Widening Experience and its Results.

With the trial of the ringleaders the rebellion was ended. After a long hearing, during which all the eloquence of an English advocate was employed in an effort to save Arabi, the rebel leader was sentenced to death. The Khedive at once commuted the sentence to one of perpetual banishment from Egypt, and, as a result of the campaign. Great Britain and France withdrew their joint control of Egypt. The Khedive resumed full authority. The administration was thoroughly reconstructed, and the British continued to occupy the country to assist in carrying out the reforms upon which Lord Dufferin, the English Plenipotentiary, had insisted.

Queen Victoria had naturally been much gratified by the high praise which the Duke of Connaught had earned from all who had personal knowledge of his share in the campaign, and, knowing that Sir Garnet Wolseley was by no means given to eulogy, she was specially impressed by his opinion, which she recorded in her journal:

BALMORAL CASTLE
30th Oct., 1882

... Sir Garnet Wolseley, who only landed on the 28th, arrived. . . . He gave very good accounts of Arthur. . . .

I saw Sir Garnet again for about an hour before dinner, and began by expressing my thanks for his kindness to Arthur. He repeated how highly he thought of him, adding, "I should say more if I were not speaking to your Majesty." On the day of the battle, Arthur had been exposed to the hottest fire Sir Garnet had ever been under. It was perfectly deafening and dreadful, and he was greatly alarmed until he knew Arthur was safe. Those who were near, and with, Arthur describe him as having been perfectly cool throughout, but he had a great deal of very harassing work.

Army hygiene had not reached its present high standard, and, owing to the climate and to scarcity of pure water, the troops suffered very much from sickness. The lessons of the Crimea had not, however, been without results, and the Army Medical Advisory Board did their utmost to cope with the difficulty. The epidemic of enteric fever was severe, and many of the men came through the fire of Tel-el-Kebir only to die in hospitals of the disease. The sufferings of his men caused the Duke great anxiety, more particularly as an unfounded rumour was current that the troops were being kept in Egypt, and thus exposed to the pestilence, longer than was necessary. He did his utmost to arrange matters for the men's comfort. He visited them in hospital as often as his other duties permitted, and he wrote very strong letters home to various administrative departments, urging them to send out more nurses and adequate supplies for the patients. He also wrote to the Queen, urging her to use her influence in the matter. As a result Her Majesty wrote to Sir Garnet Wolseley:

The Queen looked back at the telegram which Sir Garnet sent her and which caused her and the Duchess of Connaught and all of us such pleasure and sends him a copy of it, as he will see he used the words, "we have suffered severely."

She is so much disturbed to-day by letters from Arthur and Sir J. McNeill speaking of the great sickness among the Guards. Arthur has mentioned it in several letters, and he fears they have complained and thinks it is his fault that they were kept there so long, which it certainly is not, and she fears she is as much to blame about that as anyone, only of course if we had known that we were getting worse we could have altered this and let them come home earlier.

Arthur says in a letter she got to-day: "I went all over the hospitals here two days ago, and I regret to say there are a very large number of sick, especially amongst the Guards. Nearly all the cases are of enteric fever, and I am sorry to say many of them have ended fatally. I have great hopes of the healthier weather of the last few days to bring about a change for the better."

Sir Garnet can imagine that the Queen is much disturbed about this. Could nothing be done to send out nurses, beds obtained, anything more for their comfort?

She spoke and wrote strongly to Gladstone and Lord Granville to see Sir Garnet without delay and to arrange about medical comforts. The representations of the Duke had the effect of procuring much alleviation of the men's sufferings, but the knowledge of this unforeseen outbreak greatly overshadowed any pleasure he had derived from his experience of active service and the high praise that he had earned.

After the fighting was over and the rebels had been disbanded the Duke spent the rest of his time in Egypt in Cairo, studying questions of administration and all matters concerning the Egyptians themselves. There is no doubt that the time which he spent in Egypt helped him materially in his Indian career. It deepened his knowledge of native races and of the administration of dependent states. During his time in Cairo he penetrated into various parts of the city and engaged in conversation with all kinds of people, both Europeans and natives, many of whom were ignorant of his identity and therefore spoke with perfect freedom. Always a shrewd judge of men, he soon gained a clear impression both of the native character and of the trend of all affairs likely to affect the future of the country. In a letter to Queen Victoria he gave an excellent summing up of Egyptian politics:

8th Oct.

The Courts Martial for the trial of Arabi and the other ringleaders have begun to sit, but although they sit ten hours a day, the proceedings are dragging along very slowly, and until the prisoners have been judged and sentenced, the Arabs will not quiet down entirely and progress towards the re-establishment of order will be delayed. I begin to doubt whether Arabi will be hung, and if he is not, I am terribly afraid that the rebellion will not be entirely stamped out, and order will only be maintained by the presence of a large English force. Although the people in this country have no affection for Arabi, they believe in him and in his power of thwarting the Europeans and the advancement of civilization. The Egyptians are a most ignorant people and positively hate the idea of being enlightened, and yet at the same time they are very avaricious and their one idea is baksheesh.

You will have heard from Sir John how well our short trip up the Nile went off. Apart from its being a very pleasurable and interesting excursion, I think it was a very good thing politically. I think the more your uniform is seen in any corner of Egypt the better; it then brings home to the inhabitants that our army is in occupation of the country and that theirs has ceased to exist.

The entertainment given to the Guards who accompanied me was to my mind the most interesting feature of our trip. It will be known all over Upper Egypt, and the fine appearance and good conduct of the men of the Grenadier and Coldstream Guards who accompanied me will be commented on in every bazaar. In an Oriental country like this there is nothing like ocular demonstration; that goes further than anything; for unless the people see a thing, you can't get them to believe it. For this reason I regret so much the line taken in forcing an English counsel to defend Arabi and the other rebel leaders on the Egyptian Government. Of course, the Court Martial is composed solely of Egyptian officers, whose education is far inferior to those of the English lawyers, who in cross-examination will be able to twist the Egyptians round their fingers as easily as possible.

I fear too that the proceedings of the Court will be thereby tremendously delayed, as the lawyers will require time to get up a tremendous 'case' and for this purpose every kind of political and international matter may be raked up.

Affairs require to settle down in Egypt before anything can be done to improve the administration of the country, but till these trials have taken place and justice has been meted out to these scoundrels, the country will remain in an unsettled state.

The present Government here are most anxious that Arabi should have a fair and open trial, but they think it very hard that they should not be allowed to manage the trial according to their own laws. Col. Sir Ch[arles] Wilson is watching the case, and it seems to me that is sufficient guarantee that nothing unfair should be allowed to take place. Should Arabi and his fellow-agitators get off, it will doubtless cause the resignation of the Khedive's Ministry, and possibly the abdication of the Khedive himself. Knowing the immense importance of the whole question and the deep interest you take in it, I venture thus plainly to put my own views before you. I have reason to know that Sir Garnet entirely agrees with what I say, and that he views the present attitude of the Government with regret and with fear for the future.

23rd Oct.

To-day is the first day of the Bairam, the great national New Year's feast, which lasts 3 days. Everybody pays their respects to the Khedive to-day, and, in company with all our officers, I am going to pay the Khedive an official visit myself.

All Europeans and loyal Egyptians take the same view, viz., that an example must be made of Arabi and the rebel leaders, and that English troops must remain for some time. If this is not done, there will be no security in this country, and all the Europeans will immediately leave the country and all the troubles must begin over again.

While the Duke was in Cairo the headquarters were in the Abdin Palace, and on September 25 the Khedive made a State entry into the capital amid scenes of much magnificence and ceremony, calculated to impress the native population. British troops lined the streets, and the Khedive was given a fine reception, in which, to the Khedive's gratification, the Duke took due part. There is no doubt that his presence with the Guards in Egypt during the time that he spent there had a most favourable influence upon British prestige.

On September 30 the Khedive reviewed the troops, and two days later, in order to make it clear that the normal life of the Palace was once more in progress, he gave a great garden-party at the Gezireh Palace. This brilliant gathering was attended by all the prominent Europeans and Egyptians in the city. It was the sole topic of conversation for several days.

The official visits which the Duke paid to the Khedive created an excellent impression. They did much to convince the people that the Khedive was always certain of British protection, and that any rebellion against the recognized authority of law and order would certainly be punished. This impression the Duke was wisely anxious to create.

The fact that the population of Cairo was so mixed gave the Duke excellent opportunities for studying native character. He encountered Mohammedans, Copts, and Jews, as well as Greeks and Armenians, and he met many representatives of different nations in the European contingent of the population. He also visited the military schools at the Abbasseeyah and the commercial and arts schools in the city. His home letters, both to the Queen and to the Duchess and his other relatives, contain many shrewd comments on every aspect of Egyptian life.

At that time the influence of the European in Cairo was manifest in the Italian opera and the French theatre. The Duke took special interest in the collection of Egyptian antiquities which had been made for the Khedive by M. Mariette and housed in the Palace of Darb Algamâmîz. The collection contained some wonderful copies of the Koran and some very rare manuscripts. He spent many hours inspecting the treasures. He also went treasure-hunting on his own account, and wearing mufti he visited the bazaars and the odd little shops in which the city abounded. There he contrived to pick up some most interesting curios to take home for the Duchess and the Queen. These included some very fine scarabs and a jewelled scimitar of magnificent workmanship, and he also secured a Roman antiquity which had been unearthed in the old Roman remains of Kasr-es-Shammah (Palace of Perfumes).

When it was clear that matters were really quietening down in Egypt it was arranged that some of the troops should be sent home, and it was suggested that the Guards should be among the first to leave. This the Duke did not wish. He and his men had shared in the campaign, and he wanted also to share in any duties that might be left for the troops to complete until Egypt was completely evacuated. When the suggestion was made to him that he might leave he refused to entertain the idea, and he wrote to the Queen giving his reasons, adding that he felt that she would fully appreciate his motives and endorse his resolution. This Her Majesty did, as will be seen from a letter from her secretary, Captain Edwards, to Mr Hugh Childers:[1]

BALMORAL
20th September
I am commanded to let you know that the Queen is most anxious that the Duke of Connaught and his Brigade should not be the first to come home. Her Majesty feels that the Guards have not perhaps been in a position to see so much actual hard work as has fallen to the lot of some other regiments, though they have fully shared in the toil and exertion of the campaign: it is on this account that the Queen hopes that any appearance of their being hurried home may be avoided; such a course might give rise to misrepresentation and occasion ill-natured remarks.

1 Then Secretary of State for War.

I am to suggest therefore that a hint might be given to Sir Garnet Wolseley to this effect.

The hint was, of course, acted upon. The Guards were not the first to come home, and, whatever foundation there may have been for Her Majesty's fear of "ill-natured remarks," no one who had the slightest knowledge of the Duke's military career could possibly have doubted his keen desire to do his full duty and to shirk nothing that might have fallen to the lot of any of the men serving with him.

Before the Duke left Cairo he witnessed the famous Procession of the Sacred Carpet, which was carried through the streets on the way to Mecca, and for the first time in history the escort for the carpet was provided by British troops. The arrangement led to some discussion among both Christians and Mohammedans, but the prevailing feeling was that it was more of a compliment than anything else.

At last the Duke felt that, in fairness to his men, he ought no longer to exert his influence to keep the Guards in Egypt, and in due course the Brigade was sent home, receiving a rapturous welcome from the people.

At Windsor Castle, on November 21, the Queen gave the medals for the Egyptian campaign, and we find this account in her journal:

WINDSOR CASTLE
21st Nov.

First came Sir G. Wolseley, on whose breast I pinned the medal, followed by the officers and men of the Navy. It was a proud moment for me when dear Arthur came up amongst the Generals, and I pinned his medal on him. . . . I stood on the fine Turkish carpet which had belonged to Arabi, and which has been taken out of his tent, after Tel-el-Kebir. Arthur slept on it that memorable night, and gave it me when he arrived.

This carpet which the Duke had brought back to Her Majesty was a fine specimen of Eastern handicraft. Its weaving represented inlaid jewel-work, and the colours were particularly harmonious, the texture unusually fine. The Queen had suggested that the Duchess of Connaught might like to have it as a souvenir, but both the Duke and Duchess thought it a fitting tribute for Her Majesty. That she should use it when presenting the medals for the campaign was the Duke's own idea.

Besides the war medal, the Khedive's Star, and mentions in dispatches for his services, the Duke received the Companionship of the Bath and the Order of the Medjidie, 2nd Class.

The battle of Tel-el-Kebir was commemorated by several pictures. The best known of them is, perhaps. Lady Butler's *After the Battle: Arrival of Lord Wolseley and Staff at the Bridge of Tel-el-Kebir*. In this Sir Garnet Wolseley and Sir John Adye are in the centre, while the Duke of Connaught is also a prominent figure. Sir John Adye mentions an interesting fact about the bridge. During the battle the Commander-in-Chief sent him with a message to the Indian troops, and on his way back he met the Duke, with his staff, on the exact spot that Lady Butler chose for the scene of her picture. Another one, now in the Royal collection, is by R. Caton Woodville. It shows the Duke on horseback at the head of his men. Yet another one, painted by Orlando Norrie, in the Royal collection shows the Queen distributing the medals. It gives an excellent likeness of the Duke.

After his return the Duke continued to take a great interest in Egyptian affairs, and the Queen frequently sent for him to discuss questions of policy affecting that country. He made several shrewd prophecies about the future of Egypt and the disaffection there, and in private conversation with Her Majesty foretold several events, almost up to the time of the disaster of Khartoum.

Though he was first and last a soldier, he was well versed in the administrative policy of his country, and on various occasions when duty has taken him to different parts of the Empire he has sent home reports of considerable value to different Government departments. A firm believer in the Empire to which he has devoted his life, his powers of diplomacy have at times enabled him, within the limitations of his own sphere, to be as much an international peacemaker as King Edward, while his wide cosmopolitan circle of friendships has enabled him to gain an insight into affairs which would have made little appeal to a man of narrow judgments or of prejudiced views.

CHAPTER XI

HOME LIFE AT BAGSHOT
(1883; AGED THIRTY- TWO TO THIRTY-THREE.)

Birth of Prince Arthur of Connaught — The Duchess in her Home — Sketches and Portraits — "The Bogey Book" — Queen Victoria as Grandmother — The Royal Order of the Red Cross — Soldiers' Families — Games for Girls — Surrey Football — Soldier or Half-back — Devotion to Lawn Tennis — Public Activities — The Other Man's Point of View — Study of Indian Problems — The Friend of the Under-dog — Interest in the Irish Question — Colonel of the Scots Guards — Trouble in Egypt and the Sudan — The Duke appointed to an Indian Command — The Duchess and the "White Man's Burden" — Farewell to Bagshot Park.

Experience of war service, the serious side of his profession, produced upon the soldier Duke the same effect as it has upon many who follow his chosen career, a wider outlook upon foreign affairs and a strengthening of individual purpose. To this aspect of his character we shall turn in due course, and meanwhile shall dwell for the time upon the happy period of home life, first at Windsor and afterward at Bagshot Park, during which, after the usual war furlough, he was reappointed in April to the command of a brigade at Aldershot.

The great event in 1883 was the birth at Windsor Castle, on January 13, of a son to reinforce the Royal Nursery, where the baby Princess Margaret had hitherto reigned supreme. By those addicted to superstition due note will be taken of the date of the small son's birthday, the 13th of the month. It was on the 13th of March that the wedding of the Duke, the most fortunate event in his career, had been celebrated, also at Windsor. The Duke has always maintained that, so far from being unlucky, the number 13 has with him been an omen of good fortune, and this belief was strengthened by the date of the safe arrival of his sturdy small son, soon afterward christened Arthur Frederick Patrick Albert (four names recording family connexions) and now well known to the world as Prince Arthur of Connaught, who has already followed in his father's footsteps to the rank of Colonel in the Army and to the post of Governor-General of a great self-governing Dominion.

As may be imagined, his birth was welcomed with joy by the Royal Family, and it is on record that the little Princess Margaret did not resent vacating her precedence as "Baby" in the nursery and that she retained throughout her life a strong bond of affection for her only brother.

The home life of the Duchess in due course resumed its normal tenor. One of her great diversions was sketching, and she would often sit in the grounds busy with her pencil, with her babies by her side and, if he were at home, the Duke not very far away. She made some very charming studies of Princess Margaret and of Prince Arthur in their infancy, and these sketches are still treasured in the family. She would also sometimes try the Duke for a model, and at Bagshot Park there are still many examples of her artistic skill.

There are, of course, many fine portraits of the Duke in existence. One of the best is by J.B.E. Detaille, and in that both the Duke and the Prince of Wales arc shown on horseback with troops in the background. This portrait hangs in the household dining-room at Windsor. Upon his return from the Egyptian campaign in November 1882 the Duke had been constantly sketched and photographed for the Press, and, snapshot photography having made less progress than it has to-day, some of the pictures were anything but complimentary. The Duchess made a collection of photographs, or rather two collections, one of the best likenesses and one of the worst ones. She pasted the very bad ones in an album she called "the bogey book," and she used to produce this for the amusement of her relatives when they visited her. The Princess of Wales once asked whether she was going to keep it. "Certainly!" answered the Duchess. "You see if Arthur ever shows signs of being vain I can show him himself as some people saw him!" Vanity never having been a characteristic of the Duke, there is no record of the threat having ever been put into practice.

The Duchess, as already mentioned, was fond of animals, and she was particularly attached to the pair of ponies which she usually drove. She would carry the infant Princess Margaret to the stables and help her to feed the docile beasts with sugar. A model dairy was also added under her directions to the equipment of Bagshot Park, and when she was not away on her many travels this afforded an interesting hobby for herself and the children.

The Duke and Duchess did a certain amount of entertaining at Bagshot, and in the season they attended many Court functions and State dinners in London. The Duchess was a great favourite in the Royal circle, and "Louischen" was always a welcome guest at Buckingham Palace. The Queen would sometimes drive down to Bagshot to pay an informal visit to her son and daughter-in-law, and she was particularly fond of the little Princess Margaret, who is said to have been able to do very much what she pleased with the august lady, who was not as a rule given to spoiling small people.

It may be that the little Princess had found her way more readily to her Royal grandmother's heart because it was in the Queen's arms that she had spoken her first word, pointing her baby finger at one of the Queen's dogs and saying "Bow," but it may be also that even the highest in the land are addicted to the proverbial habit of the very strictest of mothers of petting the children of the second generation, for whose upbringing they are not responsible.

In her public capacity the Duchess always gave her most enthusiastic support to the Red Cross. The Queen was the Patron of the Society when the English branch was first formed. The Empress Frederick, the great friend of the Duchess in her girlhood, had been a firm supporter of the Society's work in Germany, the Prince of Wales was President, and the Duke of Connaught was one of the Trustees. When Her Majesty instituted the Royal Order of the Red Cross (R.R.C.) on St George's Day 1883 the Princess of Wales and the Duchess of Connaught were among the first to become members.

The Duchess continued to take the greatest personal interest in her husband's military career, and she was always ready to enter into any scheme for the improvement of the lot of the soldiers' wives and children or for the welfare of the soldiers themselves. In later years she became President of the Aldershot Branch of the Soldiers' and Sailors' Families' Association, an office that was also held by Lady Audrey Buller, with whose husband, Sir Redvers Buller, the Duke was constantly associated during his military service and at manoeuvres.

The Duke took a great interest in all forms of sport, both in military circles and in civil life. Throughout his career he has always advocated the encouragement of games as a part of training in adolescence, and he was so firmly convinced of the great advantages of physical exercises that from early days he was a staunch upholder of sports for girls, even at a time when Victorian sensibilities were inclined to be shocked at the idea of a girl revealing the fact that her legs extended upward from the ankles.

As a Surrey resident he became President of the Surrey Football Association, and he was always a keen critic of the game. A good story is told about his knowledge of Association football. In his first years at Bagshot he was walking across a field in Surrey when he came upon two teams of urchins playing the game with a rather dilapidated ball and with coats to mark the goal-posts. They were engaged in a heated dispute about a point in the rules, and they appealed to the Duke, whom they did not know, to act as referee. He good-naturedly agreed, and a little later showed them some passes.

"Are you a footballer, guv'nor?" asked one admiring youth.

"Er — no. I'm a soldier," answered the Duke, with a smile.

"A soldier! What a waste! When you might 'ave played 'alf-back!"

Almost from the time when lawn tennis in its present form was first introduced the Duke was an enthusiastic player. He played as often as his duties permitted, and during his visits to Windsor he always made a point of playing on the courts there. The Queen and the Duchess would look on, commenting critically on his strokes. Owing to his long residences abroad, he plays best on hard courts, and in his younger days he was a redoubtable opponent, with a service very difficult to return. The game has always appealed to him strongly, and up to the present day he follows the championships closely, often attending the finals at Wimbledon when he is in England and sometimes presenting the prizes at the Riviera tournaments.

To the youthful part of the population of Bagshot it was always a great disappointment that the Duke did not wear his uniform when he was at home. Small boys would peep longingly through the palings of the Park in the hope of catching sight of him in the full panoply of a general officer. "I suppose he only puts it on for the Duchess to see in the evening," one urchin remarked ruefully after he had waited long by the lodge gates, only to be rewarded by the sight of the Duke riding out in the dress of a country squire.

In his public life the quality which has most endeared the Duke to those with whom he came into contact has been perhaps a genial sympathy and faculty for seeing the other man's point of view. This quality he shared in generous measure with his eldest brother. King Edward. Both men knew how to uphold their Royal dignity and to prevent any attempt at familiarity; both knew how to unbend when it was desirable to do so, and they were both cosmopolitan in the best sense of the word.

At about this time there occurred an incident which illustrates well the Duke's ability to see all sides of a question. It happened when a Member of Parliament of strong Labour views gave vent in his presence to some rather pointed opinions. A brother officer of the Duke's, as strongly Conservative as the Member of Parliament was the reverse, criticized his remarks afterward in no measured terms. "I admire the man for standing up for his class," said the Duke. "He has as much right to do that as we have to defend ours, and I believe it is better for a man to hold wrong convictions than to hold no convictions at all."

Work with his Brigade and other military activities took up a very great deal of the Duke's time during this year. There were many reviews, field-days, and similar ceremonies at which he was required to be present while the Army was settling down to its peace routine after its war experience. It goes without saying that his duties were performed as conscientiously as usual and that he never allowed the claims of his private life to interfere with his military responsibilities.

Though he was anxious to go abroad again, he and his wife had felt their previous separation so keenly that they hoped that when next the Duke served abroad she would be able to accompany him. It was not, however, this consideration which kept the Duke at home so long; he was prepared to take the rough with the smooth, and he sought no more preferential treatment as a member of the Royal Family in the selection of appointments than he had in such matters as personal honours and salutes in his military capacity.

The Duke and the Prince of Wales had had many talks about India, in which country the Prince had taken the greatest interest ever since his visit, and the Duke had thus been inspired with a wish to follow in his eldest brother's footsteps and to see for himself the Eastern Empire which was deemed one of his country's greatest triumphs. So far no fitting opportunity had offered itself, and the Duke was content to wait until his time to serve in the East should come in the ordinary course of affairs. The idea that he would one day go to India was, however, always in his mind, so during that year at Bagshot he read much of Indian history, finding in its past glories, its traditions, and its great antiquity a topic of absorbing interest. He also began to learn Hindustani, a study in which the Duchess joined. They passed many hours together in their Surrey home mastering the elements of the language.

In the Royal Family it was considered very unlikely that, after his various experiences in other countries, the Duke would settle down to a military command at home, and he himself had never intended to do so. Apart from his great fondness for travel, he felt that, as a representative of the Throne, he could do more good and promote the interests of the Empire better if he were stationed in one of the dependencies of the Mother Country.

In the meantime, during a very useful year with the troops, his popularity in the Army grew on account of the many unobtrusive ways in which he increased its efficiency and cared for its comfort. Full of zeal as an officer, he was by no means a harsh disciplinarian. Like many wise commanders, he was always ready to make allowances for genuine mistakes or for errors of judgment due to inexperience and not to lack of keenness. For this reason he was always inclined to defend unfortunate Generals who by failing to obtain spectacular successes might incur the criticism of a public over-ready to condemn, while unfitted to judge of the conditions of strain and stress under which decisions were formed, of Charles Kingsley's "pestilence, want of shoes, empty stomachs, bad roads, heavy rains, hot suns, and a thousand other stern warriors who never show on paper," but who sometimes decide the issues in war. On more than one occasion he interceded for men who had made a mistake, and he was always quick in the defence of anyone, officer or man, whom he believed to have been unjustly condemned.

The Duke continued to take much interest in the Irish question, and he consulted with the Queen on several occasions about the Government's policy in Ireland. In so doing he was aided by the knowledge that he had gained personally of the Irish people and of Irish administration.

During the previous year the country had been horrified by the Phoenix Park murders in Dublin, which had been followed, in 1883, by the doings of the gang of Irish Americans who came over with the object of terrorizing the British Government, and who, as a part of their campaign of outrage, exploded nitro-glycerine at the offices of the Local Government Board in Charles Street, Westminster, and at the *Times* office in Printing House Square.

On April 9 the Home Secretary, Sir William Harcourt, introduced a Bill to deal with what he termed "the pirates of the human race," and he assured the House of Commons that the danger was so grave that the Bill must take the unprecedented course of passing through all its stages on that day. The Duke of Connaught, who in due course had taken his seat in the House of Lords, was so much impressed by the gravity of the situation that he made a point of being present when the Bill was read a first time and passed through all its stages in the House of Gammons within the hour, and also when it was taken to the Upper Chamber and there passed at once. Queen Victoria gave her assent on the following day.

On June 24, 1883, the Duke became Colonel of the Scots Guards, an appointment which he held until May 1904, when he was transferred to the Colonelcy of the Grenadier Guards on the death of the Duke of Cambridge.

In the later part of 1883 trouble again broke out in Egypt and the Sudan, where Mohammed Ahmed, a religious fanatic and at the same time a skilled military leader, proclaimed himself as national redeemer and stirred up much disaffection. The Duke, who had continued after his return to study the Egyptian question, advised a strong British policy and wanted to take part himself in another expedition, but this the English Government vetoed, and in course of time there followed, two years later, the tragedy of Gordon's death at Khartoum.

Toward the end of the year there seemed a possibility that the Duke might be wanted to serve in India. As soon as he was aware of this he made every effort to make the appointment certain, eager to visit the country which the Prince of Wales never wearied of praising. In due course his ambition was fulfilled, and on November 26, 1883, he was appointed to a Major-General's command in Bengal. Thus his long association with India began.

It was arranged, to their mutual satisfaction, that the Duchess should accompany him. At first Her Royal Highness hesitated, knowing that she would have to face separation from her children for long periods. This, the great tragedy of the "white man's burden," has been borne by the wives of soldiers and officials in India for centuries, and, as a soldier's daughter and wife, she knew that the sacrifice had to be made. She consented to accompany the Duke in his new appointment.

Queen Victoria herself undertook to see that the young Prince and Princess missed their parents as little as possible during the periods when they were parted from them, while the Princess of Wales, with whose family the habits were great favourites, promised to write long accounts of the progress of the children.

Preparations began at once. There were many sad leave-takings, as the Duchess had become much attached to the English home to which her husband had brought her as a bride, and she had grown fond of her English relatives. To leave so happy a home for a strange country for an indefinite period presented a prospect which few wives and mothers could regard without poignant regret. It was faced with courage, and whatever grief she felt from leaving so much that she loved behind the Duchess contrived to conceal from all but her husband. The sympathy between them was too complete and intricate for such concealment. By the Duke, equally devoted to his home, the enforced separation was as severely felt, but he had as compensation the knowledge that at the time much good might result from the presence of a representative of the Royal House in India. Neither he nor the Duchess had any idea how long their stay in India was destined to be. Seven years were to pass before the Duke returned from India to a home command, ten before he obtained one (at Aldershot) in close proximity to the Bagshot home.

CHAPTER XII

FIRST INDIAN COMMAND
(1883-85; AGED THIRTY-THREE TO THIRTY-FIVE)

Parting from the Children — Situation in India — The Russian Menace — Arrival of the Duke and Duchess at Bombay — A Royal Reception — Visit to Allahabad, Calcutta, Benares, and Lucknow — Meerut — Popularity of "the Connaughts" — Rawal Pindi, Peshawar, the Khyber Pass — A Tour in Kashmir — With the Maharajah — Sport and Sketching — The Divinity of Royalty — A Visit to Delhi — The War Scare of 1885 — Penjdeh — Lord Dufferin's Durbar — The Ameer of Afghanistan — Executioners and Flower-vases — Historic Ceremonies and Political Issues — Sir Frederick Roberts — The Energy of the Duchess — Return to England — Settlement with Russia — Death of Prince Frederick Charles of Prussia.

The Duke of Connaught's command of a Brigade at Aldershot came to a close at the end of September 1883, and his rest was destined to be a short one. Only a few weeks elapsed before he embarked with the Duchess in the S.S. *Bengal*, and on November 22 they first sighted the country in which they were to spend so many interesting and eventful years. As has been said in the previous chapter, it had been necessary, to the deep distress of the Duchess, to leave the children in England. Princess Margaret was less than two years old, Prince Arthur only nine months, when their parents left, and Queen Victoria definitely refused to allow them to go out. She took charge of them herself, and kept them with her practically all the time, at Windsor, Osborne, Balmoral, or wherever the Court might be.

In India the year 1883 had been marked by an acute controversy over a Criminal Procedure Amendment Bill which was in conflict with the wishes of non-official Europeans and the Army, the opposition coming to a head at Calcutta and finally resulting in Europeans being allowed to claim trial by a jury either wholly or partly European. In the internal situation the popularity of the British Raj was strengthened by an era of abundant food and prosperity, but already on the far frontier of Afghanistan were to be heard the preliminary mutterings of the storm which was to culminate in the Penjdeh incident and Russian war scare of 1885. A Russian army had for some months been conducting a victorious advance, and the surrender of Merv to Russian troops under General Komaroff was ultimately announced in February 1884. Such was the military situation on the arrival of the son of the Queen-Empress to take up his command at Meerut, now the headquarters of a military district and of the 3rd Indian Division in the Indian Eastern Command, then the headquarters of the "Meerut Division" (General Orders of September 29, 1883).

The arrival of the vessel carrying the Duke and Duchess had been eagerly awaited by vast crowds assembled on the shore, and as soon as she was sighted a squadron of the Bombay Yacht Club set out to meet her and to escort her to the allotted berth.

The Royal party landed at about four o'clock in the afternoon, and were greeted on shore by an assemblage of various notabilities, who offered a formal welcome to the strains of the National Anthem. This was the Duke's first experience of being decked with a garland, a great rope of fragrant flowers, which was placed round his neck in accordance with Indian custom in doing honour to distinguished visitors, but he supported the ordeal with his usual dignity, as if to the manner born.

Many official functions followed, his arrival being made an occasion for the advancement of numerous philanthropic and social projects in which he was invited to assist. One of his first public acts was the laying of the foundation-stone of the Cama Hospital, presented by an eminent Paxsee. There was a great fair on the Maidan, to which the Royal party drove. All the way the streets were thronged with enthusiastic crowds of Indians, who cheered the Duke and Duchess as they passed, mingling their native cries with quaint scraps of broken English, meant to be complimentary but not lacking in humour to European hearers.

The illuminations that night were magnificent. Every building up to the Clock Tower showed a blaze of lights, some of them electric, a form of public illumination then comparatively new. The decorations everywhere were in Oriental profusion, and the whole setting was typical of Eastern colour and scents. In the evening a State banquet was held at Parel. Then there was a reception at which many of the highest English and native notabilities were presented to their Royal Highnesses.

The Duke and Duchess were both anxious to see as much of India as they could, but to travel without ostentation and with as little parade of their rank as possible, so, had it not been for the decorations with which all the streets were hung, a stranger would have seen little indication of a royal progress.

After a brief stay in Bombay they journeyed to Meerut, and from there to Allahabad and Calcutta. Then on to Benares, thence to Lucknow, and so back to Meerut, obtaining a preliminary glimpse of a small fraction of the vast Empire in which their new home was to be established. At Meerut the Royal party stayed at the house of the Maharajah of Behar, and directly after his arrival the Duke reported himself to the Commander-in-Chief, Sir Donald Stewart, in whose command he was to serve.

There followed the usual peace routine of soldiering in India. No opportunity was afforded for the Duke's personal participation in active service; on Christmas Eve there was some raiding trouble by Akhas in Assam, but this was settled by the first week in January 1884, a month which marked, far away in the Isle of Wight, the second birthday of Princess Margaret and the first of the baby Prince Arthur, celebrated with the Queen at Osborne.

In September and October there was further trouble from Pathans in the Zhob valley, settled by November. In December Lord Dufferin succeeded Lord Ripon as Viceroy.

Both the Duke and Duchess became popular at once, and were soon generally referred to in conversation as "the Connaughts," an informal indication of universal popularity. The Duke was always as approachable and sympathetic in India as he was elsewhere, and eager to understand the problems of the government and administration of the country. He made a deep impression on Europeans and Indians alike, showing unfailing courtesy toward all with whom he was brought in contact either officially or otherwise. He soon grasped the difficulty of the task with which those responsible for Government administration were charged, and he also developed an unusual insight into the workings of the mysterious Eastern mind which enabled him successfully to combine great tact with dignity at all gatherings which he attended.

It is hardly necessary to add that the natural grace and character of the Duchess was as much appreciated in India as it had been in

England. They both took their due share in the social life of the station, and attended the numerous dinners, balls, and other functions which are a feature of Anglo-Indian communities at all places where large garrisons are stationed. At the same time the Duke showed the same devotion to soldiering and to punctual attendance to his military duties as he had at Aldershot.

The autumn of 1884 was spent in travel, in order that as much of the country and of its people as possible might be seen. With this end in view the Duke and Duchess toured in Kashmir, travelling as private individuals and without state or ceremony of any kind. They were accompanied by Lord and Lady Downe, Sir Michael Biddulph, and Colonel Stevenson, with which party they travelled northward from Rawal Pindi. There they had received an enthusiastic welcome, the whole place being illuminated and decorated in their honour, while the population turned out in crowds to cheer them whenever they passed.

On the evening of September 29 they left for Peshawar and the Khyber, visiting Jamrood and travelling up the famous Pass to the Chagai Heights. The Duke had been eager to take this journey, since from the heights he could see toward Ali Musjid and obtain a good view of a country which had been the historic scene of war and disturbance.

The Duke was much impressed by his stay at Peshawar and by the welcome which was extended to him and to the Duchess. He found much to interest him in the place and its history, and a family association was touched when the Royal party was shown a silver centre-piece which the Duke's grandfather, the Duke of Kent, had presented to the old 54th Regiment, now the 2nd Battalion of the Dorsetshire Regiment, which at that time formed part of the garrison. Kohala, on the Kashmir border, was also visited, and from thence the travellers went to Srinagar, where they remained for two days before leaving for the Lidar valley. An interesting feature of the tour was a return visit paid by the Duke to the Maharajah of Kashmir at Jummo at the end of October. The Royal procession passed through dense crowds of enthusiastic spectators, who had flocked in from all the surrounding districts. During the visit there was a review of the Maharajah's troops, an impressive spectacle which the Duke much appreciated. Every possible honour was shown to their Royal Highnesses during their stay, and when they left the crowds followed their carriage for miles, tossing flowers upon it until it looked like a huge moving bouquet.

The Duke and Duchess both enjoyed their tour in Kashmir (the Happy Valley, or the Abode of Snow, as it is sometimes called), and they explored it thoroughly. As they were anxious to see everything they crowded as much into each day as possible. They spent three weeks there, travelling every day, and they moved so constantly and fast and covered so much ground that the Duke became anxious lest the Duchess should be over-fatigued. She was, however, able to accompany her husband throughout the tour, and she rode the whole way, though the road was very bad and dangerous in places, dropping sharply down precipitous slopes. Travel was by no means comfortable, and it became so difficult at times that she had the misfortune to sprain her ankle when descending a hill.

During their stay at Jummo Palace the Duke was shown some sport with bear and wild boar. He also secured a fine stag. While he was in camp in Kashmir a wild boar wounded some neighbouring villagers, and one of their relatives ran into the camp crying out to the Duke for protection. He started without delay to track the animal on foot through a difficult country with thick bush and patches of cover. He got the boar in the end, and it proved to be a heavy one, weighing nearly three hundred pounds. The natives were much impressed by his prowess.

In parts of the country suited to it the Duke also became proficient in pig-sticking, claimed by Anglo-Indians to be the noblest of sports for the horseman, and in this he followed the experience of his eldest brother, the Prince of Wales, during his visit to India. During his whole time in the country he was also credited with true sportsmanship in objecting to increasing the number of the bag by the indiscriminate slaughter of immature stags and of hinds.

During the visit to Kashmir the Duchess, fox whom active exercise was impossible on account of her injured ankle, filled in much of her time by sketching. She did some very interesting work, filling a large sketch-book with mementoes of the visit.

The meeting between the Duke and Duchess and the Maharajah and his sons afforded an impressive pageant, full of Eastern colour and ceremony and staged with the true Oriental flair for such spectacles. The scene has been commemorated in a fine picture by Oliver.

There is no doubt that these and other such visits by the Duke did a great deal of good. They made an impression which can only be estimated when it is borne in mind that the natives of India look upon personages of royal blood as being almost divine, ranking far above the most exalted of lesser degree, however high a position they may fill in the social hierarchy. This was manifested in their keen anxiety to catch even a glimpse of the Royal party. They would travel for amazing distances when it was known that the Duke was to be in a certain locality. They would then wait with extraordinary patience for indefinite periods to see him pass, feeling well rewarded if they saw as much as the top of his helmet.

The kindly bearing of both the Duke and the Duchess, not always an attribute of those in high place in Eastern realms, made the happiest impression upon the native mind, and in every village community were spread tales of the courtesy and the unfailing amiability of the Royal travellers. These tales reached even the ears of the children. In all his travels the Duke made a point, if possible, of visiting the Indian quarter, and on one occasion, as he was passing a row of native dwellings attended only by his A.D.C., a little girl of five rushed out to stare at him. Then, crying out that the Duke was so beautiful that he must be a god, the small worshipper produced a flower and offered it to him. The Duke readily accepted the flower, placed it in his buttonhole, and delighted the donor with a smile and a military salute.

The Duke and Duchess finished their tour at the end of October. In a comparatively short space of time they had contrived to see much of the country, having visited Lahore, Rawal Pindi, and Peshawar, and explored the whole of the Kashmir Valley.

Late in the same year they added to their experiences by a visit to Delhi, thoroughly exploring that historic city, the seat of the Mogul Dynasty in India until the close of the eighteenth century and the scene of terrible tragedy and of great heroism in the Indian Mutiny. At Delhi they were entertained by Lord Reay.

In order to see and understand as much of native life as possible, the Duke made a point of attending all the native fetes that chanced to take place in his vicinity, and he thus took every available opportunity of gaining a real insight into the characters of the vast congeries of races and sects that go to make up the Indian people. He set a good example to all who were concerned in the administration of Indian affairs by passing the lower standard in Hindustani soon after he arrived in India, and he continued his study of the language throughout the whole of his stay in the East. Upon all, whether responsible military and civil authorities or irresponsible critics of Indian administration, he impressed the absolute necessity for gaining a working knowledge of the language of the people subject to the British Raj, maintaining that it was impossible to have any real knowledge of the thoughts and aspirations of Indians without the ability to converse with them in their own language.

During his time at Meerut the Duke took his usual marked and unfailing interest in the private soldier, both in problems that touch his Army service and in those that arise when he returns to civil life. He concerned himself specially with the question of civil employment for soldiers, and he spoke on the subject at several meetings, always impressing the need for finding for the men who had given the best years of their lives to serving their country suitable work when their Army service was over.

On New Year's Day 1885 the impression was prevalent that the Duke would leave India on April 3 to take up a home appointment, and it was announced that the arrangements for him to leave Bombay with the Duchess on that date were complete. We can imagine the joy with which the Duchess anticipated rejoining her children. The Court news of January 13 reported that, as it was the small Prince Arthur's birthday, he and Princess Margaret were taken to see a detachment of the Seaforth Highlanders parading at East Cowes to mark the occasion.

The year 1885 was, however, to prove one of the most momentous in Anglo-Indian relationship since Meerut had, in 1857, been the scene of the outbreak of the great mutiny. The mutterings of the storm on the north-western horizon beyond Afghanistan were increasing in intensity. They rose to a climax in March, when a Russian army under Komaroff attacked and defeated an Afghan force near Penjdeh, a place which, since 1840, had been assured by Britain to Afghanistan.

On April 1, after many delays and postponements, it was announced that

His Royal Highness the Duke of Connaught was called back to the command of a division on the North-West Frontier of India. The Queen is very much disappointed at this postponement of His Royal Highness's return to England, but has sanctioned the appointment of the Duke to this important post.

Britain prepared for war, strongly supported by the whole Empire and by the Indian Princes who govern the vast portion of Hindustan which is not included in 'British' India. An army of 30,000 under Sir Donald Stewart was assembled at Quetta, and the Ameer Abdur Rahman of Afghanistan came to Rawal Pindi in April to meet Lord Dufferin, the Viceroy. Sir Frederick (afterward Lord) Roberts, the Commander-in-Chief designate, was also in attendance. Matters were so serious that the Prime Minister (Mr Gladstone), in the course of a speech in the House of Commons, had said:

> The House will not be surprised when I say, speaking with measured words in circumstances of great gravity, that to us . . . the attack on Penjdeh bears the appearance of an unprovoked aggression.

In April he asked the House for a vote of credit for £11,000,000.

Sir Frederick Roberts, who was serving in India, was on his way to Lord Dufferin when he received a telegram telling him that he was to command an Army Corps which was then being mobilized in case it should be necessary to declare war. Happily, the danger was ultimately averted, but throughout the time of the Durbar, the occasion of the Ameer's meeting with the Viceroy, the outlook was still most menacing. Every Russian war-vessel on the high seas was being shadowed by a British cruiser.

The gathering at Pindi was a brilliant one. Besides the Viceroy, the Duke and Duchess, and Sir Frederick Roberts, the ruling officers of the Punjab, the chief Government officials and native Princes from all over India had assembled. The Duke and Duchess stayed in the camp with the Dufferins, this experience of life under canvas not being improved by the fact that it rained in torrents during the first part of their visit. The ground became a quagmire, interfering seriously not only with the comfort of the guests, but with the official arrangements for the Durbar and the military review. The weather became so bad that on one occasion the Duchess had to be carried to dinner because it was impossible to walk across the sodden ground between the tents except in waders.

The Ameer, a fine-looking man who had a penchant for uniforms with astrakhan trimmings not unlike those of his aggressors, the Russians, was not displeased by the wet weather, since the natives consider rain a good omen and prefer to have it as a prelude to any of their ceremonies. Like so many Eastern potentates, he was, according to European standards, a man of very mixed character. When he was in his own territory he had a strong bias in favour of capital punishment. He always travelled with his executioner in attendance, a picturesque official of fearsome appearance, clad in red velvet and equipped with axe and strangling rope, but as, on this occasion, the man's 'official' services were not in request, he did no more than lend a helping hand in erecting the tents, being treated, however, all the time with marked respect by those with whom he worked. In contrast to his arbitrary methods of destroying human life, the Ameer possessed a passionate love for flowers, and he would spend hours daily arranging them with great taste. He ordered large supplies to be sent to him while at the camp, and he would sometimes fill as many as forty vases in a morning, an occupation which seemed to afford him sincere pleasure and to satisfy a genuine aesthetic sense.

The Duke and Duchess dined with their host and hostess in the great Durbar tent, the biggest one of its kind in India. It was lined with blue and white, lit by great chandeliers suspended round white and gold pillars, and fashioned in all ways to suit the requirements of the huge gatherings which it was destined to accommodate.

For the first two or three days of the gathering it was not possible to carry out the arrangements for the military review. Every one was forced to go about in waterproofs, and even when passing from one princely tent to another it was necessary to dress as if for a thunderstorm, but on April 2 the weather cleared and the preparations began in earnest.

As some of the lesser chiefs could not remain away from their provinces for the great Durbar, it was decided to hold one on a smaller scale specially for them, and this took place in the *shamiana* on April 4. Though lacking the magnificence of the one that came later, the assembly presented a fine sight, and everything went off well. In the evening there was a dinner with about seventy guests, including many of the rulers for whom the morning's ceremony had been arranged.

Two days later came the great ceremonial march past, in which 20,000 troops took part. This afforded a most impressive military spectacle. The Duke and Duchess of Connaught were present with Lord and Lady Dufferin, and in those days of Presidency armies there were no fewer than three Generals Commanding-in-Chief, Sir Donald Stewart, Sir Frederick Roberts, and Sir Arthur Hardinge. After the review the Duke and the Duchess, whose energy was the subject of admiring comment, went for a long ride on their horses. In the evening there was a State banquet at which, after the son of the Queen-Empress, the Ameer was the guest of honour. He brought with him his personal attendant, a boy of sixteen, who stood behind his master's divan throughout the meal, smoking cigarettes. At the conclusion of the dinner the Ameer made a short speech, which was followed by three good British cheers.

Lady Dufferin had arranged for a reception to be held after the ladies retired at which many presentations were to be made to the Duchess, but every one was so anxious to speak to her at the same time that she was in some danger of being mobbed. Only the entry of the men saved her from the pressing attentions of a friendly but somewhat embarrassing crowd. The entertainment was brought to a conclusion with the lighting of great bonfires and the performance of native dances, a spectacle in which she took great interest until it was cut short by an unrehearsed effect produced by a heavy thunderstorm and torrents of rain, not, however, before a very full day of functions had been put in by the tireless Royal party.

On the day following the Ameer was publicly received in Durbar by the Viceroy. For this great occasion, which was purposely attended with as much ceremony as possible, the great Durbar tent and the surrounding space were thrown into one enclosure, and a great dais was erected with three thrones, to accommodate the Duke, the Viceroy, and the Ameer, who, of set purpose, was placed on the Viceroy's right. His Royal Highness, a dignified figure in the scarlet and gold of a general officer and wearing his many decorations, sat on the left.

After much ceremony there followed the customary presentation of gifts of all kinds to the Ameer, some of them of great value. They included State dresses and trays loaded with a wide variety of presents likely to appeal to the taste of the recipient. Then, as a final presentation, came the formal offering of a sword of honour, carried in state on a velvet cushion and personally offered by Lord Dufferin himself. The giving of the sword caused the Ameer to burst into a vehement and most martial speech, in which he professed himself the firm supporter of England and the enemy of all her foes. He concluded with the words, "With this sword I hope to smite every enemy of the British Government!" Solidarity to meet the Russian menace and to secure the integrity of Afghan territory was thereby established. Nearly thirty-five years were to pass before, as an aftermath of the

Great War, that solidarity was destined, only for a few months, to be broken.

The Ameer's speech naturally pleased his British audience, and the Duke led the applause with which it was greeted. The Viceroy proclaimed that Britain and Afghanistan would stand side by side. The Ameer had the most profound belief in the good faith and loyal support of the British Empire, for when, on that night, the Viceroy told him that he had received news of the Russian attack upon Penjdeh, he received the tidings with complete unconcern. He seemed more interested in his ambition to receive a British decoration, and after consultation with the Duke it was agreed to confer upon him, unofficially, the Grand Cross of the Order of the Star of India. With this and his gifts he departed in high content.

The Durbar ended on April 12, and the Ameer's faith in British protection was subsequently completely justified. Sir Frederick Roberts left the Durbar fully expecting to be called upon to take up the proffered command, but matters were eventually settled.

The Duke and Duchess stayed at the Viceroy's camp for three days after the Durbar, and during that time there were several reviews and similar ceremonies, in all of which the Duke bore his full part. The Duchess, as usual, was a general favourite. Her energy and vivacity seemed in no way to suffer from a climate which many find destructive of these qualities. It was rumoured that some of the less robust of her suite experienced no little difficulty in keeping up the pace, and a story is told of one occasion when, as the guests of Sir Thomas Baker, the Adjutant-General, the Duke and Duchess made an expedition to which the party went in jinrickshas. On the way back the Duchess suggested they should walk, and this they did, much to the discomfort of one member of the party, who was handicapped by a pair of tight boots but did not like to suggest riding when the Duchess walked on ahead without the least sign of fatigue.

The future plans of their Royal Highnesses remained for some days in the balance. On April 19 *The Times* reported, "The Duke of Connaught will take four months' leave and accompany the Duchess to England, but return to India at once if his services are required." On April 25 the Duke left Simla, but he was summoned back owing to bad political news. "Should the Duke go on active service, it is believed that the Duchess will remain here."[1] Things dragged on, and on May

1 This and the two following quotations are also from *The Times*.

10 it was announced that the Duke would take two months' leave and that he would spend this leave in Simla. On May 18: "The Duke and Duchess will leave for England on the 26th, for two months' leave, but their plans have been so often changed that the public will not be surprised to hear of yet another change."

However, the war cloud had definitely lifted, and they really did sail in the *Sutlej* on the 26th, with the understanding that the Duke "returns home for two months to see the Queen and to attend the wedding of his sister. Princess Beatrice."

So, in peaceful soldiering, in travel, and in social functions, and in participation in one great historical ceremonial conducted with all the pomp and panoply of "the gorgeous East," was passed the first period of service of the Duke of Connaught in India. In June a change of Government took place in England, Mr Gladstone being succeeded by Lord Salisbury. By September the Anglo-Russian dispute was settled, and shortly afterward the frontier with Russia was delineated on lines satisfactory to the Afghans.

We read that at Windsor before the Duke and Duchess left India, the Queen received the old colours of the 1st Seaforth Highlanders, and that "Prince Arthur and Princess Margaret were present" (one of their first official appearances). We can imagine the Duchess's joyful anticipation of the reunion with the children, but a tragedy was destined to throw a shadow over the meeting. On June 14 the Duke and Duchess landed. On the next day there came the news of the death, very sudden and unexpected, of the Duchess's father. Prince Frederick Charles of Prussia. They went straight to Potsdam for the funeral, and did not return to Windsor until June 28.

CHAPTER XIII

BRIEF REST AND RETURN TO INDIA— THE JUBILEE
(1885-87; AGED THIRTY-FIVE TO THIRTY-SEVEN)

High Policy — The Duke's Future — Queen Victoria's Differences with the Cabinet — Birth of Princess Patricia at Windsor Castle — Appointment to Rawal Pindi — The Military Situation in India — The Duke and Duchess return to the East — Visit to Simla — Illness of the Duchess — The Duke visits Kashmir — The Duke appointed Commander-in-Chief in the Bombay Presidency — Move to Poona — The Duke as a Freemason — Treatment of Indians — Policy of Conciliation — Language at Polo — Activities of the Duchess — Jubilee Celebrations in Bombay — The Jubilee in England — The Royal Mother and Son.

Before proceeding farther with our narrative it is necessary to recall some matters of high policy connected with the military career of the Duke of Connaught which were discussed at several Cabinet meetings during the Premierships of Mr Gladstone and Lord Salisbury. The former held office up to June 1885, and between February and July 1886, and the latter from June 1885 to February 1886, and from July 1886 until after the period which this chapter covers. The Duke's duties in command of the troops were purely military, and it was Queen Victoria's wish that he should be transferred to a higher command in the Bombay Presidency, which carried with it a seat on the Governor's Executive Council and, therefore, participation in political as well as in military affairs.

Her Majesty was much annoyed when the Cabinet, for political reasons, would not sanction the appointment. She expressed her opinion plainly in entries in her journal:

17th *Aug.*

I . . . asked privately of Lord Dufferin, through Lord Salisbury, as to Arthur's fitness for Bombay, which has been answered in a most satisfactory manner, by Lord Dufferin giving the opinion of Sir D. Stewart and Sir F. Roberts; the latter has succeeded the former as C.-in-Chief in India.

11th Oct., 1885

A good deal annoyed at hearing from Lord Salisbury, that, in spite of the opinion and wishes of Sir D. Stewart, Sir F. Roberts, Gen. Hardinge and the Viceroy, the Cabinet has decided that Arthur should not have the command at Bombay, this on political grounds only. They fear cases might arise in which he might have to give his vote on political questions, which would not be fitting for a Prince of the Royal Family. I consider this absurd, and saw Sir H. Ponsonby about it. Arthur is, of course, a good deal disappointed, but takes it calmly and well.

Her Majesty continued to press the question, but for the time being her wishes did not prevail with the Cabinet. Lord Salisbury told her in a letter written on December 14:

The Cabinet then took into consideration again the question of the appointment of the Duke of Connaught to the command at Bombay in obedience to Your Majesty's letter. They examined the question carefully, but they came to the conclusion that the former grounds for the advice they humbly rendered still remains valid, and that H.R.H. the Duke of Connaught should be appointed for the present to Rawal Pindi rather than to Bombay.

There, for the time, the matter had to rest, though, as we shall see later, the Queen eventually had her way. The Duke and Duchess returned to England in the autumn of 1885. In that year, on July 23, the Duke's youngest sister, Beatrice, had been married at Whippingham Church, Isle of Wight, to Prince Henry of Battenberg. In March 1886 a second daughter was born to the Duke and Duchess at Buckingham Palace. Christened Victoria Patricia Helena Elizabeth, she was destined to be affectionately known in the family circle as "Patsy." Her birthday was St Patrick's Day (March 17), and, her father's third name being Patrick, there could be little doubt about at least one of the names to be selected, or about the one most likely to obtain favour for general use, and that was Patricia. Destined to become one of Britain's most popular Princesses, she is now the Lady Patricia Ramsay.

Of other events during those months in England while the future of the Duke's military career was in doubt there is but little to write. It was finally decided that he should return to India to take over the District command at Rawal Pindi, his appointment to which was dated September 27, 1886, but, as matters turned out, Queen Victoria obtained her wish by the end of the year, so the appointment was only held until December 8.

The military events in the year 1886 in India had included a great military review by the Viceroy at Delhi and the annexation of Upper Burma by proclamation in the month of January. In Afghanistan the joint Delimitation Commission completed its work on the Russian frontier in July and was dissolved in September. Sir Joseph West Ridgeway's Commission received a warm welcome at Kabul in October.

During the brief period of the Duke of Connaught's second appointment in the rank of Major-General in India he contrived to widen his knowledge of the country and of its people, and he set the seal upon a popularity which has never since waned throughout the Empire. For the second time, accompanied by the Duchess, he landed at Bombay from the S.S. *Bengal*, and on landing, conspicuous in white uniform, he again met with a most cordial reception. From Bombay they went to Poona, where they remained for some days, during which the Duke witnessed a great military review and attended an exhibition of the products of India, in which both he and the Duchess took a great interest. They made a prolonged inspection, and asked numerous questions about the articles displayed.

As a special compliment to the Duke the Reay Market was rechristened the Connaught Market, and everywhere festivities and *fêtes* were held in honour of the Royal visitors, who as usual gave great pleasure by their willingness to attend every possible function.

During the whole journey to Simla, which was next visited, the progress took the form of a Royal procession. At Simla itself a reception was held in which the military element predominated, and though this and other similar receptions at the end of long and wearisome journeys must have been a great strain upon them, the Duke and Duchess never appeared to be anything but pleased with their welcome or cut the ceremony short by as much as a quarter of an hour. Had he consulted his own personal inclinations, the Duke would doubtless have preferred to be treated as an Army officer rather than as a Royal Prince, but in these matters the atmosphere of the East differs from that of Aldershot, where it had been possible to carry out his wishes.

On October 9, amid scenes of great enthusiasm, the Duke opened the Town Hall, of which he had previously laid the foundation-stone. The central room is still known as the Connaught Hall, and it contains a life-size portrait of the Duke in Major-General's uniform which was presented by Queen Victoria. In the address which was offered to the Duke a phrase was introduced which aptly summed up the Indian attitude toward those of Royal blood:

> An ancient Indian saying goes that the touch of a Prince is the benediction of the Almighty; and now we have the truth of that saying realized in the ceremony to-day. The touch of your Royal Highness consecrated the first stone of this edifice, and it has in so short a period reached its completion.

Unfortunately, the Duchess contracted fever at Simla and also suffered from erysipelas, so she was obliged to remain behind for a while when the Duke left to take up his command at Rawal Pindi. He soon paid another short visit to Kashmir, where he enjoyed the princely hospitality of the Maharajah, who showered his highest honours upon his Royal guest.

At the end of the year. Queen Victoria having obtained her wish, the Duke was appointed Lieutenant-Governor of Bombay and Commander-in-Chief in the Bombay Presidency, with his headquarters at Poona. He succeeded Sir G. G. Arbuthnot, who was transferred to the command of the Madras Army. The Duke's appointment, which was dated December 14, carried with it the rank of Lieutenant-General. While in some narrow Army circles there was a little criticism over the displacement of General Arbuthnot, it was generally considered, in the Army and elsewhere, that the Duke's appointment was sound policy. It raised his official status, bringing it nearer in accord with that which he held in Indian estimation, and his influence, already great, would become still greater in his new position. In any event, his widespread popularity made him supremely fitted for his new and higher command.

The Duke and the Duchess, who by this time had recovered, left Rawal Pindi on December 9, and on their way down were joined by

Prince Leopold of Prussia, who was then touring in India. He accompanied them to Bombay, and they reached Poona at the end of December.

Lord Reay was Governor of the Bombay Presidency at the time, and the relations between him and the Duke were most cordial. The Duke's broad views, and the ideals which he had conceived of Empire statesmanship on the British model, qualified him to help nationally in advancing the policy of fostering the growth of friendly relations between British, Anglo-Indian, and Indian views, and between the India Office and the Government in India, two administrations that were not always in accord. Both by precept and example His Royal Highness did much to discourage the 'inferior race' attitude once in vogue in certain European classes in India toward an ancient civilization highly sensitive to the behaviour of those set in authority over it. On at least two occasions he administered stinging rebukes to those whom he considered to have failed in justice or in courtesy. Working in support and in conjunction with Lord Reay, whose administration was highly successful, he used his influence to break down the barriers of racial exclusiveness, which had hitherto done much to prevent a really helpful understanding between the European and the many Indian races.

As District Grand Master of the Presidency of Bombay and a keen believer in the Craft, it was natural that the Duke should do his utmost to spread Freemasonry among the Europeans in India. There had been a certain amount of rivalry between the English and Scottish Constitutions which perhaps had prevented the spread of the sentiments for which Freemasonry stands, so he made it his object to bring the two branches together. With his usual tact, combined with his high standing as a Mason, he succeeded in linking the responsible authorities in the two sections in a common desire to second his efforts for the good of Freemasonry as a whole. Excepting in this policy — Freemasonry and its mysteries being confined to the male sex — the Duchess, as usual, supported her husband in all his public activities. She helped him in his efforts to extend the social amenities to the higher-class Indian, and, like Lady Reay, she was always ready to attend suitable functions or to co-operate in any scheme which had for its purpose the promotion of friendliness and goodwill. How far they succeeded is best known to those who witnessed their unfailing efforts and to those who have had the opportunity of studying their beneficial results.

The Duchess had a very high conception of her duty as the wife of a General Commanding-in-Chief, and for that reason, as well as on account of personal inclination, she made a point of attending all sports and similar events connected with the Army. She was fond of watching polo, in which she took a genuine interest, and she attended every match. The story goes that in those days the language of Army polo-players when they were excited over a match somewhat resembled that for which their ancestors were celebrated when serving in Flanders; in fact, before the Duchess came the use of expletives during an exciting chukka was so universal as to create the impression that the practice was a part of the game without which it would lose quite a typical feature. After one match it was reported to the players by some authority, veracious or otherwise, that the Duchess had told a friend that she had had to leave the ground on account of the language. However that may have been, the informant was wise in the event, as from that time forward the rule of abstention from lurid metaphor during a game was invariably observed, and the Duchess was a constant attendant.

Reference has already been made to her energy, and this was a constant subject of surprise to those Europeans who were accustomed to take life more easily under Indian skies. Nothing seemed to tire her. She would go for a walk in the morning, attend some social function or play tennis with the Duke in the afternoon, and then go to a ball in the evening, dance most of the dances, and usually stay to the very end, much to the gratification of her hostess.

Once, when she was the guest of honour of a high official, the whole party rose at seven and attended a paper-chase, and when they returned, most of them tired out, she announced that she wanted some exercise and would explore the grounds.

The Duchess often went out with the Duke at hours when most Europeans were taking a siesta behind drawn blinds. They would hunt for curios, explore the Indian quarters, or inspect the buildings in the town. Her energy nude a great impression on the Indian attendants, about whom a typical story is told. In one of the rooms of the Commander-in-chief's house there was a favourite clock belonging to the Duchess. One morning a servant who was cleaning the room found that it had stopped, so he sought out the Duchess's maid and conducted her to the clock, explaining reprovingly that it was "unwinded." There followed a long pause, and then there came the admiring statement, "The Great Lady she never unwinded."

The year 1887 was marked by the Jubilee which celebrated the fiftieth year of Queen Victoria's reign. The ceremonials and rejoicings in England were to take place in June, but the celebrations were held much earlier in the year in India in order that they might be completed before the advent of the hot weather, which would have interfered seriously with the programme and entailed the exclusion of many important items. It was naturally very desirable that the Duke should participate in the gathering of the Royal Family in England, and the dates arranged enabled him ultimately to be present at both the Indian and the British celebrations, but for that to be possible it was necessary for special legislation to be passed. Under the terms of his high office in chief command of the troops in the Bombay Presidency he could not legally leave the country without vacating his command. The necessary machinery was therefore put into motion, and in course of time the House of Commons passed a short Bill to deal with the situation. It provided that

> The Government of India and the Governor-General in Council may authorize His Royal Highness Prince Arthur Duke of Connaught and Strathearn to return to England, for the purpose of being present at the celebration of Her Majesty's Jubilee, and for that purpose to be absent from the Presidency of Bombay for such period, not exceeding three months, as may be fixed by the Governor-General in Council, and the return of His Royal Highness, so authorized, shall not be in law a resignation, or avoidance of his office as Commander-in-Chief in the Presidency of Bombay.

There was some talk of possible opposition in the House, but the Bill became an Act in due course without any dissentient vote. In the meantime the Duke attended the Indian celebrations.

The ceremonies in the Bombay Presidency began early in February, the chief of them taking place on the 16th. They began with the 'proclaiming' of the Jubilee by Lord Reay from the steps of the Town Hall. The proclamation was followed by a fanfare of trumpets and a salute of a hundred and one guns, and the population of the city then indulged in every kind of rejoicing with a wholeheartedness that had never been surpassed. A special service, attended by practically every European in the place, was held in the Cathedral, and all the lavishly decorated streets were thronged with merrymakers.

The Duke and Duchess of Connaught arrived in the afternoon from Poona, where the Duke had inspected the troops, who had given an Imperial salute, fired a *feu de joie*, and given three hearty cheers for the Queen-Empress. They rode through the city in the evening among enthusiastic crowds, who mingled their cheers for the Queen-Empress with greetings for their Royal Highnesses, to whom they tossed flowers as they passed. The illuminations were magnificent. Bombay had never offered so brilliant a spectacle as it did on that night, with its myriads of many-coloured lights, its illuminated crowns and emblazoned messages which greeted the Duke and Duchess during their triumphal progress.

The only other incidents, outside the usual routine, which occurred during this period of the Duke's service in India were visits paid by him to Indore and to Aden, at which places he, as usual, contrived during a visit of a few days to learn more about the people and their surroundings than many tourists have either the will or the opportunity to gather during visits of several weeks. He sometimes discomforted officials by his determination to get below the surface of things and to extend his knowledge of local problems of government and of social conditions.

When the time came for the departure for England General Carnegy was appointed to take over the Duke's responsibilities as Commander-in-Chief of the troops in the Presidency. The Royal party then left on the *Sutlej*.

Forty-two years have passed since the Jubilee which marked the fiftieth year of Queen Victoria's reign, and the ranks of those who can recall the splendour of that wonderful summer in England are rapidly being depleted. The weather was perfect. The epithet 'jubilee' was conferred upon everything from atmospheric conditions to advertised articles of male and female attire, and upon every prominent personality from the greatest of the great to the poor 'jubilee juggins' who won, and lost, a great fortune by gambling on the Turf and at Monte Carlo. The thoroughfares of London bristled with Venetian masts, with brightly coloured streamers and fluttering flags. Triumphal arches, garlands, newly erected stands smelling of freshly cut pinewood and covered with crimson baize, windows decked with flower-boxes and bunting, gaily apparelled spectators everywhere, filling the windows and crimson stands and crowding even the roofs of buildings — these were all features of the routes of processions, and even the meanest home in the slums showed some little scrap of decoration. By night the clubs and large buildings blazed with the gas-jets of set-pieces, and the windows of houses showed rows of coloured fairy-lights if they could be obtained, bare candles or night-lights if they could not. Fortunes were made by the letting of windows commanding the routes, and by the 'cornering' of fairy-lamps!

All over the country the meadows were glorious with golden buttercups, and the towns, villages, and hamlets vied with the metropolis in their keeping of the festival.

This is not the place to describe in detail the Queen's Thanksgiving Service in Westminster Abbey, where the great procession followed her up a carpet of Garter blue to the High Altar, or her progress up Whitehall in the gold State coach drawn by cream-coloured horses, preceded by ranks of Royalties, British and foreign, mounted on showy chargers. In these, and all other great occasions of State, the Duke of Connaught bore his full part.

Looking back now for nearly half a century, we seem to see a set purpose beneath the surface of all the pageantry and enthusiasm, a spontaneous drawing together, by loyalty to the Royal House, of all the forces of the Empire to meet the great menace of the future. During that brilliant summer there was held in London the first of the Imperial Conferences which culminated in the formation of the great Army that the free peoples of the Empire who owe allegiance to the same Sovereign contributed to victory in the conflict of 1914-18.

When the Duke arrived in England he was at once immersed in the preparations for the great Jubilee. Before the ceremony itself he attended many functions, and took part both in State celebrations and in private conferences, one of which may be recalled. Queen Victoria had determined to cling to her deep mourning, though the occasion seemed to demand a less funereal attire. Even on so great an occasion in her life she was still disposed to wear black, and, as this was felt to be unsuitable, a family conclave was held to discuss the subject. When the Queen mentioned her intention of wearing black velvet it was the Duke who exclaimed, "Now, Mother, you must have something really smart!" His persuasion really overcame the Queen's first intention, and induced her to wear the toilette which she finally selected, a lavender costume and a bonnet made in the form of a coronet.

While the Duke attended the Jubilee primarily as a son of Her Majesty, he went also as a kind of envoy from India, and in this *rôle* he presented to the Queen the Poona Jubilee address and casket, and also the Bombay Masonic address.

Before the 21st of June, which was the anniversary of the Queen's coronation and therefore had been selected as 'Jubilee Day,' various entertainments were given to the Indian officers and potentates who had come over for the ceremony, and in these the Duke played a prominent part. On June 18 the Indian officers went down to Windsor and lunched there, and afterward were presented to the Duke. He said a few words to each of them in Hindustani the excellence of which seemed to please as well as to surprise them, and then the Duke brought in the little Prince Arthur to speak to them and to shake hands with each of them in turn, a touch that was much appreciated.

The Queen herself came to see the officers, and after Captain Muir, who was in charge of the contingent, had been presented to her by the Duke, each of the Indian officers offered the hilt of his sword to her as a token of loyal homage. The Queen, following the usual custom, accepted their tribute by touching each sword in turn, and the Duke then explained to Her Majesty the rank of the selected representatives of units in the Indian Army and such of their exploits as had come under his notice.

The Duke's tact was well displayed in all his dealings with the Indian potentates who came over for the Jubilee, and whose services to the Empire and loyalty to the Crown it was so desirable to recognize. One incident can be taken as an illustration. Sir Pratap Singh was shown much honour on his arrival in England. He was gazetted as an Honorary Lieutenant in the British Army, and was placed on the staff of Her Majesty. Soon after his arrival Sir Pratap was present while the Indian Princes offered their gifts to the Queen. He had thought that he would have another opportunity of offering his own gift, so he had brought nothing for the occasion, and in consequence was much embarrassed when his name was called. He was equal to the occasion, and, taking the *sirpesh* (a golden ornament set with gems) from his turban, he bowed low and handed it to the Queen, who took it and passed it on to the Duke of Connaught. The Duke, who had seen the whole incident and guessed at the Prince's embarrassment, asked the Queen to wear the *sirpesh* that night at the Royal banquet. She did so, much to Sir Pratap's gratification, and she summoned him to her side and told him that, as he had presented the gift with his heart's esteem, so she wore it in the same spirit.

While the Duke was in England for the Jubilee celebrations he had several conversations on Indian affairs with the various Government departments affected thereby, and he was able to give some valuable information and advice about the administration in different states, much of which was afterward of service. The Queen, who had always valued his opinion, was interested in all that he had to tell her, and she questioned him constantly both about the country and about its administrators. The Duke naturally had much to say both of places and of people. Standing as he did above all petty ambitions or tendencies toward intrigue, and being an excellent judge of character, certain to set down naught in malice, his judgments were proved in the event to be singularly accurate.

CHAPTER XIV

BACK TO INDIA AND THE HOMEWARD TOUR
(1887-90; AGED THIRTY-SEVEN TO FORTY)

More Jubilee Celebrations — A Great Review — Departure for India — Investiture of Lord Reay — The Duke injures his Knee — Freemasonry — The Duchess and the Children — "Missy Sahib" — Visit of the Duke and Duchess of Oldenburg — Memorial Service for the German Emperor William I — Ceremonial Visit to the Nizam of Hyderabad — Great Procession of Elephants — Indian Princes and their Status — Cholera among the Suite — A Visit to Agra — A Maharajah sings John Peel — The Taj Mahal — Back to Poona — Children's Parties — Visit to the Viceroy at Calcutta — His Royal Highness the Duke of Clarence — Nautch Dances and Conjuring — Bareilly — Entertained by the Rifle Brigade — The Duchess indisposed — Final Scenes and Functions at Poona — Farewells at Bombay — The Return Voyage — Ceylon — Singapore — Hong-Kong — Procession of Dragons — Chinese Hospitality— Canton — Home via Shanghai and Japan — The New Canadian Pacific Railway.

While interest centred in Queen Victoria's great Thanksgiving Service in the historic setting of Westminster Abbey on June 21, London for many days resounded with the huzzas of multitudes as processions passed to various functions. The decorations continued to be centres of attraction to visitors from all parts by day, and by night horsed vehicles carried loads of sightseers of all classes to view the illuminations. All over the country bonfires showed tongues of flame on every eminence, as they had in the days of the Spanish Armada, and rockets illumined the sky at intervals.

At Spithead the Queen reviewed her great fleet, Britain still being universally claimed as Mistress of the Seas without rancour or challenge, and the Royal yacht, with her standard flying, passed through apparently endless lines of ships amid the booming and heavy clouds of smoke from saluting guns. At Aldershot, in the Long Valley, Her Majesty witnessed for hours the march past of about 70,000

Regular troops and volunteers, trampling through clouds of dust under a blazing sun. When a Royal Prince held the Colonelcy of a passing unit he rode forward, usually distinguished by the broad ribbon of the Order of the Garter, to lead his regiment or battalion, rejoining the throng round the Royal Standard when his command had passed. The soldierly figure of the Duke of Connaught was in evidence on this, as on all other military and State occasions during the summer of the Jubilee.

As records of the thanksgivings and rejoicings there remain certain pictures, one, by T. S. C. Crowther, of the ceremony in Westminster Abbey, another, by L. Tuxen, now in the Royal collection, of the gathering of the Royalties. In this there is an excellent portrait of the Duke standing beside the Princess of Wales, afterward Queen Alexandra, while the children, the young Prince Arthur of Connaught and the Princesses Margaret and Patricia, are grouped round the Queen's knee.

With a Jubilee Ascot, Goodwood, and Cowes, all celebrated in bright sunshine, the summer passed away. The foreign Royalties returned to their realms, and the Duke of Connaught to India, alone on this occasion, to resume his command, and Bombay General Orders were again issued under the name of "H.R.H. the Commander-in-Chief, Bombay Army." The closing months of the year were marked by practical demonstrations of loyalty to the Throne by the Indian Princes of whom the Duke had seen so much. The Nizam of Hyderabad offered twenty lakhs of rupees (£600,000) for three years toward the defence of the North-West Frontier, the Rajah of Kapurthala five lakhs and his army, the Rajah of Nabha four lakhs, and other Indian Princes further sums. Such was the atmosphere which prevailed when the Duke returned, and in creating it he had borne his part. He arrived in India in September and went at once to Poona, and then there began a long round of public ceremonies in which he took a prominent part, laying foundation-stones, opening various institutions, and fulfilling with his usual zeal and good humour the duties, some of them wearisome, which fall to the lot of those in high places.

A ceremony which gave him much pleasure was the investiture of Lord Reay with the insignia of a Knight Grand Commander of the Indian Empire. This took place in the Council Hall at Poona, and it was attended by all the notabilities of the neighbourhood.

When he had finished the long round of functions at Poona the Duke began a tour of military inspection which concluded at

Mahabaleshwar, a hot-weather station for Bombay troops. Up to this time his health had been excellent, but in the autumn of 1887 he had had the misfortune to injure his knee rather badly, being in consequence obliged to walk with a stick. He continued to suffer much inconvenience from this cause for the remainder of his time in India. To a man of his active temperament this check to his movements was naturally irksome, though he tried his best not to allow the mishap to interfere with his duties.

In November he was installed as the District Grand Master of the Bombay Freemasons in recognition of the great impetus that he had given to the cause of the Craft in India, where a spirit of brotherhood is perhaps even more essential than it is in any other country in the world.

The Duchess and the children joined the Duke at Poona later, but, as Princess Margaret and Prince Arthur after the first separation had been with their parents during much of their time in India, it was felt in the spring of 1888 that it would be better for them to be away from the climate during its most trying period. They were sent to Europe in charge of Sir Howard and Lady Elphinstone, the former of whom had been tutor to the Duke.

The Royal children had become great favourites with every one. The natives were naturally charmed by the fair little Princess, and they would throng places where the children were taken for their airings in the hope of catching sight of the "Missy Sahib," to whom they would offer flowers as she passed. The children were away all the summer. In the autumn came their very welcome return, and both the Duke and Duchess met them on their arrival at Bombay.

It was during this year that the Duke of Oldenburg and his Duchess (the Duchess of Connaught's eldest sister) came to India on a visit, and while they were there the Royal party went on several short tours, the Duke trying to show their guests as much of India as was possible during their stay. Unfortunately, the visit was overshadowed for both hosts and guests by the knowledge that the Crown Prince Frederick of Germany, brother-in-law to the Duke and cousin to the Duchess, as well as the husband of the great friend of her childhood, was suffering from an illness which was known to be incurable. A gigantic figure, clad in white, with a silver helmet surmounted by the wings of an eagle, he had stood out conspicuously among the foreign princes who had ridden up Whitehall doing honour to Queen Victoria during the previous summer, but already he was a stricken man, and even at the time his father, the old Emperor William, died it was well known that he would not live long to occupy the throne.

On the day of the Emperor William's funeral in Germany a special service was held in the Cathedral in Bombay. The Duke and Duchess of Connaught, Lord Reay, and the principal European residents attended. Much solemnity was added to the occasion by the knowledge that the shadow of death hung over the kindly prince, Frederick William "the Noble," who died three months later.

The Duke and Duchess of Oldenburg remained in India long enough to accompany the Duke and Duchess of Connaught to Hyderabad in January 1889. There they were the honoured guests of the Nizam who had made so magnificent a contribution to Indian defence. He met them in person at the railway-station. The populace gave them a warm welcome, and as they drove to the Nizam's residence the Duke's hand was perpetually at the salute.

The Nawab Syed Hosein Bilgrami presented an address, in which he offered a "right royal welcome to His Royal Highness as a loved and honoured son of the great and powerful Imperial Ruler," and added:

> In the old days of Royal Oriental rule it was the custom to strew the paths of Royal visitors with presents of rice. We cannot venture to proffer, and your Royal Highness would not care to accept, such paltry gifts. We offer you instead the true love and loyalty of our hearts.

There was a State banquet in the evening, and on this occasion the decorations at the Nizam's palace were unusually magnificent, even for India. The windows of the edifice all glowed like jewels in the darkness, while festoons of coloured lights surmounted the towers and twined like ropes of fire round the pillars. After the dinner the Nizam proposed the healths of the Queen-Empress and of his illustrious guests. The Duke in reply assured the Nizam that he would tell the Queen of the "felicitous and loyal terms" of his speech, and ended by asking the company to drink the Nizam's health.

The day concluded with an unusually brilliant and varied display of fireworks, so much enjoyed by the Royal visitors that they stayed until the conclusion.

One of the most interesting and picturesque features of their stay at Hyderabad was a great procession of elephants through the city, an imposing spectacle which Europeans, used only to the sight of single elephants, can hardly picture. The procession extended for quite a mile and a half. The elephants numbered 110, and on the first fourteen the Duke and Duchess of Connaught and members of their respective suites rode in places of honour. In front of the first elephant was borne the Nizam's standard. Behind this marched a cavalcade of fifty camel-sowars and fifty standard-bearers, while the elephant bearing the Duke was surrounded by a body of over a thousand Arabs, who played on native instruments and chanted their national songs as they marched, armed with spears and swords. Even after the Duke's long experience of Indian customs it was something of a novelty. The great procession moved through streets black with people, and every balcony and housetop showed clusters anxious to catch a glimpse of the Royal party, upon whom they showered compliments freely mingled with prayers and blessings.

The Duke took the opportunity during this visit to dine with his old regiment, the 7th Hussars, who were then stationed in the vicinity. He also reviewed all the British troops within reach, and attended a picturesque parade of the soldiers of the Nizam.

At Hyderabad he had some good shooting and also took part in a panther-hunt. At this, much to his chagrin, he was unable to ride a horse on account of the injury to his knee, and had to be carried on an elephant. The Nizam rode beside him on horseback, so well mounted and riding with such a good seat and hands that the Duke paid him a special compliment on his exceptionally fine horsemanship.

It may be mentioned here that Indians of all classes, like other Eastern races, are excellent judges of character. They are not deceived by politeness or by formal speeches. They may not be able to understand a word of the language of those set in authority over them, but they do grasp their true motives, and often have an uncanny insight into their real feelings. An Indian of some education who was in Government employ once remarked to a member of the Duke's suite, "Some of your big men, they come, they talk with their mouths, and we hear with our ears, and this is finished; but your Prince speaks with his heart, and it is with our hearts we listen," which gives a clue to the popularity of the Duke in all parts of India, and to the amount of good his stay there effected.

This visit to Hyderabad has been dwelt upon at some length because of a popular fallacy which causes so many people to talk of "India" when they mean only British India, thus ignoring the vast territories ruled over by the Indian Princes. They now have a Chamber of their own, which affords facilities for collective expression of their opinions, even perhaps on such subjects as the influence upon India as a whole of the development of British India in the direction of 'Dominion status.' With these deep matters of State we are only concerned in so far as they are affected by the excellent impression which was produced among the rulers of states by the long sojourn in India of the soldier Duke, son of the Queen-Empress.

The visit to Hyderabad was one of the most successful functions that the city had ever known, but, unfortunately, directly after leaving for Poona, whither they journeyed in the Nizam's special train, some of the Duke's party were attacked by cholera. The Duke of Oldenburg caught the complaint, but not seriously. Surgeon-Major Keith took it in its worst form, and died at Poona, much to the Duke's distress.

In March of the same year their Royal Highnesses visited Agra, where they were entertained by the Maharajah Rana of Dholpur, who presented the Duchess on their arrival with a wonderful bouquet of white roses and pansies. After the usual State banquet, at which the Maharajah gave as the only toast "The Queen-Empress," there was a concert at which, much to the Duke's amusement. His Highness sang *John Peel* and gave an excellent rendering of that old English hunting-song.

The Royal party made many excursions to places of interest in the old city, which was built by a Mogul Emperor. The Duke devoted much attention to the old fort, which was built in 1566, while, as can be imagined, the Duchess was lost in admiration for the famous Taj Mahal, the loveliest and most wonderful monument ever raised to the memory of a woman. They visited the white marble tomb by moonlight, and on that occasion the Taj was illuminated by blue lights. These gave so exquisite an effect that the Royal visitors for whom it had been arranged felt reluctant to leave the scene and remained till a late hour.

They also visited the famous carpet factory and the Pearl Mosque and other beauties of the place. Agra, apart from its beautiful monuments, must have held a special interest for the Duke, as the place withstood a siege for several months in the days of the Mutiny.

A pleasing feature of the life at Magdala House, their Poona residence, on their return there was the children's parties, at which their own children were, of course, resent, and in which they themselves took an active part. One such party was given on the

Duchess's birthday in 1889. It was for the children of the non-commissioned officers, their parents also being invited. These parties were always highly successful, being conducted with a complete absence of formality. It was understood in Poona that these children's entertainments were marked by an abundant supply of every delicacy dear to the heart of the young, and fond mothers, while delighted at the honour done to their offspring, would await their return with anxiety, not to mention supplies of the 'Gregory powder' of Victorian days.

In July 1889 Poona was the scene of a Masonic installation at which the Duke was present as Grand Master. He made a good speech, in the course of which he mentioned his pleasure at finding brethren of so many different nationalities present. He also regretted that his bad health had prevented him from attending as many Lodges as he would have wished, which records the unfortunate fact that their last year in India had, for both their Royal Highnesses, been somewhat spoiled by their indifferent health.

In 1890 the Duke held a special parade of a large number of troops to mark the anniversary of the proclamation of the Indian Empire when Queen Victoria assumed the title of Queen-Empress, and the Duchess brought the children to witness the great pageant, at which they were present from start to finish.

Early in January their Royal Highnesses went to Calcutta, where they were the guests of the Viceroy, to meet the Duke's nephew. Prince Albert Victor, Duke of Clarence, who had just arrived from England for an Indian tour and for whom many entertainments were arranged. One, of a public nature, was given on the Maidan, with native dancers, native actors and conjurers, and every kind of side-show likely to appeal to the spectators. Special native dances were performed for the Royal party, so the Duke of Clarence witnessed the nautch and a *kuttak* dance for the first time. The extraordinary and mysterious conjuring for which India is famous interested the Duke more than the dancing. Some of the tricks have never been explained. On this occasion the conjurer concluded his performance with a ring and stick trick, and he was much honoured when the Duke offered to hold the stick while the ring was being conjured on to it. It may be mentioned that he had hoped by holding the stick to learn the secret, but he failed to do so either with this or with another trick in which the leaves on a twig turn into scorpions.

After the conjuring there came a native theatrical performance from *Sakuntala*, a Sanskrit play, a Tibetan dance (a weird and picturesque performance, in which some of the players wore animal masks as they did at the British Empire Exhibition on a recent occasion), then another kuttak dance by sowars and sepoys from the North-West Frontier who had been the torch-bearers in the Royal procession. Wearing high turbans, they danced round huge bonfires to the accompaniment of native music, somewhat discordant, perhaps, to the ears of Europeans, who in those days had not been inured to post-War 'jazz.'

For the Royal party the programme ended with dinner at the Bengal Club and a ball at Government House, at which the Duke and Duchess of Connaught and the Duke of Clarence were present.

It had been arranged that the Duke and Duchess should leave India for good when the Duke relinquished his command in March, so, with this prospect in view, they spent their last Indian leave in tours, beginning in January. Bareilly was visited first, and they stayed there with Colonel Hildyard. They were met by a special Guard of Honour of the Rifle Brigade, with full band, and after Colonel Hildyard had received the Royal visitors a parade of the regiment was held. The Duke and Duchess lunched afterward at the Officers' Mess. They attended a garden-party in the afternoon, and a dinner-party, given by the officers of the regiment in their honour, in the evening. There was another parade the following day and many other functions, so on this, as on the other visits which were paid during the final leave-taking, the Duke and Duchess put in a very strenuous time. A still more extensive tour had at first been arranged, but this had to be abandoned on account of the ill-health of the Duchess, and a somewhat less exhausting itinerary was planned. The Duke made a military tour of various places, during which he inspected regiments, attended parades, and took leave of the commanding officers, returning to Poona on February 10.

The Duke had always taken much interest in the Artillery and Poona Boat Clubs, which in compliment to His Royal Highness afterward changed their name to the Duke of Connaught Boat Club (the Royal Connaught Yacht Club). In February he presented the club with a special flagstaff. The Duchess came to witness the ceremony, bringing with her Prince Arthur (then aged seven), who, as the Duke made the presentation, unfurled the Royal Standard of England and the flags of all nations, an incident which much pleased the onlookers.

In his speech of thanks the club secretary said that he hoped that it would not be long before the Royal Standard was again unfurled to welcome the return of His Royal Highness, and many years later his hopes were realized. When the Duke revisited India in 1921 he paid a special visit to the Boat Club, where he was received with enthusiasm.

At Poona there were many farewell entertainments, including one given by the Freemasons, and everywhere sincere regrets were expressed at the departure of the Duke, whose stay in India had been productive of so much good and was destined to have far-reaching results. While in Poona he had taken considerable interest in the racing which takes place there, and had become an excellent judge of the Indian ponies. Those which he owned had to be left behind, and both he and the Duchess were specially sorry to part with Golab, a particular favourite.

The departure from Poona took place on February 23, and they had hardly arrived at Bombay before they were engaged in assisting Lady Reay with a Fancy Fair. The Duchess, who was still rather lame from a recent illness, took charge of a stall, which she arranged personally, spending several hours in the process. She made a fine display of her stock, much of which she had ordered from Europe. She had taken a lively interest in all philanthropic schemes during her residence in India, and by her support contributed to the successful working of Lady Dufferin's celebrated movement, started in 1885, for providing female medical practitioners and nurses to work among native women. Later she became a special Patroness of the Up-country Nursing Association for Europeans in India, which she continued to support long after she returned to England.

The Freemasons gave the Duke a great farewell entertainment as a mark of their appreciation of his interest in the Craft. The Duchess also was present, "to show," as the Duke remarked, "the interest that my wife takes in the work that I, as a Mason, have been carrying on in this Presidency." The Bombay Yacht Club also gave a farewell dinner, at which there were many speeches, the Duke's being notable for its outspokenness and absence of formality. An official farewell address, presented at Bombay, contained the words:

As Commander-in-Chief you have always laboured to promote the comfort and well-being of your officers and the soldiers under your command. The Duchess has been a most worthy co-operator in this.

The Duke and Duchess were both visibly moved at the leave-taking, and he made a sincere farewell speech of thanks, alluding gratefully to many who had worked under him, specially mentioning how much he had enjoyed co-operating with Lord Reay. He then bade a reluctant farewell.

On their way home from India the Duke and Duchess paid a visit to China, where they spent an interesting time. Leaving Bombay on March 13 (the anniversary of their wedding-day) in the P. and O. *Kassar-i-Hind*, they stopped first at Colombo. They went up to Kandy and were received by the Governor, Sir A. H. Gordon. After a brief visit they returned to Colombo. There the Duke held a reception which was largely attended by native chiefs in marvellous costumes, who came in to offer their homage to the son of the Great White Queen.

After leaving Colombo they touched at Penang and reached Singapore on the 25th. There they were received by the Governor, Sir Cecil Clementi Smith. The ship was late in arriving at Hong-Kong (so late that some wag nicknamed their ship the "Kaisar-behind"), but on March 31 she steamed slowly into the harbour at about 2 p.m. greeted by guns of H.M.S. *Impérieuse*.

The Acting Governor, Mr F. Fleming, received them on landing, and after the usual ceremonies the Duke and Duchess drove to the City Hall, where an address of welcome was presented. After the ceremony the Royal party went on to Government House, where they were to stay during their visit, and there the Duchess found a nice compliment in the form of a beautiful bouquet, bearing a ribbon on which were embroidered the words, "A welcome from the German ladies of Hong-Kong."

In the evening there was a great dinner and a reception, at which many presentations were made. On the following day a sham fight, in which the Duke was much interested, was staged by the garrison, and in the evening both he and the Duchess attended a military tattoo for which the music was provided by the band of the Argyll and Sutherland Highlanders.

An interesting feature of their Royal Highnesses' stay at Hong-Kong was provided in the form of a procession of Chinese dragons. This took place on April 2. The dragons were enormous, several hundred feet in length, and they were supported by a number of Chinese bearers, completely hidden, who contrived to make the monsters twist and wriggle in most fantastic contortions. Both the Duke and Duchess were interested and amused by the novel spectacle, and the Duke took several photographs of the dragons.

They attended many functions and assisted in various ceremonies, including the inauguration of the Praya reclamation scheme, after which the local lodge of Freemasons presented the Duke with an address. They also visited the Docks, afterward lunching on board the *Impérieuse*, where they were received by Admiral Sir Nowell Salmon.

A novel entertainment in their honour was given by the Chinese community, entirely on their own initiative. The entertainment, which followed very much the lines of a present-day *cabaret*, went on while the meal was in progress and was entirely Chinese. On the top of the menu was inscribed:

> A good digestion to you all, and once more
> I shower a welcome to you. Welcome all.

The choicest Chinese dishes, which, though they sounded and tasted somewhat peculiar to the European guests, constitute a normal Celestial banquet, were included. As a compliment to their hosts the Duke and Duchess did their best to use the chopsticks, and among other dishes which they negotiated there figured birds'-nest soup, sharks' fins, *bêche-de-mer*, fish-gills, fried marine delicacies, sweet lotus soup, carambolas, rose dew, and rice wine.

The dramatic entertainment had been prepared with great care, in order to pay special honour to the Royal guests. An episode entitled Promotion, which was only acted when a person of very high rank was present, was included. In due course the actor entered in sumptuous robes, and, looking at the guest of honour, unfolded a scroll on which was inscribed, "May you rise in office and be promoted in rank!" He then looked upward and pointed to the roof, signifying that the promotion would be as high as the sun when it is in its zenith. The other items on the programme were entitled *Congratulations of the Eight Genii*, *The Fair Wife*, and *The Visit to the Moon*.

On the next day the Royal party went to Canton, and they spent an interesting time there, seeing the Chinese sights and visiting many of the public buildings. They returned to Hong-Kong on the following day, and, after many farewells, they left in the P. and O. Ancona for Shanghai and Japan, and so back again to England.

They left Japan on May 8 for Vancouver, and when the Duke arrived at Victoria, British Columbia, he said, in answer to an address of welcome, that he had taken the Canadian route home as he was most anxious to see that all-important new link between the West and the East, the Canadian Pacific Railway, by which he would travel. They crossed the Rocky Mountains by the C.P.R., and during the run across the Rocky Mountains the Duke and Duchess were enchanted with the magnificent scenery along the railway. At different points the train slowed down to enable the Royal party the better to view the panorama. At the various stations groups of settlers assembled to give the distinguished visitors a cheer. They stopped at Banff, Regina, the capital of the North-West Territory, and at Winnipeg, where they stayed at Silver Heights with the Lieutenant-Governor. The Royal party then travelled to Ottawa along the northern shore of the lake. The Duke expressed himself as highly gratified by the loyalty everywhere, and as being amazed at the railway and at the progress which Canada had made in every respect since he was there last. They had a great reception at Toronto, where once more the Duke expatiated upon the " marvellous railway trip." They visited Niagara and went to Montreal, sailing from Quebec on June 12, and arriving at Liverpool on June 21.

Through communication between Vancouver and Montreal by the Canadian Pacific Railway had been opened as recently as 1886, but communication with New York was not established until 1891. On this, as on so many other occasions, we find that the Duke of Connaught was destined to be in close touch with great Empire developments — at this particular time with an important strategic link between East and West, one of the great conceptions of the Canadian statesmen of Victorian days.

CHAPTER XV

THE PORTSMOUTH AND ALDERSHOT COMMANDS
(1890-98; AGED FORTY TO FORTY-EIGHT)

High Place — The Riflemen's New Headdress — The Duke appointed to the Southern Command — A Visit to Potsdam — The Duchess as a Colonel — The Duke's Prospects — Death of the Duke of Clarence — Tattoo at Osborne — A Royal Marriage — The Connaught Princesses as Bridesmaids — The Duchess and her Children — The Kaiser at Cowes — Death of Duke Ernst of Saxe-Coburg-Gotha — Succeeded by the Duke of Edinburgh — A Visit to Austria — Army Manoeuvres there — The Aldershot Command — Press Criticism — Not justified by Results — The Duke's Activities at Aldershot — Queen Victoria's Visits — The Empress Frederick of Germany — The Shahzada Nasrullah of Afghanistan — Army Reforms — Manoeuvres in 1895 — Scarlet versus Khaki — Death of the Hereditary Princess of Oldenburg, Sister of the Duchess — A Visit to Saint-Cloud — Retirement of the Duke of Cambridge — The Queen's Wishes — Lord Wolseley appointed Commander-in-Chief.

Only a small selection from the public and social functions in which the Duke took a prominent part as a member of the Royal Family during his long sojourn in India has been noticed in the preceding chapters, and we have endeavoured in making that selection to draw a varied picture of the country and its peoples during the eighties of last century. It must be borne in mind that attendance at so many great ceremonials, public functions, and social engagements brings a heavy strain upon the leading participants, however inured they may be to them by experience, and that with the Duke they were superimposed upon all the work which falls normally upon a general officer holding high military appointments such as his. We are thereby reminded of Bacon's saying that:

> Men in great place are thrice servants: servants of the sovereign or State; servants of fame; and servants of business; so as they have no

freedom, neither in their persons, nor in their actions, nor in their times. It is a strange desire, to seek power and to lose liberty.

Power was not sought by the Duke; it came to him naturally in the first instance, through his Royal descent, but, however it may have come, the duties and the mode of life attached thereto during those years in India caused some measure of weariness in both him and the Duchess, and even on the voyage home there were functions at the ports of call.

In spite, however, of the strenuous time that he had experienced in India, the Duke was no sooner back in England than he began at once to take an active part in Army affairs. On August 9, 1890, he inspected the 4th Battalion of the Rifle Brigade at Parkhurst, in the Isle of Wight. This inspection was marked by the first appearance of the new headdress, and, as we have already noted, it was through the personal influence of the Duke in high quarters that Riflemen, at that time, were delivered from the unpopular, ugly, and uncomfortable helmet under which most of the British Army suffered for so many years.

On August 25 the Duke took over the Southern Command, becoming as well Lieutenant-Governor of Portsmouth, where his headquarters were situated — an appointment which met with unanimous approval both from military and civil authorities. Upon taking over the command he crossed from Osborne to Portsmouth, the flagship saluting him as he arrived at the Dockyard, and drove straight to his headquarters, where he took over the command from General Sir Leicester Smyth.

Soon afterward the Duke visited Potsdam with the intention of witnessing German naval and military manoeuvres. Accompanied by the Duchess, he arrived there on September 6, and they stayed with the mother of the Duchess. In due course the Duke went to Berlin, accompanied by four British officers, for the manoeuvres of the 5th and 6th Army Corps in Silesia.

As the Duchess was Honorary Colonel of the 8th Brandenburgers, the officers of that regiment gave a dinner on October 25 in honour of Her Royal Highness. She drove to the dinner in a carriage that had been filled with beautiful flowers for the occasion, and, as a compliment to the regiment, she wore a tailormade jacket of the colours of the uniform, and made an attractive martial figure as she was escorted to the seat of honour.

Owing to the Duke's devotion to his career and in consideration of what he had achieved in the military appointments that he had already held, there was some suggestion as early as 1890 of his promotion to a higher command. It had been suggested that Lord Wolseley might take over the chief command in India from Lord Roberts, but he refused this and wrote in a letter to Mr Edward Stanhope:[1]

> I will only add this: in the event of my not going to India, I presume it will be offered to Sir Evelyn Wood. Aldershot as well as Ireland would thus become vacant for His Royal Highness the Duke of Connaught to take either of these two commands as might be arranged between himself and the Cabinet. I should be perfectly content to serve in whichever command the Duke of Connaught might leave open.

Three years later Lord Wolseley again stressed the Duke's qualifications for the Aldershot Command, but until then the appointment at Portsmouth held good, and Roberts remained in India.

Early in 1892 the Royal Family was plunged into deep mourning by the untimely death of the Duke's nephew, the Duke of Clarence, who was one of the victims of the serious epidemic of influenza which swept over the country at that time. Tragedy was added to the young Duke's death by its occurrence shortly before the date which had been fixed for his marriage with Princess May of Teck, our present Queen, and the blow to his relatives was severe. In the autumn of the same year, when the Court was no longer in mourning, a Grand Tattoo was held at Osborne under the direct command of the Duke of Connaught. At this spectacle, which was of unusual splendour, the Queen and many members of the Royal Family were present.

During the summer of 1893 it was rumoured that the Duke was about to relinquish the Southern Command, and that the garden-parties given at Portsmouth by their Royal Highnesses were in the nature of a farewell entertainment. These rumours were contradicted, and it was then announced that His Royal Highness would retain his command for the usual period of five years. This arrangement was soon altered, as the Duke was promoted to the chief command at Aldershot in October of the same year.

1 At this time Secretary of State for War.

The summer of 1893 was a very gay one, marked by many interesting social events. The chief of these was the wedding of our present King and Queen, which took place on July 6 at the Chapel Royal, St James's. The Princesses Margaret and Patricia of Connaught were both bridesmaids, and charming portraits of them in this role are included in the picture of the ceremony by L. Tuxen, now in the Royal collection. In that picture the Duke and Duchess of Connaught also figure prominently.

The Duchess was at Portsmouth on the occasion of her birthday (July 25), and the day began for her with a serenade from a military band. In the afternoon, accompanied by the Duke, she visited Queen Victoria at Osborne, travelling in the Royal yacht *Alberta*, and remaining for a dinner-party the Queen gave specially in her honour.

In those days the children spent a good part of their time at Osborne, where they were the playmates and companions of the children of Princess Henry of Battenberg. They romped in the gardens and held childish tea-parties in the same little chalet where their father had played as a child.

The Connaught children were charming, unaffected little people, great favourites with all who knew them, and they were very popular with the wives of the soldiers under their father's command. A corporal's wife to whose baby they had once carried some playthings remarked of them, "They're just as simple and nice as they can be, those little girls. I'm sure you'd never think they weren't the same as any of us, as common as good bread." A homely simile, yet if understood in its entirety it goes far to explain the widespread popularity of "the Connaughts."

The season at Cowes was an exceptionally brilliant one that year, and it is doubtful whether the town had ever contained so many people. The German Emperor was there on his yacht *Hohenzollern*, upon which he gave regal entertainments, and in return was much entertained. He often attended functions at Osborne, where the Queen was in residence. On August 4 (ominous date!), which on that occasion was a glorious day of unclouded sunshine and promise, he gave a great reception which both the Duke and Duchess of Connaught attended, finding the yacht wonderfully decorated with a touch of Imperial splendour. Queen Victoria did not go on board the yacht, but she steamed in the *Alberta* through the lines of escorting German warships in the evening, and the German Imperial standard was dipped as she passed, making her progress something in the nature of a great sea ceremony.

The social season of that summer had been extremely gay, and the Duke and Duchess had taken their full share in the festivities. In the autumn the Duke undertook a mission that contrasted sharply with the gaiety of those preceding months. After a reign of nearly half a century the Duke Ernst of Saxe-Coburg-Gotha died, and he was succeeded by the Duke of Edinburgh, the Duke of Connaught's elder brother. The Duke went to Coburg to attend the funeral on August 26, and he found the city in deep mourning, the whole place presenting a most gloomy appearance. The massive old gates of the city were heavily draped in black; black-and-white standards lined the streets, black obelisks were at every corner, and the fronts of the houses were all covered with black cloth. It seemed a veritable city of the dead. The obsequies were celebrated in sombre magnificence. Twelve of the Duke's foresters carried his coffin to the hearse, which was drawn by six horses with trappings of silver and black. Behind the coffin walked the Duke of Connaught, with the Prince of Wales and the new Duke Alfred (the Duke of Edinburgh). After them came an endless procession of mourners.

In the afternoon Duke Alfred issued a proclamation in which he swore allegiance to the German Empire and to its Emperor. In later years there arose the question of the Duke of Connaught's succession to the Coburg throne, to which the Duke replied, with frank directness, "England is good enough for me."

When the Duke returned to England he and his family went to London, where they stayed at Clarence House. In September the Duke and Duchess accepted a special invitation to stay with the Emperor of Austria at Guns, in order that the Duke might attend the Imperial Austrian military manoeuvres, in which he naturally took much interest. Before the manoeuvres several days were spent with the Emperor in Vienna, and the Duke explored that beautiful city before travelling to Güns, where by September 17 a large and distinguished party including many Royal guests had already assembled. The manoeuvres were on an impressive scale. Five Army Corps had been concentrated, and for so keen a soldier as the Duke valuable knowledge was to be gained in witnessing the handling of troops massed on the Continental scale. On the first day he rose at six, so as not to miss any incidents in a cavalry fight which lasted from that hour until noon. At the end of his visit he was made an Honorary Colonel of the 4th Regiment of Austrian Hussars, one of their crack regiments.

After a very rough passage the Duke and Duchess arrived in England on September 22, and they travelled at once to the old home at Bagshot, where the children were waiting to give them a joyful welcome.

Queen Victoria, always ambitious for the Duke, had never ceased to press his claims for the Aldershot Command when opportunity offered, and she was much gratified when he was given this command in the autumn of 1893.

Before leaving Portsmouth for Aldershot the Duke was entertained at a farewell dinner by the staff. Major-General Geary presided, and His Royal Highness left a farewell message that he would always remember with pleasure the three years when he commanded the Southern District and would continue to take the greatest interest in its welfare.

At first the new appointment was criticized in some quarters because Sir Evelyn Wood, the previous commander, had done so much to improve matters at Aldershot, where the influence of the intense conservatism of the old Duke of Cambridge at the Horse Guards had previously done much to retard Army, progress. Sir Evelyn Wood's command had been very popular and productive of progress, and, much to the Queen's annoyance, there were some murmurs at the selection of a member of the Royal Family to succeed him. These *The Times* summed up in a leader commenting on the appointment:

> When we bear this [the great reforms of Wood] in mind, some anxiety may be felt how far the change of commanding officers at Aldershot is likely to endanger the continuation of Sir Evelyn Wood's policy. Apprehension on this score does not necessarily imply mistrust of the capacity of the Duke of Connaught. We have cordially approved the Duke's appointment as fairly earned by service and warranted by the high opinion formed of his abilities by competent judges. Aldershot is quite as much a school for the General as for the troops under him. . . . Each newcomer has his spurs yet to win. But without in the least reflecting on the Duke of Connaught's abilities, it is a fair observation to make that, to the Army and the public generally, he has as yet given no clue to his professional sympathies. It is hardly conceivable that he should have formed none, but whether they lean to the side of the party of energetic progress or to the party which is content to advance

slowly, no one can say with certainty. It is not premature, therefore, to feel some uneasiness whether the good work accomplished by Sir Evelyn Wood is to be carried on in the same spirit and with the same adviser or advisers with the same capacity for work. . . .

Any signs of relapse into the old easy-going ways from which Aldershot has been so happily delivered would produce profound dissatisfaction. Sir Evelyn Wood leaves a standard to which for long all commanders at Aldershot will be expected to approach.

It is hardly necessary to mention that the Duke had been only a short time at Aldershot before it was proved beyond all dispute that he was fully prepared and thoroughly competent to carry on the good work of his predecessor and to emulate Sir Evelyn Wood's zeal and energy. He introduced several reforms on his own initiative, and kept up a high standard of discipline throughout the command. In the care for the man in the ranks which was a notable feature of all his commands his criticisms were directed against methods, rather than against those who suffered under them, especially when those methods bore too hardly upon the young soldier not yet inured to Army life, in the days when 'welfare' was not studied as it is in these times.

Health, as we noted during his time at Gibraltar, was always a special hobby with the Duke, as it was with Nelson. There was one occasion at Aldershot when the troops were likely to be inconvenienced by a sewage-farm, and he took a strong line on their behalf, entering himself into every detail of the arrangements, and making sure that nothing that the local authorities could do for the sake of the soldiers was left undone. One officer who was serving in his command at the time stated that "The Duke is not to be silenced when the comfort and health of the men is concerned," and this gives us a key to his method of procedure.

As on former occasions, he made the welfare of the soldiers' wives his special care, and at Aldershot he inaugurated a scheme for giving instruction in cookery to the married women in the camp. The instruction was free, and it was highly successful in promoting the well-being of the husbands thus provided with well-cooked food as economically as possible.

The Church of England had for years been doing yeoman service in providing accommodation for healthy indoor recreation for men off duty, and soon after his arrival the Duke was the principal guest at one of their anniversaries at their soldiers' hut. In all ways he promoted schemes for recreation, and he was glad when he was given an opportunity of opening the "Walker" Billiard Room in the camp. He made a speech at that ceremony, and took the opportunity of recording the immense improvement which had been effected in such matters during the eleven years that had passed since he had last served at Aldershot.

His official residence at Government House, Farnborough, was only a few miles from his home at Bagshot Park. Queen Victoria went over for a few days on several occasions. She took every opportunity of watching the reviews, military tattoos, and other displays which were held under the direction of her soldier son, and she always took a great interest in the proceedings. She reviewed the Aldershot troops in May and July 1894 and in July 1895.

In their early days at Aldershot the Duke and Duchess were visited by his eldest sister, the Empress Frederick of Germany. After having luncheon with her brother and sister-in-law she drove round the camp with an escort provided by the 9th Lancers, seeing everything of interest and gaining a good insight into the Duke's life and surroundings. On a later occasion (June 1895) Aldershot was visited by the Shahzada Nasrullah, son of the Ameer of Afghanistan, in whose honour 1 8,000 troops were paraded for review and marched past.

The Duke served for his full term of five years (October 9, 1893, to October 8, 1898) in chief command at Aldershot, but peace-time soldiering in those days differed materially from what it is in these. There was more pomp and circumstance, more parade and ceremonial, and very little of the constant and progressive annual training which has been introduced as the result of experience gained in the Anglo-Boer War of 1899-1902 and the Great War. Manoeuvres and 'sham fights' (well named!) were more of the nature of 'set pieces,' as less ground was available for training purposes. In these circumstances there was more monotony and less incident to record, so it is only possible to give a few selected examples of the Duke's activities to promote Army efficiency.

Mobility in those days depended mostly upon the selection and condition of horses and upon the marching powers of the infantry battalions. To both of these matters the Duke paid special attention. From the first he saw as much as he could of the cavalry and artillery horses, and he took care that the mounted units received the progressive training which his predecessor. Sir Evelyn Wood, had inaugurated. The infantry spent the winter in constant marches, carrying full equipment. After his first manoeuvres he commented adversely upon the marching, and especially upon the weight carried by the soldier on long marches, and was instrumental in lightening the men's burden considerably. In this he anticipated the present-day tendency in the British Army, resulting from war experience.

In his first year he complained that few tactical lessons could be learned on familiar manoeuvring ground, and set himself to introduce schemes covering wider areas. He also ordered long-distance signalling by visual methods, which were destined so soon afterward to be put to the test in South Africa. In one scheme communication was established between London and Guildford and other centres.

Subject to the limitations mentioned above, which existed before his time, the various manoeuvres and sham fights in his early years at Aldershot were highly successful, according to the standards of the day, and there was a special improvement in scouting work after the Duke's adverse criticisms. In 1895 he was partly responsible for a manoeuvre scheme over new ground in Surrey and Hampshire, in which about 15,000 troops were engaged. Sir William Butler and Sir Charles Warren were among the subordinate commanders. The scheme was very successful, and useful lessons were learned and recorded. On several such occasions the experience for commanders in leadership had been spoiled by lack of secrecy. The Duke introduced an improvement in this matter. Other smaller but interesting items before the manoeuvres began were orders to the men to have their hair cut before leaving the camp and not to indulge in excessive smoking, which would have an adverse effect upon their fitness and marching powers. An outstanding point was the stand made by the Duke against the old practice of wearing conspicuous scarlet and blue on such occasions. Apart from the fact that their appearance in such guise was ruined by a march of a few miles along hot, dusty roads, it was obviously undesirable for them to be unnecessarily conspicuous in the days of increasing ranges of lethal weapons.

The Duke earned the deep gratitude of the British Army for having, in conjunction with Lord Wolseley, been one of the pioneers in introducing a service dress of khaki colour. He lost no opportunity, when in a position to do so, of bringing to the notice of the military authorities the need for introducing a uniform suited to men on active service. His activities in that direction after the Egyptian campaign have already been noted. He carried them on in connexion with peace training.

In September 1895 the Duke and Duchess left England on a sad errand, that of attending the funeral of the Duchess's sister, the Hereditary Princess of Oldenburg, who had stayed with their Royal Highnesses in India, and at whose wedding they had first met. After the funeral they took a house in the Parc de Montretout, at Saint-Cloud, for a few weeks, where they were joined by the young Princesses Margaret and Patricia and their governess. Mile Damont.

On the retirement of the Duke of Cambridge, at the age of seventy-six, from the post of Commander-in-Chief in November 1895, it was rumoured that the Duke of Connaught would be appointed as his successor. There is no doubt that the Queen, who was always anxious that her son should rise to the very top of his profession, promoted his candidature vigorously. The news reached the ears of Lord Wolseley, who stood every chance of being offered the appointment himself, and he immediately let it be known to the Queen that he would be strongly averse to blocking the way for the Duke, of whose military qualities he had the very highest opinion. Despite the views of Her Majesty and of the Prince of Wales, who also wished his brother to be Commander-in-Chief at the Horse Guards — a position of great power in those days, but now in abeyance — the claims of the Duke were not considered officially, though Lord Lansdowne, as a member of Lord Salisbury's Coalition Government, mooted the idea of sending Wolseley to Berlin as Ambassador and thus clearing the way for the Duke. This proposal was eventually dropped. It was decided that the Duke was somewhat junior in the Service for the supreme command, and Lord Lansdowne appointed Lord Wolseley to succeed the Duke of Cambridge (the last Royalty to hold the office) as Commander-in-Chief of the British Army at the Horse Guards. The Duke of Connaught's godfather, the Duke of Wellington, was Commander-in-Chief, but his successor, Lord Hill, was made General Commanding-in-Chief. The Duke of Cambridge held a similar title until the Jubilee of 1887, when he was made Commander-in-Chief by patent. The office was abolished in 1904.

CHAPTER XVI

ALDERSHOT AND AFTER
(1896-1900; AGED FORTY-SIX TO FORTY-NINE)

The Aldershot Command — Activities of the Duke — Coronation of Tsar Nicholas II — A Catastrophe at Moscow — The Diamond Jubilee — Autumn Manoeuvres, 1897 — A Polo Match — The Queen at Aldershot — *The Times* on the Soldier Duke — Autumn Manoeuvres, 1898 — A Visit to Wilton House — French Army Manoeuvres — "Great Britain likes the French Army" — Farewell to Aldershot — A Foreign Tour — Reception by the Pope — Egypt — The Duke lays the Foundation-stone of the Assuan Dam — Up the Nile — Atbara and Khartoum — The Saxe-Coburg Succession — Prince Arthur's Views — The Question of Lord Wolseley's Successor.

In preceding chapters we have stressed — we hope not *ad nauseam* — the Duke's keen interest in the individual soldier, as this gives the keynote both to his personal inclination and to his system of command. While he was in command at Aldershot he issued instructions directing that special attention should be paid to the training of the individual soldier with a view to helping him to think and to act for himself, and there is no doubt that this training did much to improve the efficiency of the troops under his command and to make his time at Aldershot extremely valuable to the Army. In such matters he was ahead of his time. The need to train the individual for responsibility and initiative, then a new idea, has since become a commonplace of Army instructions.

His Royal Highness made many other innovations, among the most popular being a competition for regimental teams for cross-country marching, the prize being a handsome shield which he personally presented.

It was while the Duke was at Aldershot that Lord Wolseley, who had often had occasion to know how keen His Royal Highness was on improving the Service, wrote to him asking for his support in a scheme for increasing the Guards. Wolseley wanted a considerable addition to

166

the Army, and he conceived the idea of adding two battalions to the Foot Guards. His proposals were agreed to by the authorities, and, feeling sure of the Queen's support if he could get that of the Duke, Wolseley wrote a long letter explaining the proposals and begging his support. As a result the increase was announced in February 1897. In 1896 Wolseley, as Commander-in-Chief, went to Aldershot to review the troops. The Duke led the march past, and Wolseley expressed his satisfaction at seeing the men in such an excellent state of fitness.

In May 1896 the Duke, who had just been made a Knight Grand Cross of the Royal Victorian Order, and the Duchess went to Russia as the Queen's special representatives at the coronation of the Tsar Nicholas II. They left London accompanied by Major-General F. Grenfell (afterward Field-Marshal Lord Grenfell) and others, and travelled in the Royal yacht *Victoria and Albert* to Copenhagen, where they stayed a few days before completing their journey. They arrived in Moscow in time for the opening ceremonies connected with the coronation, which began with the proclamation *urbi et orbi* of the date of the great occasion. The programme began within the walls of the Kremlin, and it was continued in various public places in the city with the pomp and pageantry appropriate to the occasion. The Imperial grand procession entered Moscow on the 21st of May, the coronation taking place on the 26th in the Cathedral of the Assumption.

From the beginning there were premonitions of the terrible disaster that was to make that Coronation Day a day of mourning in a thousand homes. The parts of the ceremonies in which the public took a share seem to have been badly managed, no proper allowance being made for the vast crowds that were flocking into the city from the surrounding districts. The proclamations were read by heralds most magnificently arrayed in crimson, black, and gold, round whom were ranged squadrons of cavalry in their picturesque uniforms. The reading of the chief proclamation was followed by the distribution of beautifully printed copies of it among the crowd, and there began a great struggle for possession of the precious documents. Many people were injured, but this accident, while it might well have served as a warning to those who were responsible for the organization of the ceremonies, was overshadowed by that which was to follow. The Duke and his suite were present at the principal reading of the proclamation, and he also attended the solemn ceremony of the blessing of the Banner of the Empire, which took place afterward in the Palace of the Kremlin.

The coronation itself was magnificent. The Cathedral of the Assumption is comparatively small, so that few could see the actual ceremony in which, according to the words of the service, the Emperor and Empress were "wedded to the Empire." The Duke of Connaught, a striking figure in his scarlet uniform, followed the service with keen attention, and remarked afterward that what had impressed him most forcibly was the Tsar's striking likeness to his cousin the Duke of York (the present King) — a likeness which increased with the passing of the years.

As the crowns were placed on the heads of the Emperor and Empress the bells of the Kremlin pealed, and a hundred and one guns thundered in salute. The Emperor prepared to descend from the dais. As he did so a ray of sunshine struck the diamonds in his crown and collar, so that for a moment it seemed as if he were encompassed by a halo, and at the time this was looked upon as a good omen. In the light of the tragedy that was to follow the superstitious may be more inclined to regard it as a foreshadowing of the martyr's crown.

Soon after came an occurrence which even then was regarded as a terrible omen for the reign that had just opened, a presage of the many and dreadful disasters by which the reign of that most unhappy ruler was destined to be marked. Moscow was overcrowded. So great was the press of people that it was dangerous to walk in the streets where the throng was thickest, and the constant incoming of country folk, eager to see something of the day's ceremonies, increased the possibility of accidents.

At the Khodinskoe Plain. a vast open space, a distribution of gifts — a gaily painted tin mug, a sausage, some gingerbread, and a few nuts, all tied together in a bright-coloured handkerchief — from the Tsar to the people had been arranged. These bundles were to be distributed from booths set up on the plain, and the crowds besieged the booths in vast multitudes. So thickly did they press that the distributors, growing alarmed, made the terrible mistake of throwing the bundles into the crowd, who at once began to fight for them. There followed one of the most ghastly scenes that even Russia can have witnessed. The panic-maddened throng fought and trampled on each other like stampeding beasts, and when at last something like order was restored the scene rivalled a battlefield in horror and carnage. Nearly fifteen hundred people were trampled to death, and nearly seven hundred were severely injured.

The catastrophe cast a deep gloom over the city. From a national point of view it was necessary to carry out certain of the ceremonies, but the Tsar and his guests were deeply affected, and after the Duke of Connaught had fulfilled his engagement to inspect the Imperial troops at Moscow both he and the Duchess were thankful to get away from a city haunted by such tragic memories.

The year 1897 was marked by the Diamond Jubilee to celebrate the sixtieth year of Queen Victoria's reign — the longest reign of any British Sovereign. On the 19th of June Colonial troops marched from Victoria Park to the Mansion House. On the 20th, which fell on a Sunday, "Thanksgiving Day," solemn services were held throughout the land. On the 21st, at a State banquet, foreign Princes, envoys, and others were received at Buckingham Palace by the Queen. On the 22nd, "Commemoration Day," Her Majesty sent a telegram to all her subjects, "From my heart I thank my beloved subjects: may God bless them!" and then left Buckingham Palace with a great procession, preceded by Colonial, Asiatic, and African contingents of troops and the Colonial Premiers, for St Paul's Cathedral, where a thanksgiving service was conducted by the Archbishops of Canterbury and York. Prominent in the Queen's procession were British and foreign Princes, the Empress Frederick, the English Princesses and their children, Lord Wolseley, the Commander-in-Chief, the Princess of Wales, Princess Christian, the Prince of Wales, and the Dukes of Edinburgh, Connaught, and Cambridge. The dream of a British Empire Army, which was destined to materialize later, was beginning to take shape. The spectacle that raised the crowds to a greater pinnacle of enthusiasm than any but that of the Queen herself was the sight of a long procession of Indian and Colonial troops, led by Lord Roberts on his favourite grey Arab charger. The Indian contingent was the subject of the Duke of Connaught's particular concern.

Good use had been made of the ten years that had intervened since the earlier Jubilee, and the seed of unity in defence of the Empire had grown. Another Empire Conference was held to promote that growth, and again the Indian Princes assembled in London to do honour to the Sovereign. The Duke of Connaught played the same part as he had at the Jubilee of 1887, making it his special mission to receive these Indian potentates, many of whom he knew well, and to see to the comfort of the Indian contingents.

For the rest, the celebrations of 1897 followed the lines of those of 1887 — illuminations and festivities throughout the land; over 2500 beacon fires from Caithness to Cornwall; receptions, banquets, and reviews of the naval and military forces, all recorded in *The London Gazette Extraordinary* of March 14, 1898. In all the pomp and circumstance, and in the personal relationships which did so much to promote unity in the Empire, the Duke of Connaught bore his full share, before undertaking the direction of the Army manoeuvres held at Aldershot between August 16 and 25.

In these operations, though he was careful to allow great freedom of action to the officers under him, he took occasion to point out that the real object of manoeuvres was to discover mistakes and to rectify them. That was in the days when the public heard more about 'who won' than they did about the lessons which had been learned. No canvas was carried, and the whole of the supplies were borne on Army transport, which did away with the former long train of contractors' carts. The troops, when they struck camp, never knew where they would bivouac.

In the autumn of that year it was possible for the Duke to report to the War Office that there was a great improvement in the Volunteers who had visited Aldershot, in camp discipline, and in the zeal shown by the men in the carrying out of their duties.

The same year marked his appointment to the Colonelcy of the 6th (Inniskilling) Dragoons, which he held until 1922.

The Duke has always been interested in polo. One of the best of the many matches that he attended during his time at Aldershot was one between the Inniskillings and the 13th Hussars which he watched together with the Duke of Cambridge and a most brilliant company. After the game the Duke of Cambridge presented the shield to the winning team, and both he and the Duke of Connaught drank from the loving-cup that was passed round. During this season the Duke also presented a cup for the winner of point-to-point races for officers in the Aldershot Command.

The Jubilee of the Emperor of Austria's reign was celebrated in May 1898, and the Duke attended this ceremony accompanied by a number of officers of the 1st (King's) Dragoon Guards, of which regiment the Emperor was Honorary Colonel, and he took part in many of the celebrations.

In July of this year the Queen paid another of her numerous visits to Aldershot, and while there she presented colours to the 3rd Coldstream Guards. She also reviewed the troops under the Duke's command. This afforded an impressive military pageant. As the Queen approached the Duke's trumpeter heralded her coming, and the line saluted as the Royal procession passed. Thirteen thousand troops took part in the review, with which Her Majesty was much pleased, sending a special letter of commendation. Certain roads at Aldershot were renamed in commemoration of the Queen's visit. The road through which she had driven was called Queen's Avenue, and those leading from it were named after various Generals who had held the command at Aldershot — one of them after the Duke.

Another ceremony in the same month was a Torchlight Tattoo. This was held on the lawn in front of the Officers' Mess of the Gordon Highlanders, with whom the Duke dined. The surrounding trees were lavishly hung with fairy-lamps, while similar lights and Chinese lanterns were used as decorations in the shrubbery, the whole presenting a fine spectacle.

Though, to the military authorities, it was increasingly evident that the Duke's work at Aldershot had more than justified his appointment to the command, there were still critics here and there who seemed to imagine that because a man was a Prince it was impossible for him also to be a zealous and expert soldier. The words of *The Times* in reply to these are worth quoting, the more so, perhaps, because, as will be remembered, it was *The Times* which had originally questioned the wisdom of the appointment:

> The full value of that work, it is to be feared, is not appreciated owing to an absurd idea that, being a Prince, the Duke of Connaught cannot be a soldier also.
>
> It has become the fashion to depreciate His Royal Highness, and some find it no doubt to their advantage to appear fashionable in this connexion, but soldiers who have watched the Duke's career, and those certainly who have had dealings with him, are well aware how able and conscientious he is.
>
> Over and over again we have heard of the wonderful grasp that His Royal Highness has shown in his endeavours to continue the system inaugurated by his predecessor, Sir Evelyn Wood. . . .
>
> If anyone doubts the practical effect produced by this course of instruction he has merely to notice the way in which any military work in the field is done by the original Aldershot troops and to compare it with the performance of troops who have not been at Aldershot. The work of the former is that of the professional, the work of the latter has a flavour of the amateur.

His Royal Highness the Duke of Connaught may be well satisfied with the development of the system he has so carefully fostered.

For the autumn manoeuvres of 1898 the Duke and Duchess of Connaught were the guests at Wilton of the Earl and Countess of Pembroke. The final feature of these manoeuvres, which took place in Wiltshire and Dorsetshire, was the march past of the two Army Corps, in which all acquitted themselves with much credit. Huge admiring crowds assembled to watch the spectacle. The Duke's work in this year was aptly commented upon thus by *The Army and Navy Gazette*:

> His Royal Highness has shown himself a General of the highest capacity. He has astonished even those who know him best as a soldier by the easy way in which he has caused work to be done and the confidence he has inspired in all about him. The Duke is no Royal amateur; he has obtained his post by study and hard work.

Throughout this period the Duchess had done her utmost, as usual, to second the efforts of the Duke for the welfare of the soldiers and their wives. She was always anxious to associate herself with any scheme for their betterment, and among many other good works she opened a hostel for soldiers. The Duke was present at the ceremony, and the edifice was named, after the Duchess, the Louise Margaret Hostel.

In September 1898 the Duke attended the French military manoeuvres, and at their conclusion the French President, M. Faure, thanked him for his attendance and conferred upon him the Grand Cross of the Legion of Honour. In reply to a speech from the President, and after the toast of the foreign officers had been honoured, the Duke said:

> Allow me to say, Monsieur President, that Great Britain likes the French Army. I say this as an officer of the British Army and a member of the Royal Family.
>
> I trust our Armies will never meet as enemies and that comradeship will always exist between us.

The French Press expressed the warmest approval of the Duke's speech, and in commenting upon it the *Débats* said:

The presence of a Prince of the English Royal Family has been a stimulus to our troops. The Duke of Connaught by his spontaneous familiarity and the way in which he entered into the life of our soldiers, tasting their soups and trying their knapsacks, has won all their sympathies.

After holding the appointment for the normal period the Duke handed over the command at Aldershot to Sir Redvers Buller, but two days before he did so there was a great farewell parade. First there was a grand march past of all ranks; then of troops formed into line, the flanks thrown forward, the right being formed of the Horse Artillery and the Cavalry Brigade and the left of the remainder of the mounted troops ; then a general advance, and finally the Royal Salute. This parade was witnessed by the Duchess and by her two daughters, who had attended nearly all the reviews and field days during the Duke's command and were familiar as well as popular figures in the camp.

After the review the Duke addressed the Generals and commanding officers, and, in an impressive speech, thanked them all for the help that they had given to him during his command. There had, he proceeded, been a great many innovations, and this had meant hard work for them all, but he felt that he could say that he was leaving the command in a thoroughly efficient state. Then came the final leave-takings. The Duke shook hands with the officers, and the Royal carriage, followed by the Duke, drove slowly toward Government House while the bands struck up *Auld Lang Syne*. The wives of the officers of the Headquarters staff presented the Duchess with a magnificent bouquet, as a token of their regret at losing her, and both she and the Duke were plainly moved by the great regret manifested by all ranks at their departure.

The Duke's farewell order was worded:

> In relinquishing command of the Aldershot District I wish to thank the General Staff and command officers. Regular and departmental officers, for the unfailing support they have at all times given me.
> Owing to the cheerful manner in which all ranks have responded to any call made upon them, the example set by warrant officers and N.C.O.'s, and the good behaviour of the men, my duties have been

made pleasant. It is with the greatest regret that I now bid farewell to those with whom I am so proud to have been associated.

ARTHUR
General

After relinquishing the command at Aldershot, and before he proceeded to his new command in Ireland in 1900, the Duke, accompanied by the Duchess, made a tour in the East. They went first to Rome, where Princess Margaret and Princess Patricia accompanied them. The Royal party stayed at the Hotel Bristol, and did a certain amount of enjoyable sightseeing.

After paying formal calls on the King and Queen of Italy the Duke and Duchess set themselves to explore the city, visiting the principal basilicas, the Sistine Chapel, the Forum, the Colosseum, which they also saw by moonlight, and all the historic marvels of the Eternal City, ending their sightseeing with a lengthy promenade along the famous Appian Way. On January 29 the Pope received the Royal party, including the Princesses, in audience. They were escorted to the Vatican by the Papal Guard, and afterward the Duke, who was in uniform, visited Cardinal Rampolla. With the Duchess and the young Princesses he then dined with the King and Queen.

At the beginning of February the Duke and Duchess went on to Egypt while the Princesses returned to Florence. Their Royal Highnesses first went to Cairo via Alexandria, and then to Assuan to take part in the ceremony marking the beginning of the great Assuan Dam, of which the Duke had been invited to lay the foundation-stone. The stone, like everything else connected with this stupendous project, was enormous. It weighed five and a half tons, and it was composed of solid granite, bearing the inscription, with the Turkish crescent and star, "This stone will be laid by H.R.H. the Duke of Connaught, Feb. 12th, 1899." Messrs John Aird and Co., the English engineers, erected the dam, upon which 500 Europeans and 5000 natives were employed. After laying the stone the Duke turned to Fakhry Pasha and said that it had given him great pleasure to lay the foundation-stone of such a colossal work. He also wrote a message, to be transmitted to the Khedive, which ran:

Having this moment completed the laying of the foundation-stone of the Great Dam at the request of your Highness, I telegraph my sincere congratulations on the occasion of Bairam.

After the ceremony was concluded the Duke and Duchess crossed the top of the cataract and explored the bazaars, returning to Assuan in the yacht which the Khedive had placed at their disposal.

They spent another month touring Egypt, and everywhere had a most cordial reception. The Duke was able to visit again the scene of his first campaign. They went to Wady Haifa and Khartoum, and they explored the battlefield of Atbara, ending their tour at Cimiez, on the French Riviera, where the Queen was staying, on March 17.

In February 1899 occurred the death of Prince Alfred, only son and heir of the Duke of Saxe-Coburg-Gotha. There thus arose the question of a successor, and Queen Victoria, who, as we have seen, was always extremely ambitious for the Duke of Connaught, inclined to the idea that he was entitled to the succession, and wanted his name to be submitted to the local Diets of the two duchies. She did not think it necessary to inform the Kaiser of her suggestion. He was not famed for tact with his senior relatives, and when he heard of it he ridiculed her choice. He went so far as to threaten her and Lord Salisbury with the veto of his Reichstag. Nevertheless the local Diets favoured the Duke of Connaught as the future ruler, but the Duke, in consultation with the Queen, promptly renounced his candidature, extending his refusal to his son, Prince Arthur.

It is said that the young Prince, who was then at Eton, where his father had been educated, held strong views on the desirability of remaining an Englishman, so when it came to his ears that there was a possibility of his being forced to become a German Prince he sought out his cousin, the Duke of Albany's son (who eventually did occupy the throne of Saxe-Coburg-Gotha), and threatened him with a thrashing if he did not at once offer himself as a candidate!

On January 9, 1900, the Duke of Connaught was appointed General Commanding the Forces in Ireland, in succession to Lord Roberts, who was leaving for South Africa to take over the command of the troops engaged in the Boer War. Later in the same year the office of Commander-in-Chief became vacant, as Lord Wolseley's tenure of office was ended. The Queen still wished the Duke to be appointed to this supreme command, but even as Lord Lansdowne had withstood her in 1895, so now Lord Salisbury opposed her views. He put forward the suggestion that Lord Roberts' South African service entitled him to the post. Still unconvinced, the Queen consulted the Prince of Wales, who, to her surprise, sided with Lord Salisbury and told her he considered Lord Roberts' claims to be superior to those of his brother. With that Her Majesty had to rest content.

'The First of May, 1851'. Queen Victoria, Prince Albert, Prince Arthur and the Duke of Wellington, engraving after a portrait by Franz Xaver Winterhalter

Queen Victoria, the Prince Consort and their family at Osborne House, 1857, Prince Arthur standing at front, fourth from left

Prince Arthur and Prince Leopold, c.1864

Queen Victoria and Prince Arthur, 1871

The Duke and Duchess of Connaught with their two elder children,
Princess Margaret and Prince Arthur (in mother's arms), 1883

The Duke and Duchess of Connaught with their children, Prince Arthur, Princesses Margaret (standing) and Patricia, 1893

The Prince of Wales, Duke of Connaught
and Duke of Edinburgh, 1893

Clarence House, London home to the Duke of Edinburgh and then to
the Duke of Connaught, 1874

*Queen Victoria, Emperor William II, the Empress Frederick and various other members of the royal family at Coburg for the wedding of Ernest, Grand Duke of Hesse and Princess Victoria Melita, April 1894.
The Duke of Connaught stands at right of the second row from back, with the Duchess in front of him*

*Prince Gustavus Adolphus of Sweden and Princess Margaret
at their wedding, June 1905*

*The Duke and Duchess of Connaught with Princess Patricia
and Prince Arthur, 1907*

The Duchess of Connaught, 1907

Rideau Hall, Ottawa, about 1918

Prince Arthur of Connaught with the Duchess of Fife and bridesmaids at their wedding, October 1913

*The Duke of Connaught with General Henry Horne and troops
In Canada, 1917*

The Duke of Connaught and generals in Canada, 1918

*The Duke of Connaught in full masonic dress as
Grand Master of England*

The Duke of Connaught in the uniform of the Highland Light Infantry

*The Duke of Connaught at the Great Imperial Scout Jamboree,
Wembley, 1924*

The Duke of Connaught in the garden of his villa,
Les Bruyères, near Beaulieu

CHAPTER XVII

DEATH OF QUEEN VICTORIA— KING EDWARD'S CORONATION AND THE DELHI DURBAR
(1900-2; AGED FIFTY TO FIFTY-TWO)

A Visit to the Empress Frederick — Kaiser William II — The Death of Queen Victoria — The Duke present at her Deathbed — Executor of her Will — The Queen's Funeral — The Duke assumes Command in Ireland — Colonel-in-Chief of the Highland Light Infantry — Command of the Third Army Corps — King Edward's Illness — The Coronation postponed — The Duke commands on the Horse Guards Parade — Queen Alexandra and the Prince of Wales — King Edward's Coronation — The Duke's Part therein — Visit to Egypt — Opening the Nile Barrage — To India for the Delhi Durbar — A Great Procession — The Gorgeous Durbar Ceremonies — The Duke and the Indian Princes — A Visit to the North-West Frontier — Another Indian Tour — Sport with Tigers — Return to Ireland.

In October 1900 the Duke and Duchess of Connaught visited Germany in order to see the Empress Frederick, who was seriously ill with the malady which eventually proved fatal. It was a sad visit, as may be imagined, but the Empress's health appeared to improve, and, more hopeful of her condition, they returned to England, intending to visit the Empress again in the following autumn.

In January of the following year the Duke paid another visit to Germany, this time in order to attend the two-hundredth anniversary of the foundation of the Prussian Monarchy. Queen Victoria was not in very good health at the time, but she had such an excellent constitution, hardly having had a day's illness in all her long life, that her indisposition was not taken very seriously. It was regarded merely as a temporary condition which the change to Osborne would very likely set right, so there was no question of it being necessary for the Duke to remain in England.

The Hohenzollern celebration in Germany was observed all over the country with the greatest enthusiasm, and the Duke took part in many of the functions. One of the most important of them was the great thanksgiving service in the Royal Chapel, Potsdam, at which the Kaiser founded a new order, the Order of Merit of the Prussian Crown.

After these ceremonies the Duke paid another visit to his sister the Empress Frederick, whose malady was then known to be incurable. He had intended to stay with the Empress for a week and then to return to Ireland, where he had taken up the command, but in the meantime the Queen's health had grown worse. Telegrams were sent to the Duke, describing her condition; on January 19 matters appeared to be so serious that he decided to return home at once.

Unfortunately the Flushing express had left, but the Kaiser, on hearing of his grandmother's illness, had decided, with typical impulsiveness, that he would accompany his uncle to England, and that they must travel in his own special train. The Kaiser's dramatic sense of his position in such matters was always strongly accentuated, and as soon as he knew of Queen Victoria's serious illness he took charge of all arrangements, including the Duke of Connaught's, ordered that all the Berlin ceremonies should be postponed, and set off with the Duke.

It may be that William II was, as he always averred, very fond of his grandmother, but it is typical that he saw himself so much the chief figure in the anxious journey that he insisted on driving the train himself and on steering the vessel in which they crossed. It was further typical of the "All-Highest" that his method, doubtless well-intentioned, of trying to relieve the Duke's anxiety was to make little jokes, saying to members of his suite, "Uncle Arthur is so downhearted we must cheer him up."

They left Berlin at six o'clock on the evening of the 19th, the Kaiser wearing the uniform of an English regiment, and, in order to return the compliment, the Duke in the uniform of the Ziethen Hussars. They reached Buckingham Palace on the evening of the following day. They were received at the Palace by the Prince of Wales, who, as the Queen seemed a little better, had been able to leave Osborne for the occasion. On the next day they all went to Osborne, crossing in the Alberta. At Osborne the Kaiser still, by over-prominence and monopolizing attention, showed some lack of a sense of proportion in surroundings of such deep tragedy, but this doubtless was temperamental, not intentional.

The Queen lived for another day after the arrival of the son of whom she had always been so fond, and, happily, she was able to recognize all her family before she passed away. Around her deathbed were gathered the Prince of Wales and the Princesses Helena, Louise, and Beatrice, besides the Duke of Connaught, and at half-past six on January 22 the tolling of innumerable church bells told the nation that the Great Queen had breathed her last. Before her death she had commanded the full details of her funeral, even to the music that was to be played. The Duke of Connaught was one of the executors of her will, together with Princess Beatrice and Lieutenant-Colonel Sir Fleetwood Edwards, Keeper of the Privy Purse, and the day after Her Majesty's death the Duke accompanied the Prince of Wales to attend to the many duties which the occasion entailed.

The sad pageantry of the funeral of the Queen on February 1 was a scene that will live for ever in the memory of those who witnessed it. The ceremony began with a slow passage in a calm sea from the Isle of Wight in the *Alberta* between the lines of warships, escorted by destroyers, British and foreign, all with flags at half-mast, the whole silhouetted against the glory of a sunset seldom equalled in England in the winter months. When the Alberta arrived at Portsmouth a brief service was held on board at which the new Sovereign and the Duke of Connaught were present. Later there came the journey to London, where, at Victoria Station, Kings, Princes, ambassadors, and great statesmen awaited, on February 2, the last coming of the Queen. The forces were fully represented. There were in attendance bands of the Brigade of Guards (massed), of the Royal Artillery and the Royal Engineers, and of the Royal Marines. The coffin was reverently removed from the train and placed on a gun-carriage, and the procession was formed for the progress through the sorrowing multitudes who thronged to the capital for the occasion.

Before the gun-carriage the bands played at intervals Chopin's *Funeral March* and Beethoven's *Funeral March in B Flat Minor*. Immediately behind the coffin rode King Edward on his charger, wearing the uniform of a British Field-Marshal, on his right the German Emperor and on his left the Duke of Connaught. In streets and thoroughfares hung with the purple of Royal mourning dense crowds paid the tribute of deep silence as the great *cortège* passed on to Paddington. At Windsor a smaller procession was formed. While on the way to St George's Chapel a small mishap occurred, which might have been more serious. A horse in the team drawing the gun-carriage became restive and kicked, nearly striking the King, who followed behind on foot. The horses were at once removed, and the great Sea

Queen was drawn to her last resting-place by bluejackets from her last Guard of Honour. So ended the Victorian Era, a period of great glory, prosperity, and extension of world influence, leaving great responsibilities on the shoulders of generations to come.

At the time of Queen Victoria's death the Anglo-Boer War had lasted for fifteen months. It had been thought that the end was in sight and that the anxiety and sorrows that she suffered would be relieved in her lifetime by an honourable peace. Lord Roberts had returned in December 1900 in that belief, but the war lasted until May 1902.

The Duke of Connaught, who had relieved Lord Roberts in the Irish Command after the "Black Week" of disaster in South Africa in December 1899, could have no opportunity of serving where his heart was, with the Army at the front. In Ireland he continued to carry out his duties with the zealous thoroughness which had characterized his rule at Aldershot, finding there, as he had elsewhere, great value in that memory for faces for which his family is world-famous. On one occasion, as he was passing through a soldiers' hospital soon after he took over the command in Ireland, he stopped beside a bed in which lay a private, and amazed the man by telling him that he recognized him as having formed one of a Guard of Honour for himself and the Duchess at Gordon's palace at Khartoum during their Egyptian tour.

In September 1901 the Duke became Colonel-in-Chief of the Highland Light Infantry. On October 1 he was given the command of the Third Army Corps in Ireland. In June 1902 he was promoted to the rank of Field-Marshal, and it was in this capacity, wearing his Field-Marshal's uniform for the first time, that he commanded two great parades of the Colonial and Indian troops on the Horse Guards Parade on the occasion of the postponement of the coronation of King Edward owing to grave illness. Both of these parades were of exceptional brilliance, and on each occasion the Duke rode up with his staff to take direct personal command. The King at the time was lying on his sick-bed at Buckingham Palace, and when Queen Alexandra appeared on the parade-ground in her carriage there was a tremendous outbreak of sympathetic cheering, which was repeated when the Prince of Wales rode up to inspect the troops. The King sent a kind message to his soldiers and to the people, "having heard the cheering with satisfaction in his sick-room." The Duke received a warm welcome, and when after the march past he gave the order "Hats off!" and called for three cheers for the King, a roar of enthusiastic shouts from the crowd mingled with those of the soldiers.

The Duke took a special pleasure in commanding the second parade, that of the Indian troops. Many of the officers were personally known to him from his long tenure of commands in India, and the varied uniforms of the East gave an added brilliance to the spectacle. On this occasion he again called for three cheers, which were given with renewed heartiness.

Lieutenant-Colonel J. Mackenzie-Rogan, in his *Fifty Years of Army Music*, gives, in connexion with these parades, an interesting example of the Duke's knowledge of Army music and its correct traditions. Queen Alexandra arrived first on the parade-ground. Then came the Prince of Wales (the present King), who represented the King, and Lieutenant-Colonel Mackenzie-Rogan decided that he would be doing the correct thing in such matters by playing six bars of the National Anthem for the Queen, as Consort, and the whole for the Prince, as representative of the reigning monarch. After the parade a question arose as to whether Lieutenant-Colonel Mackenzie-Rogan had acted correctly. On the following day the Duke of Connaught rode up to where the bands were waiting and complimented them upon their performance, whereupon Lieutenant-Colonel Mackenzie-Rogan seized the opportunity to ask His Royal Highness whether his decision about the National Anthem had been correct. "What you did was perfectly correct," said the Duke promptly, and the decision remained the rule until King Edward's coronation, when he gave orders that all Guards of Honour should play the National Anthem for the Queen exactly as they would play it for himself.

It was at this time that the Duke visited the Indian troops at Hampton Court, and gave them their South African and China War medals. He spent some time with them, chatting with many of the officers. Soon afterward he presented medals to the Colonial troops at Alexandra Park. Even as the Crown links together the peoples of the Empire, so has the Duke of Connaught represented on many occasions the link between the Empire's armies.

On July 13 the Duke was at the station to meet Lord Kitchener on his return from South Africa after the Peace of Vereeniging, and he was also present at the great banquet given in Kitchener's honour at St James's Palace, at which the Prince of Wales took the chair.

The great event of the year 1902 was the recovery of the King, who, in an intimate letter to his people, wrote from Buckingham Palace on August 8:

The postponement of the ceremony owing to my illness caused, I fear, much inconvenience and trouble to all those who attended to celebrate it; but their disappointment was borne by them with admirable patience and temper.

On the following day the coronation of King Edward VII and Queen Alexandra took place in Westminster Abbey with great pomp and ceremony. Many of the Empire's statesmen from India, the Dominions, and the Colonies were present, and there were heartfelt and thankful rejoicings throughout the Empire. A few days later the King received the Indian Princes and Dominion Premiers at Buckingham Palace, and held an investiture parade of the Colonial and Indian troops.

The Duke of Connaught was entrusted with the whole of the military arrangements for the great ceremony in the Abbey, and these he superintended with the thoroughness which has characterized him in the whole of his military career. From early in the morning he drove from point to point in a motor-car, accompanied by Sir Henry Trotter, attending to the numerous details which such a ceremony involved. The Duke was in his Field-Marshal's uniform, carrying the baton of his rank, and whenever he appeared the crowd which had lined the streets since dawn cheered him heartily. He obtained special recognition from the London crowd, as he invariably did (and does) even when quite alone and not in uniform. On this occasion the Duke's car was held up by the traffic at one point, whereupon an agitated onlooker in the crowd cried out, "'Urry up, your Grace! You'll be late for the show!" He was not late, and at the magnificent ceremony in the Abbey he occupied, together with the Prince of Wales and the old Duke of Cambridge, a conspicuous position seated on a chair covered with crimson near the King's Throne.

Though the coronation service was, in the main, conducted in accordance with old tradition, there was one interesting innovation in which the Duke was directly concerned. A slight alteration was made in the ' Homage.' This had formerly been the same for the Princes of the Blood Royal as it was for other peers of the realm, but on this occasion the Royal Princes removed their coronets, knelt in their places, and, with the Prince of Wales leading, repeated the Homage, each in his own name, in these words:

I, Duke of Connaught, do become your liege man of life and limb and of earthly worship and faith and truth. I will bear unto you, to live and die, against all manner of folks. So help me God.

There had been one mishap among the troops lining the route. The horse of Trooper Oburn, of Driscoll's Scouts, fell on him, injuring him severely, and it was characteristic of the Duke's care and thought for men in the ranks that, before returning to Ireland thirty-six hours later, he found time to call personally at St George's Hospital in order to inquire after Oburn, whom he was relieved to find a little better though not out of danger.

At the end of the year the Duke and Duchess of Connaught again visited India, this time as representatives of the Royal Family at the State Durbar and proclamation of King Edward at Delhi, a spectacle as magnificent as any that even India can number among her State pageants. They left England on November 30 in the Renown, which was met at Genoa by the remainder of the Royal Party. Besides attending the Durbar, the Duke had other duties to perform in the course of his tour, one of the chief of these being the inauguration of the great Nile barrage, the foundation-stone of which he had laid when he visited Assuan on his Egyptian tour.

Their Royal Highnesses arrived at Port Said on December 6, and they travelled straight up to Cairo. As they entered the train the Duke took care to ascertain when they would be passing Tel-el-Kebir, as he wanted to show the Duchess the scene of the battle in which he took part in 1882. At Cairo an escort of the Rifle Brigade awaited them, and during his stay the Duke made a special inspection of the regiment at the Citadel. In the course of an address delivered to the men he spoke feelingly of the vacancies left in the ranks by their losses in South Africa, where the regiment had greatly distinguished itself, and he presented the war medals.

On leaving Cairo the Duke and Duchess went up the Nile, where the inauguration of the barrage took place on December 10. Special trollies were used to convey the party along the top of the immense dam, and the Duke and Duchess were deeply interested in the vast enterprise, asking many questions about its progress since their last visit. The Duke having laid the first stone, it was suggested that the Duchess should lay the last. This she did, and the Duke then opened the lock-gates. The Khedive opened the sluices of the dam, so letting the water through. It was a wonderful ceremony, only to be fully appreciated by those who had seen the great enterprise in the course of construction, and in their speeches both the Duke and the Khedive congratulated the engineers on the magnificent result of their labours.

Their Royal Highnesses stayed for a few days in the neighbourhood, exploring Assuan and Assiut. They also paid a visit to the wonderful Tomb of the Kings at Luxor, where they were introduced, not for the first time, to the marvels of ancient Egypt. They had an enthusiastic reception wherever they went, and among the many tributes paid to them was a quaint one from the donkey-boys of Egypt, many of whom, to the great amusement of the tourists, promptly rechristened their steeds "Duky Conart" or "Duchessy Conart," in accordance with their usual practice of using the names of celebrities to advertise their mounts.

When the Duke and Duchess got back to Cairo many dinners, balls, and similar functions were given in their honour as well as several reviews, which the Duke attended in his military capacity, and after a brief stay they again boarded the Renown and went on their way to India.

At Bombay they had their third experience of a magnificent reception, which was repeated wherever they went, India having good cause for welcoming "the Connaughts" with affection. All those who had in any way been brought into contact with their Royal Highnesses during their previous sojourns in the country flocked together in crowds in the hope of being able merely to catch a glimpse of them as they passed.

The Duke and Duchess arrived at Delhi toward the end of December. Lord Curzon was Viceroy of India at that time, and Lord Kitchener Commander-in-Chief. As the direct representative of the King-Emperor, Lord Curzon took precedence before the Duke, but, owing partly to their previous knowledge of him and all that his command in their country had stood for, and partly to the fact that he was of Royal blood (to them an almost divine attribute), it was the Duke whom the people were most anxious to see, and, as *The Times* remarked:

> To the native crowd especially the moment of the appearance of the Duke of Connaught was always that of the most interest. All eyes arc raised with reverent curiosity towards the brother and sister-in-law of the Sovereign, towards the personality of the Duke which has

that combination of soldierly dignity, personal charm and good looks which give him great prestige amongst them.

No verbal description can do justice to the splendour and magnificence of the great Durbar held in the New Year, 1903, the most spectacular ceremony of its kind, and it was surpassed only by the Durbar which was held nine years later, when their Majesties King George and Queen Mary visited India in person.

The great ceremonies began with the State entry of the Viceroy and the Duke and Duchess of Connaught into Delhi on December 29. This entry was made on elephants, gorgeously caparisoned. There were over seventy of these great beasts, preceded by two, larger even than their fellows, which had been lent for the occasion by Indian potentates. As the elephants came in sight the troops presented arms and the massed band struck up the National Anthem. The first mighty creature carried a golden howdah of wonderful workmanship containing the Viceroy and Lady Curzon. On the second great elephant, lent by the Maharajah of Jaipur, were the Duke and Duchess of Connaught in a silver howdah, while on both animals magnificently embroidered saddle-cloths with golden fringes swept to the ground. Then came over fifty Indian Princes, all mounted on beasts of ceremony, and all clad in their robes of State, on which there flashed and sparkled jewels worth an Emperor's ransom. Along six miles of streets, lined with troops, every inch packed with spectators, this procession passed in waves of brilliant colour, a glittering spectacle befitting even the greatness of the occasion. And here we can take note of the aftermath as embodied in a book entitled The British Crown and Indian States : an Outline Sketch drawn up on behalf of the Standing Committee of the Chamber of Princes in India,[1] in which the points are made that the native rulers still have no voice with regard to naval movements in Eastern waters and that there is no impartial tribunal to decide disputes with the Government of British India. There can be no doubt that such questions will be settled amicably and by sympathy and goodwill, sentiments in the development of which the Duke of Connaught bore a full share.

On the next day the Arts Exhibition was opened, and on January 1 the great Durbar itself.

1 Published in 1919.

In the centre of the horseshoe-shaped arena was placed the dais, on which were two thrones, that of the Duke being slightly lower and somewhat less richly ornamented than that of the Viceroy. There Lord Curzon and His Royal Highness took their seats, the Duke in the uniform of a Field-Marshal and wearing many Orders, while the Duchess sat with Lady Curzon, slightly in the rear of the dais. First came the proclamation of the King-Emperor. This was read by the Herald, Major Maxwell, of the 6th Prince of Wales's Bengal Cavalry, who made a most impressive figure wearing golden raiment and mounted on a jet-black charger with satin tabard embroidered, back and front, with the Royal Standard. His voice rang out clear and full, and as the last word was spoken the trumpets sounded and the King-Emperor's standard was unfurled. Then Lord Curzon read the King's message, which was given full weight by the dignified and impressive tones of the speaker. After this came the ceremony of receiving the Indian Princes and potentates, the Viceroy and the Duke taking an equal part in the reception. This presented an imposing spectacle as each Indian ruler came to the dais offering his message of congratulation to His Majesty on his coronation.

On January 3 a grand investiture was held in the Diwan-i-Am at Delhi, and in this the Duke again figured conspicuously, a most impressive presence that excited the admiration of the Indian and European spectators. His Royal Highness wore the insignia and robes of the Star of India, and his pale blue mantle was upheld by two dark-eyed little pages, scions of Indian princely houses. Delightful little figures in their shining raiment, they were fully sensible of the honour done them, and so desperately anxious lest they should fail in the least of their duties that more than once they brought a twinkle to the eyes of the Duke. Knowledge of the language was again of service to him on this occasion, as it enabled him to talk to many of the Indian rulers in their own tongue, which caused much pleasure, and he renewed in the pleasantest fashion many of the acquaintanceships that he had formed during the years of his Indian commands.

The Duke took special interest in the great procession of the Indian Princes' retainers. That, in its way, was almost as attractive as the experience of the Durbar itself. Each set of retainers made a point of having something to distinguish it from the rest. One, for instance, chose a huge Noah's Ark, painted in gold and drawn by two elephants, with a baby elephant following in the rear. The procession included numerous elephants, many of them richly painted. One of them, painted wine-colour, caused something of a sensation (much to the delight of its owners) by stopping at the saluting-point, rearing up on its hind legs, and saluting with a great trumpeting.

When the Durbar ceremonies were all over, and the "great city of tents" began to disappear, the Duke and Duchess left Delhi and travelled to the North-West Frontier. There they visited once again the Khyber Pass, Peshawar, and many of the places which were familiar to them during their previous tours. The Duke also took the opportunity of visiting Malakand and scenes of the comparatively recent battles of 1895 and 1897, and he naturally was specially interested in hearing the details of the fighting on the actual spot where it had taken place.

Then they turned southward, and at many places, including Gwalior, the Duke enjoyed some excellent shooting, being lucky enough to secure several very fine tigers.

This tour, which the Duke had of set purpose made as extensive as possible, left an excellent impression in India, and it renewed all the old loyalty which the former presence of the Duke had inspired, as well as convincing many of the chief rulers that their services to the State were not forgotten by the son of the great Queen-Empress whom they had learned to know so well ten years before.

On returning home their Royal Highnesses reached England on March 27, and they left at once for Ireland, where the Duke resumed his command.

CHAPTER XVIII

THE IRISH COMMAND
(1902-4; AGED FIFTY-TWO TO FIFTY-FOUR)

The Royal Family and Ireland — King Edward's Visits — Popularity of King Edward and Queen Alexandra in Ireland — The Views of a 'Jarvey' — Review in Phoenix Park — The Duke and the Naval Brigade — The Queen's Doves of Peace — Prince Arthur's Illness — Inspections and Reviews — No 'Eyewash' — Sport in Ireland — The Duchess plays Hockey — A Month in London — The Duke on the Irish — Marriage of Princess Alice of Albany — A Brilliant Dublin Season — Charm of the Young Princesses — Colonel of the Royal Army Service Corps — Colonel-in-Chief of the Royal Dublin Fusiliers — Leaving Ireland — The Duke the First Inspector-General of the Forces — Colonel of the Grenadier Guards — The King and Queen visit Dublin again — Funeral of His Royal Highness the Duke of Cambridge — The Duke of Connaught and the Bandmaster.

In previous chapters some references have been made to the intimate connexion between the Duke of Connaught, the "Prince Pat" of earlier years, and Ireland. Additional proofs will in due course be furnished of the affection borne for him by the people of Ireland, but meanwhile some further notes on the subject of the relationship between Ireland and the Royal Family in Victorian days may be found of value in considering the atmosphere which surrounded the Duke during the years when he was in command of the British Army in the "disthressful country." Even the troublous years of the Boer War did nothing to diminish the Duke's popularity. His third name and the name of his younger daughter may have constituted a claim upon the affections of the Irish, but, apart from any such consideration, the whole family had always been accorded a special place in their hearts. During this period of the Duke's command even the Nationalist papers gave frequent accounts of the cordial receptions that were given to them wherever they went.

The period was marked specially by a visit to the country of King Edward, who was also, from previous acquaintanceship, a strong favourite with the Irish. He had first visited the country with his parents in 1849, and after this visit Queen Victoria wrote in her journal:

> I intend to create Bertie Earl of Dublin as a compliment to the town and country. He has no Irish title, though he was born with several Scotch ones.

In 1853 the "Earl" again visited Ireland. He was nearly twelve at the time, and he wore a sprig of shamrock in his buttonhole, much to the delight of the crowd. At the age of seventeen he spent a holiday at Killarney, where he charmed the people with his gay good-humour and his open admiration of their beautiful country. On that occasion Colonel Herbert of Muckruss placed his eight-oared barge at the Prince's disposal, and while he was being rowed near Innisfallen he saw a fine root of shamrock and sent one of the oarsmen ashore to dig it up for him. The Prince sent it back to Osborne with injunctions that it should be planted in his own garden, where it flourished exceedingly.

Subsequently he underwent some military training at the Curragh, and in 1868 he and the Princess paid their first visit together. On that occasion the Prince gave great pleasure to the Irish people by expressing a wish that on the occasion of their public entry into Dublin the troops should be withdrawn from the streets. Both the Prince and the Princess of Wales met with a most enthusiastic reception. The courtly Irish called the Princess " the Rose of England," and flocked to catch a glimpse of the lady whose beauty and grace captivated all hearts. The Princess visited Alexandra College, where the girl graduates strewed her pathway with flowers. In memory of that visit her portrait still adorns the college hall. During the same tour the Prince was installed as a Knight of St Patrick, the ceremony, in which both Catholics and Protestants participated, taking place in the Cathedral of St Patrick on April 18.

The Prince and Princess again visited Ireland in the spring of 1885, in spite of the fact that, owing to the prolonged trouble over Home Rule, the Irish Nationalists strongly disapproved of the visit, and there were dark hints of the dangers that might arise if it were carried out. The people, however, proved more reasonable than their leaders, and the Prince and Princess were given the warmest welcome everywhere. It was on this occasion that the Princess was made Doctor of Music and the Prince a Doctor of Laws by the University of Dublin.

Warm as had been the welcome given to their Royal Highnesses on those occasions, their reception was even more cordial when, as King and Queen, they revisited Ireland in 1905, when the influence of the prolonged residence of the Duke and Duchess of Connaught in Dublin had done so much to increase the popularity of the whole of the Royal Family. Even the weather favoured the visit, and glorious sunshine prevailed throughout the whole of their Majesties' stay in the Emerald Isle. There were many State functions, balls, and receptions, and the King and Queen also paid many private visits to various institutions and charmed every one with their sympathetic interest in the places which they visited and in the people with whom they were brought into contact. Without escort they visited poor houses in the back streets of Dublin, and the fame and popularity of this procedure travelled to the far west to Bantry Bay, where the 'jarveys' of outside-cars that carried naval officers when on shore told their passengers that a King who did that was "all right."

A great ceremonial review, under the Duke of Connaught's command, was held in Phoenix Park, and there an observer remarked upon an incident which illustrates the Duke's thoughtfulness. A naval brigade, from the Fleet at Kingstown, was on the right of the line. At the conclusion of the ceremony the "Officers' Call" was sounded, for the Duke to deliver a message from the King. The troops covered a wide expanse and the naval and Marine officers were on foot, all others being mounted. The Duke, noticing this, sent a message to stop them and rode himself to the naval end of the line to deliver the King's message there.

Some Irish ladies at this time presented Queen Alexandra with a white dove as an emblem of peace, and this the Queen had carefully caged and taken back to Sandringham. There, a mate having been found for the bird, a glass dove-house was erected near the kennels, and whole families of the pretty creatures were reared. Her Majesty's Irish doves were cared for and attended by her for the remainder of her life.

The Duke and Duchess of Connaught lived during their stay in Ireland at the Royal Hospital in Dublin, where they entertained largely after the year 1901, when only the necessary official State functions were held, owing to the long period of mourning for Queen Victoria.

Prince Arthur of Connaught, who had followed in the footsteps of his father by choosing the Army as a profession, had obtained a commission in his father's old regiment, the 7th Hussars. He went with them to South Africa, but unfortunately contracted dysentery in a severe form and in consequence was invalided to England. His condition naturally caused his parents some anxiety, and when he reached London early in January 1904 the Duke crossed from Ireland to meet him and to bring him to Dublin to regain his health. There he celebrated his twenty-first birthday on January 13, by which time he had practically recovered.

As Commander-in-Chief in Ireland, as well as in the office of the commander of the Army Corps stationed there, the Duke had naturally to travel all over the country for inspections and reviews. It goes without saying that he carried out these duties with the thoroughness typical of his work throughout his military career. On January n he attended an inspection of the troops at Armagh, speaking to many of the men, questioning them about their past service, and asking them how they liked the Army. This was a question which the Duke often put to the men under him. He held that it was only by arriving at the real views of the private soldier that military abuses could be discovered and corrected, and by degrees the men in the regiments under his command grew to understand that they could answer the Duke's questions truthfully and that the conventional evasions or 'eyewash' of inspections were by no means required of them. It was this policy on the part of the uke, his determination to get to the bottom of things, that enabled him to do so much to improve matters in the Army and to add greatly to the welfare of the men in the ranks.

During the same inspection at Armagh he saw signalling work, drill, and gymnastics, and everything else that was to be seen, by thorough inspection of barracks and quarters, of the standard of cleanliness and comfort that was being maintained.

The popularity of the Duke and his family was naturally enhanced by the fact that they were all fond of horses and rode well (a great virtue in Irish eyes), and liked dogs and sport in general. The Duke, often accompanied by the Duchess and their daughters, attended all the great sporting events, at which his genuine keenness and the enthusiasm that he displayed made him a prime favourite with the crowd. They never omitted to acknowledge his appearance by a spontaneous burst of cheering.

The Duke had some good shooting while he was in Ireland, particularly when he stayed at Boyle with Lord Dudley, the Lord-Lieutenant, but also on the occasions of other visits. At these large crowds would assemble at the railway-stations to cheer the Duke and Duchess on their arrival and departure.

As with all other sports, the Duke and Duchess and the Princesses took much interest in hockey while they were in Ireland, and they attended all the principal matches that were played in Dublin. The Duchess got up a "Royal Hospital" team, in the progress of which she showed much interest. It usually acquitted itself very creditably. Once, with the Duke and the Princesses, she took part in a match in the Royal Hospital ground, when her team beat the Kildare team opposing them with ease. After the game she entertained the Kildare team at the Hospital, and won their allegiance by the personal charm which had done so much to endear her to the Irish people at large.

The Duchess still retained to some extent the shyness which had been one of her characteristics as a girl. She never allowed it to interfere with any of the duties which were part of her position, and it lent an added attraction to her manner and helped materially to put at their ease people who, shy themselves, were specially self-conscious in the presence of Royalty.

On January 20, 1904, the Duke and his family crossed over to England and went to Windsor to attend the memorial service to Queen Victoria, which was held there on the 21st of the month. They remained in London for nearly a month, residing, as was their wont, at Clarence House. During that time they attended several important functions, including the inaugural dinner of the Ireland Club, at which the Duke took the chair. The Ireland Club had been founded by Lord Charles Beresford, who had intended to take the chair himself. A severe accident prevented him, however, from being present, and the Duke kindly consented to act for him. After the dinner the Duke made a telling speech, in which he expressed his hopes for Ireland and his admiration for many of the qualities of her people. He said:

We want to see Ireland in the position she ought to hold. We hope that a club like this will do a great deal to break down political barriers, to bring all classes of Irishmen together. We want to recognize that Ireland is a great nation. The Irish are very gifted, they have talents which probably far exceed the talents of other parts of the

United Kingdom. They have charm and a strong sense of humour and wit which we all love and admire.

He then proceeded to pay high tribute to the Irish troops, whom he knew so well:

> As a soldier myself, I should like to refer to the splendid services that Irish soldiers and their officers have rendered to the Empire for many a long day. I respect the energy, courage, and devotion that our Irish regiments have shown; I feel the greatest love and admiration for the heroism and humanity shown by Irish soldiers.

This speech was freely reported in Ireland, and there it did much to increase the deep affection felt for "the Connaughts," who had striven so hard to understand a race often misunderstood and to give to that race due credit for its many fine qualities.

The Duke and Duchess were in London for the marriage of Princess Alice of Albany to Prince Alexander of Teck, on February 10, 1904. Princess Margaret and Princess Patricia were both bridesmaids, and they were much in request for several important weddings, where their grace and beauty made them conspicuous.

Soon after their return to Ireland the Duke and Duchess and the Princesses attended a State ball at Dublin Castle. The Duchess, who looked specially well in a becoming toilette of pale green and black, danced the first quadrille with the Lord-Lieutenant, and the young Princesses, both in white with some exquisite Brussels lace, danced nearly all the dances. One warm-hearted spectator proclaimed that they grew prettier each time they made a public appearance. The amount of flattery that they received during their stay in Ireland might have turned any girl's head, but they remained quite unspoiled, simple, natural girls, great favourites with all who knew them, not only for their attractive appearance, but just as much for the sterling characters with which they were endowed.

On February 23 their Royal Highnesses gave a great ball themselves at the Royal Hospital. Though many of the functions given there had been on a suitable scale, this one was specially noted for its pomp and ceremony and for the lavish beauty of the decorations. These were under the direct supervision of the Duchess, and they were both novel and effective. Over each of the many windows the Union Jack was entwined with the Royal Standard, the spaces in between being occupied by clusters of lances, hanging pennons, and gleaming bayonets arranged as shields against the wall. A similar arrangement was carried out in the great hall, which glittered with weapon-trophies and blazed with colours. It was there that the dancing took place. (Note may here be taken of the fact that the Royal Hospital has since been shorn of the collection of weapons, some of great antiquity, which used to adorn the walls. They have been transferred to York and to other headquarters of Army commands in England.)

Another ball was given on March 1. About 600 guests were invited, and this also was talked about in Dublin for weeks for its splendour. During the same week a Viceregal Drawing-room was held at the Castle, at which the Duke and Duchess and the Princesses were present. The Princesses again wore white, and were dressed exactly alike. At the time that was their usual custom. They were so much attached to each other, and resembled each other in so many ways, that the Duchess sometimes remarked that they ought to have been twins.

The Dublin season of that year promised to be one of exceptional brilliance, but soon after the Drawing-room the Lord-Lieutenant had the misfortune to lose his brother, and this put an end to the festivities for the time being.

On September 2, 1902, the Duke had been appointed Colonel of the Royal Army Service Corps, which had gained much prestige in South Africa, and on November 7 of the next year he became Colonel-in-Chief of the Royal Dublin Fusiliers. His command in Ireland ended in April 1904, and on his fifty-fourth birthday, the 1st of May, 1904, he was appointed Inspector-General of the Forces and President of the Selection Board. This was a new position, and its creation had been recommended by Lord Esher's War Office Commission ("the Triumvirate"). It was felt that, in view of his wide experience and the improvements which had been effected during his various commands. His Royal Highness could most worthily fill the new appointment. The office of Commander-in-Chief at the Horse Guards, which Queen Victoria had hoped that her son might hold, was at the same time abolished (February 1904). The announcement of the new appointment gave some idea of the duties that it would entail:

> The duties of Inspector-General will be those of review and report upon the practical results of the policy of the Army Council within the financial limits laid down by the Cabinet. His field of action will cover

the United Kingdom and those portions of the Empire where troops under the Home Government are stationed.

On the same day (May 1, 1904) the Duke became Colonel of the Grenadier Guards.

Bagshot Park was at about this time being overhauled, and many of the rooms were being redecorated. Residents in the neighbourhood took it as a hopeful sign that once again they would have the Duke and Duchess with them, but though, in the usual course of events, the Duke would have left Ireland in April, the fact that the King and Queen intended visiting Ireland again in that month caused him to postpone his departure until May, when it was arranged that he should take up his new appointment. During that second visit as Sovereign King Edward laid the foundation-stone of the new buildings for the Dublin Royal College of Science.

The Duke came to England for the funeral of the Duke of Cambridge, which took place on March 22, a few weeks after the office at the head of the Army which he had once held for so many years was abolished. In some ways the old Duke's funeral was a touching spectacle. As all the world knows, the Duke had contracted a morganatic marriage which had been supremely happy, and, with the strong prejudice of her day, Queen Victoria had refused to receive the lady who proved so devoted and loyal a wife to her cousin. The Duke of Cambridge had lived in perfect happiness with his wife until her death, and he had expressed a wish that he might be buried with her at Kensal Green instead of in the Royal tomb where in the ordinary course he would be laid to rest. King Edward, with the warm-hearted and broad-minded sympathy which always characterized him, saw to it that the old Duke's wish was respected, and, after the great service and the pageantry of the military obsequies at Westminster Abbey, the actual interment took place at Kensal Green. That funeral marked the passing of an epoch in the history of the British Army. The old Duke had been Commander-in-Chief for nearly forty years. He began as a reformer, exercising his great influence in the direction of progress. As increasing years affected him he gradually became too strongly conservative to move with the times, but he was always a good friend of Tommy Atkins, and those who are at all familiar with his speeches on military topics will remember that, for many years before his death, he was constantly alluding to the inadequacy of the soldiers' pay and advocating its increase.

The funeral was attended by detachments of cavalry. Royal Artillery, Royal Engineers, and Infantry of the Line, and six battalions of the Foot Guards. Lining the route there were Life Guards, Lancers, Royal Artillery, Foot Guards, Infantry of the Line, Departmental Corps, Yeomanry, and Volunteers. The massed bands of the Brigade of Guards played the *Dead March in "Saul"* from the Abbey to the Horse Guards, and Chopin's *Funeral March* at the cemetery gates.

The sad occasion afforded yet another example of the thoughtfulness of the Duke of Connaught for others, even at a time when his feelings were deeply moved and there were matters of great moment on his mind. When the military bands paraded outside Buckingham Palace under the Bandmaster (nowadays Director of Music) the Duke remembered that that officer had recently been granted his commission, so he left the Palace and walked toward the bands. The Bandmaster (Lieutenant-Colonel J. Mackenzie-Rogan) called the musicians to attention. The Duke made a sign that he wished to speak to him privately. "Rogan," he said, "please let the bands stand easy. I have only come across to congratulate you on being gazetted to commissioned rank. I do it most heartily. I think that no one deserves it or has earned it more than you have."

In such little ways the Duke earned the abiding loyalty of all who served with him in the Army.

CHAPTER XIX

ARMY REFORM AND FAMILY AFFAIRS
(1904-6; AGED FIFTY-FOUR TO FIFTY-SIX)

The Story of Army Reform, 1850-1904 — The Futility of Commissions — The "Triumvirate" Committee recommends Drastic Changes — The Duke as Inspector-General — Home Life at Bagshot — Wedding of Princess Margaret to Prince Gustavus Adolphus of Sweden — Her Life in Sweden — A Cordial Reception — "She kisses the babies" — Birth of a Son — Becomes Crown Princess — Her Love of Flowers — A Royal Poet — The Duke at the German Manoeuvres in 1906 — The War Menace — The Family at Bagshot.

While the death of the old Duke of Cambridge marked the close of an era in the history of the British Army, the Duke of Connaught's fifty-fourth birthday, the 1st of May, 1904, marked the opening of a new one, and, in order to place his military life up to this period in its true setting, it will be well for us at this stage to recall some outstanding events affecting the British Army during the years which had intervened since his birth.

The Crimean War, which broke out in 1854 just before his fourth birthday, revealed many abuses in the Army, which led to considerable alterations in the Articles of War and in the Mutiny Act, which had been in force since 1689. In 1857 came the Indian Mutiny, which was followed by some improvements in soldiers' quarters and hygiene and a partial abolition of flogging (which was, however, destined to endure until 1868, when it was abolished altogether for times of peace). In 1867 service in the Army, hitherto a lifetime employment, was reduced to twelve years. It was in 1868 that the Duke joined the Army, and the next six years (1868 to 1874) were marked by the initiation of its reform on drastic lines by Cardwell, the great War Minister of the Gladstone Administration which covered those years. Appointment and promotion by purchase were abolished in 1871, after desperate opposition by the 'die-hards' and much impetus was given to Army training, as distinguished from the 'drill' which had hitherto been the order of the day, by the Franco-Prussian War. The first manoeuvres (in Hampshire) were held in the same year, with the Duke of Cambridge as an umpire and the Prince of Wales and the Duke of Connaught (then Prince Arthur) engaged with the troops. Autumn manoeuvres in various areas were in vogue for some years after, and attention was turned to the military education of officers and to the practical side of field tactics, most of the strategy being based upon the assumed invasion of England by Continental armies. At that time and for many years later much of our military organization and training was based, in face of the experience of centuries, on the doctrine that invasion was the greatest menace. An Intelligence Department was first established at the War Office in 1873. During the first fifty years of the Duke of Connaught's life the Army had participated in overseas wars in India, China, Persia, Abyssinia, Ashanti, and South Africa, besides the Egyptian War of 1882, which was followed by wars in the Sudan and the Anglo-Boer War of 1899-1902. In connexion with that war, the extent to which military problems had been studied in advance could be gauged by the telegram, "Dismounted men preferred," which was dispatched to Dominions offering to send contingents to a country in which mounted men were destined to settle the issue.

This and other important wars disclosed great faults in our Army administration and system, and the practice was to meet public criticism by the appointment of Royal and other Commissions, which reported long after popular indignation had died down. Little, if any, action was taken. The Hartington Commission, which reported in 1888, and several Royal Commissions which immediately followed the South African War can be taken as examples, and it was not until the Triumvirate — Lord Esher, Sir John (afterward Lord) Fisher, and Sir George Clarke (now Lord Sydenham) — was appointed in November 1903 that real progress was made. Drastic reforms recommended by this "War Office (Reconstitution) Committee," which reported in February 1904, included the strengthening of the Committee of Imperial Defence by invariably having the Prime Minister as its head, the establishment of an Army Council and of a General Staff, and the abolition of the office of Commander-in-Chief, then held by Lord Roberts.

In March the Duke of Cambridge died, and in the same month the Triumvirate Committee issued a final report stating that if the recommendations of the Hartington Commission had not been ignored many thousands of lives and many millions of money would have been saved in the recent South African War. This statement arrested public attention, and it was then obvious to all that the whole future of the Army would depend upon the personal question, upon all Army appointments, from the highest to the lowest, being filled by officers loyal to the spirit of reform, and upon promotions being made without fear, favour, or social influence. At the end of April the new Army Council prohibited all private applications by officers to the War Office on official personal matters, and prescribed conditions under which interviews would be granted.

One of the recommendations of the Triumvirate had been that, on the abolition of the office of Commander-in-Chief, an Inspector-General, occupying a new office, should preside over a Selection Board to make appointments and to recommend promotions.

It was at this critical time in Army history, and for work of such great moment, that the Duke of Connaught assumed his new office. On his work in connexion therewith we shall touch in due course, and in the meantime turn our attention to an important family event which occurred a year after he assumed his new duties.

As Princess Margaret and Princess Patricia grew from girlhood to womanhood there were many rumours concerning their betrothal, and the names of many eligible young Princes were coupled with those of two of England's popular Princesses, but neither rank nor wealth made any appeal to the daughters of parents who had themselves experienced the deep happiness of a marriage which was a true union of hearts.

The Princesses were very attractive, and at this time Princess Margaret, known to the family circle as "Daisy," looked even younger than her years, with her delicately rounded features and childlike innocence of expression. Her appealing charm claimed many victims, but it was not until a young Prince from the North entered the lists that her heart was at all touched.

When Prince Gustavus Adolphus, eldest son of the Crown Prince of Sweden, was first presented to her the attraction was mutual, and their affection ripened until, in February 1905, their engagement was publicly announced.

There were no political or social considerations to be studied. It was entirely a love-match, and those who were privileged to know them pronounced the young couple to be ideally suited to each other. Prince Gustavus was a young man of fine intellect, as popular in his own country as his bride-elect was in hers, so both in England and in Sweden the match was welcomed as a union likely to make for the sincere happiness of both parties.

Though the Princess had of necessity passed the greater part of her girlhood in Court circles, her tastes were simple, and her natural manner was one of her most striking attributes. She had excellent tastes in literature, and for so young a girl she was unusually well read, while the amount of travel that she had undertaken with her parents had helped to make her a good conversationalist.

Prince Gustavus was a prince after the Swedish people's heart. Having been brought up in the simple, rather strict manner which is the custom in the Swedish Royal household, he had developed into a virile and energetic personality, and was fond of athletics, as his muscular build proclaimed. He had a keen interest in his country and in all questions pertaining to the welfare of its people, and possessed, too, an interest in the arts which formed an additional bond between him and the English Princess whom he had chosen for his bride.

Their marriage took place in St George's Chapel, Windsor, where the Duke and Duchess of Connaught had been married, on June 15, and in its atmosphere of youthful romance and promise of a happy future the ceremony was one of the most beautiful that the Chapel of many memories had witnessed.

The weather smiled on the bride and bridegroom, and the day was worthy of the month of roses; for Princess Margaret it was "roses, roses, all the way." With all its pageants, Windsor had never witnessed a more joyous occasion, and the people flocked in their thousands to greet the young couple on their passage through the streets. The atmosphere of youth abounded, since, with her usual thoughtful sympathy, the Princess had begged for a holiday for the boys at Eton, who, as a token of their gratitude, rose to the occasion with much cheering. The Princess naturally drove to the Chapel with her father, and the welcome accorded to them must have surprised even such popular Royalties, used as they were to acclamation. The Princess showed quite clearly her pleasure at the good wishes that were shouted to her from all kinds of people in the crowd.

The Chapel contained the brilliant gathering of visitors common to such occasions, but the wedding service itself had the great charm of simplicity. The Duke, looking, as usual, a soldierly and impressive figure in his Field-Marshal's uniform, gave his daughter away. The colour of the ribbon of St Patrick, which he wore across his tunic, was repeated in the dresses of the bridesmaids, as the Princess had chosen 'St Patrick's blue' for their attire as a delicate compliment to the country where during many happy years she had experienced the warm affection of a people whom she had not forgotten. She herself wore white satin, and her bouquet was little more than a simple bunch of Madonna lilies. She made a beautiful bride, shy yet composed, with her delicate colour slightly heightened by the excitement of the occasion, her expression radiant as she glanced from the figure of her young bridegroom to her father and from him to the Duchess, who smiled rather wistfully at the daughter whom she was to lose. There were four bridesmaids. Princess Patricia, Princess Mary (now the Countess of Harewood), Princess Ena of Battenberg, and Princess Beatrice of Saxe-Coburg, making a delightful group in their blue frocks with white wreaths crowning their hair. An air of youthfulness pervaded the whole ceremony.

After the wedding breakfast the young couple left for the little country village of Saighton, where the first part of the honeymoon was to be spent in quiet simplicity. The bride 'went away' in a white frock and a hat with a blue feather — a graceful figure as she waved again and again to acknowledge the farewells of the cheering crowds.

Thus passed the day that marked the first real break in the family circle. The Duke and the Duchess felt keenly the loss of their daughter, though they both rejoiced in the assurance of her future happiness. Marriage inevitably meant taking up a new life in her husband's country and an almost entire separation from her English home. Throughout the vicissitudes of the Duke's attachment to his home and family had if possible been strengthened, and so permanent a severance from his elder daughter left him sorely disconsolate.

Princess Margaret settled down in her new home and in her new country with surprising rapidity, and the people of Sweden speedily accorded her a warm place in their hearts. Though many aspects of the national life are entirely different, there was much that was similar in the Court life of the two countries, noticeably in their purity and traditions. The official etiquette of the Swedish Court was strict, but the home life of the Royal Family has always been as simple as is that of our own Royal Family, so she found little essential difference. The Court circles were prepared to offer a warm welcome to the charming English Princess whose natural simplicity accorded so well with their own Royal traditions, and she set herself to do her best to get to know the people who were henceforth to be her own.

The Swedish people are endowed by nature with good manners, so they much appreciated Princess Margaret's graceful courtesy to every one with whom she was brought in contact and her genuine wish to understand the Swedish temperament and to adapt herself to her new environment. She soon became a great favourite when she and her husband settled down in the beautiful capital which, with its imposing public buildings set amid its waterways, with numerous picturesque little islands on its outskirts, is one of the most attractive cities in the world.

Princess Margaret mixed freely with the people in her anxiety to explore her new country. Often, under suitable escort, she travelled incognito, and during these expeditions she sometimes had amusing little encounters with people who, not knowing who she was, talked to her sometimes of their new Princess. She made good progress with her study of the language, but at first she did not speak it well enough to be taken for a Swede, so people usually guessed her nationality, though not often her rank. One old woman, with whom the Princess chatted as she sat by the shores of a lake, asked her whether she had seen the new Princess. "Have you?" asked the Princess. The old woman shook her head, and said, "No, I have not, but my daughter has, and she says she does not think she can be English, for she smiles much, and often she kisses the babies!"

The year after her marriage the Princess had a baby of her own to kiss, a son being born to them on April 22, 1906, who in due course was named Gustavus after his father.

In the upbringing of her little son the Princess had excellent traditions to follow, from both her own and her husband's family, as the nursery has always played a very important part in Swedish Royal circles. So it was with education. Her Royal father-in-law and his brother attended Swedish public schools, where, at the express desire of their parents, no difference was made between them and the other pupils, and the Prince's upbringing had been equally hardy. It was a maxim of Queen Sophia of Sweden that "the world's history is made in the nursery," and the Swedish Royal children had always been trained most carefully.

Princess Margaret devoted herself to the upbringing of her small son and, in later years, of the three brothers and the sister who followed him. There was, of course, the usual nursery staff, but the Princess herself spent a great deal of her time with her babies, seeing that they were brought up according to the most modern ideas of infant hygiene. And it was not only for her own children that she could feel affectionate concern. She took much interest in all philanthropic schemes for infant welfare throughout the country, and she was always ready to extend her patronage to any institution for the care of orphans or the relief of suffering among young folk.

Two years after her marriage her father-in-law ascended the throne, and her husband then became Crown Prince. This event naturally widened the Princess's sphere. She found that her State duties increased, and that the calls upon her time became considerably more numerous, but nothing was ever allowed to interfere with the home life of the Crown Prince and Princess, which was one of undiminished happiness. In its simple joys and family affection it set an admirable example to the Swedish nation, which responded with a most sincere affection for both the Royal parents, repaid by the devotion of their lives to the welfare of the nation.

Princess Margaret resembled her mother in her great love for flowers, and wherever she was her room was always filled with them. She always arranged the vases for her own special rooms herself, including one that invariably stood on the Prince's desk with the portraits of his wife and children.

The Crown Prince's palace at Stockholm, known as Gustaf Adolf's Torg, is a rather barrack-like building, but the Royal couple's country homes were charming, and whenever she visited these Princess Margaret would return with her carriage filled with flowers. The people knew of her love for every kind of bud and blossom, and when on gala occasions she drove in procession with the Crown Prince they would toss flowers into her carriage. Once they threw them in such profusion that the carriage had to be stopped, for the little Princess Ingrid, who was driving with her mother, was in some danger of being smothered by these tokens of regard.

King Oscar of Sweden, the Crown Prince's grandfather, wrote excellent verse, and during his lifetime a book of his poems was sold widely in Sweden. One of his poems is a great favourite with the Crown Prince, who translated it for his young wife as a picture of their family life. King Oscar's verses can be freely rendered:

These are two favourite rooms. Here the flowers are bathed in sunshine. There is no sweeter freehold than this she has chosen for herself. An awning covers the veranda, whence, as we rest, our eyes overlook the ocean spread beyond. And round about is room for my children's sports, to learn, and for the night repose ever near the mother — for such is our custom. Could I desire more? We are peaceful under a peaceful roof, our days filled with art, science, poetry.

This gives us a peaceful picture of their happy domestic life, and one which is by no means overdrawn, as all who visited the Royal Family at Stockholm can fully testify. Throughout her life Princess Margaret remained deeply attached to her own family in England. She kept up a voluminous correspondence with her father and mother, with her brother, and with Princess Patricia, and many happy visits were exchanged between the two families.

After her marriage the Duke and Duchess of Connaught continued to live at Bagshot Park, and the Duke spent as much time there as the duties of his new appointment as Inspector-General of the Forces and President of the Selection Board would permit. In September 1906, now known to have been the year of the "Schlieffen" plan for the invasion of Belgium which was put in force in 1914, His Royal Highness visited Germany to attend the Imperial Army manoeuvres, at which he wore the uniform of a German Hussar regiment of which, at that time, he was Colonel. The German Emperor made him a Prussian Field-Marshal — the highest military compliment in his power.

It may not be out of place to mention here that, for some years before the Great War broke out in 1914, the Duke had premonitions of the disaster. His military experience, combined with his personal knowledge of his Imperial nephew, did much to cause him to fear the outbreak of hostilities, and he dropped more than one hint to the authorities that war with Germany, if not inevitable, was at least highly probable. Nevertheless, until almost the last day he hoped, in common with many others whose knowledge was as wide as his, that the German people, with their good sense, might have the will and the power to avert the calamity. At no time did he believe much in the Kaiser's ability to take control at moments of crisis, and he had had many opportunities of holding conversations with his elder sister, the Empress Frederick.[1] As all the world knows now from her recently

1 *Letters of the Empress Frederick,* edited by Sir Frederick Ponsonby (Macmillan).

published letters, she had estimated her son's character with great thoroughness.

At this time, however, the war-clouds on the horizon were visible only to those with sufficient technical knowledge to gauge the menacing importance of the railway-construction work which was obvious to all observers near the Belgian frontiers, and all that the Duke could do was to use his utmost endeavours to effect improvements in the Army to make it a really efficient fighting machine. Both by inspections and by exercising his influence on the Selection Board in favour of the most efficient officers, he did much to prepare the material which Lord Haldane had forged into the wonderful army of "Old Contemptibles" which took the field in the great emergency.

For two years after the wedding of Princess Margaret the family resided principally at Bagshot, with the exception of Prince Arthur, who was often away with his regiment, the Scots Greys, following in the footsteps of his father as a public favourite. The fact that his only son was a keen soldier like himself was naturally a source of great pleasure to the Duke, and this was increased by the knowledge that, besides his soldierly qualities. Prince Arthur had inherited diplomatic abilities which were to cause him in later years to be entrusted with various important missions to foreign countries.

During that period Princess Patricia became a familiar figure in London Society. She increased the popularity which she had gained when she first came out, before and after the Duke's Irish appointment had taken the family away from England, and almost every month rumour provided a new consort for the admired "Princess Pat"; but she held decided views on matrimony, and, as future events proved, preferred to form her own opinion on matters of such moment to herself, rather than to leave them to others.

CHAPTER XX

THE DRAMA OF ARMY REFORM
(1904-10; AGED FIFTY-FOUR TO SIXTY)

The Passing of the old Army Regime — The Triumvirate Reforms — Establishment of the Army Council — The Duke of Connaught its "Eyes and Ears" — Inspector-General of the Forces — President of the Selection Board — Field-Marshal Commanding-in-Chief and High Commissioner in the Mediterranean — Lord Kitchener and the "Fifth Wheel in a Coach" — Social Duties in Malta — A Holiday in East Africa — Death of King Edward.

In course of time it may be that some competent historian, worthy of his theme, will be inspired by the great human interest in the drama to write of Army Reform in the decade that opened in the year 1904.

The early months of the year were marked by the death, on March 17, of the old Duke of Cambridge. It has been written of the post that the Duke formerly held that the story of the office of Commander-in-Chief is to a large extent the story of the struggle between Parliament and the Crown for control over the military forces of the State, and that during the last years of his service (1888-95) he had enjoyed powers greater than those of any Commander-in-Chief since Monk, who became General-in-Chief at the Restoration. The early months of the year were marked also by a painful occurrence in the life of Lord Roberts of Kandahar, the great-hearted "Little Man" beloved by the Army, who was compelled at scant notice to relinquish the same high office, of which the utility was thought to have lapsed. Lord Wolseley, the previous Commander-in-Chief (1895-1900), who in his day had been constantly in conflict with the old Duke, was eating his heart out for lack of employment. Thus there had passed from the stage the actors of the old regime, when, on his fifty-fourth birthday, the Duke of Connaught was called upon to bear his part in the reforms. In order to gain a proper understanding of the nature of his work as Inspector-General of the Forces and President of the Selection Board during the years 1904-7, it is necessary for us now to consider further some of these reforms, of which the one with the most direct influence upon the Army was the establishment of an Army Council and of a General Staff.

First and foremost the Army Council was an administrative body, not exercising the functions of command, which were deputed to the Generals Commanding-in-Chief in the military areas. As far as personal knowledge of the Army went, the new Council was at that time blind and deaf. In the words of the reports of the Triumvirate Committee[1] the Inspector-General of the Forces was "to provide the Secretary of State and the Army Council with eyes and ears." The methods which he should adopt to perform these functions were specified in detail:

> To form a judgment, either personally or through his staff, as the Army Council may direct, on the efficiency of officers and men, on the handling of the troops, on the standard and system of the training, on the suitability of equipment, and generally on all that affects the readiness of the Forces for War.

As an additional suggestion it was recommended that he should act as umpire at all large manoeuvres. Hardly could more important work have been allotted to any individual at that crisis in the history of the Army, and of that note will doubtless be taken by our future historian. The permanency of the post (its duration was to be for five years) tended, if due account was to be taken of the Inspector-General's reports, to support the object for which the Duke of Cambridge had fought so hard: the prevention of military patronage from passing into the hands of a Minister who would change with every successive Government. It was fortunate for the nation that it possessed at that crisis, in the person of His Royal Highness the Duke of Connaught, a Royal Prince, set above all social or political intrigue, who for over thirty years had served as a soldier in all arms and under varied conditions of service and command, in Britain, in India, and in Ireland.

Of the performances of the other actors in the great work of Army reform (which was completed just in time to face the ordeal of 1914) much is already known; of the unobtrusive part played by the Duke of Connaught very little. The leading characters in the initial stage were Mr H. O. Arnold-Forster, the War Minister, who, after a lifetime study

1 Parts I-III, col. 1932-68, January 11-March 9, 1904.

of Army matters, had with untiring zeal laid laboriously the foundations of reform, on which, between 1906 and 1914, the late Lord Haldane — our best War Minister of modern times — erected his great edifice, and Mr Arthur (now Lord) Balfour, who devoted his great brain-power and persuasive oratory to studying and exploiting our problem of defence as no Prime Minister had ever done in time of peace. By providing "eyes and ears" for the Army Council, which carried out the reforms under these leaders, the soldier Duke bore no mean part in ensuring their success. His field of action was originally defined as covering "the United Kingdom and those portions of the Empire where troops under the control of the Home Government are stationed," and, with the Duchess and Princess Patricia, he travelled as far as Ceylon, Singapore, Hong-Kong, and Egypt on tours of inspection.

Many difficulties were expected when the appointment was made. It was thought that the effect might be to derogate from the influence and the authority of the executive Generals Commanding-in-Chief; and, again, that the Inspection Department might grow into a bureaucracy or develop into a revived Horse Guards, where the former office of the Commander-in-Chief was situated. These pitfalls were all avoided by the tact and discretion of the Duke. Whether he found his new duties to his taste is doubtful. There is some evidence to the contrary. So keen a soldier must have preferred active command, of which, by the deep interest which he took in the efficiency and welfare of all ranks, he had made so great a success, but, whatever his own personal inclinations, the Duke never at any time allowed them to interfere with what he considered his duty. Though it may be that he looked back regretfully at his really military commands of Aldershot and Ireland, he did excellent work in his new position.

The story of the Duke's activities between 1904 and 1907 would be incomplete without some further reference to the Selection Board, over which he presided. Before his time the Selection Board was presided over by the Commander-in-Chief. The members were the Adjutant-General, the Quartermaster-General, the Inspector-General of Fortifications, the Director-General of Ordnance, the Military Secretary, and the Director of Military Training. These officers, as well as special representatives of the different arms of the Service, were summoned by the Commander-in-Chief to sit on the Board only as he thought necessary. There was also a Promotion Board, to lay before the Military Secretary the names of colonels considered fit for promotion or employment. In the Duke's day the Selection Board at first included only the General Officer Commanding-in-Chief and the Military Secretary to the Secretary of State. The members of the Army Council were not put on the Board until later. These notes will suffice to show the importance of the work which was performed, under the Duke's *régime*, without fear, favour, or prejudice.

He held his important dual appointment until December 20, 1907, when he became Field-Marshal Commanding-in-Chief and High Commissioner in the Mediterranean, with his headquarters at Malta. We have few data to enable us to judge upon the policy which underlay the initiation of such an appointment. We can only take note of certain self-evident points, within the knowledge of the public, which serve to indicate the need for tact on the part of a "Field-Marshal Commanding-in-Chief and High Commissioner" in the Mediterranean. The British troops in that area at the time were the garrisons of Gibraltar and Malta, where there were Governors, who were representatives of the Sovereign, and Commanders-in-Chief, small detachments in Cyprus and in Crete, the British force in Egypt and the Sudan under a General Officer, and the Egyptian and Sudanese forces under a Sirdar (and a Governor-General in the Sudan) responsible for those forces under the direction of a British "Agent and Consul-General" in Egypt. If friction and loss of prestige had been feared on behalf of the Generals commanding troops in the United Kingdom when an Inspector-General visited their commands, it was clear that, unless the holder of the new office was exceptionally endowed with tact, far greater difficulties would arise in the widely scattered Mediterranean forces under a new "Field-Marshal Commanding-in-Chief." It suffices to add that no friction arose under the *régime* of the Duke of Connaught.

His duties were thus defined in a Memorandum by the Secretary of State for War on the Army Estimates for 1907-8:

> For many years the Commanders-in-Chief at Malta and Gibraltar have also been charged with the responsibilities of the civil government of those Colonies; and it has been necessary to provide a complete staff, general, administrative and personal, on a liberal scale at each station. At the same time these two commands, as well as the third Mediterranean command of Egypt, have been entirely independent of one another, without any provision for co-ordination except through the War Office itself. In view of the progress made with

decentralization from the War Office, it has been decided to appoint a purely military Commander-in-Chief, with no civil duties, for the Mediterranean as a whole, to be stationed at Malta. No increase in cost of any kind will result from the new arrangements.

This was supplemented by a statement in Parliament (August 8, 1907) that

all matters of local military administration, except the more important cases of discipline, would continue to be dealt with by the Governors of Gibraltar and Malta and the General Officer commanding in Egypt.

Some further light is thrown upon the nature and duties of the appointment in a letter from Lord Kitchener, written when he was asked if he was willing to succeed the Duke:

I think it rather hard on me, as I wanted a time to myself and had no wish to replace the Duke of Connaught in a billet which he himself found fifth wheel in a coach, but I do not see that I could have done anything else. I hope the Duke will understand that it has been no wish of mine. It would be costing every interest I have to follow him to the Mediterranean.

During the time he held the Mediterranean appointment the Duke lived at San Antonio Palace — one of the residences of the Governor. There he and his family took up their residence, speedily becoming as popular as they had been elsewhere, and for over two years he and the Duchess and Princess Patricia were prominent figures in the social life of the island.

The Duke held this post until July 1909, when he resigned the appointment, and during the next year he was able to carry out a long-cherished project and to set out, with the Duchess, Princess Patricia, and Prince Arthur, on a shooting expedition to East Africa.

From the first it was understood that the expedition was purely a private one and that no details were to be issued to the Press. The Royal party did not travel incognito, but they wished to undertake the journey in their private capacity, without the official receptions and similar functions which had hitherto marked their tours. They went in the German steamer *Admiral*, landed at Mombasa on February 10, and went on to Nairobi without delay. There they were delayed for twenty-four hours, pending the collection of the *safari* material, *personnel*, and equipment. When this had been arranged they pushed on to the actual camping-ground. Their object was to shoot big game in Kenya Colony, and they had some excellent sport, living in camp, spending long hours in the saddle, and exploring the country thoroughly.

They had arranged originally to return to England together in May, but Prince Arthur came home in advance of the others. The Duke was already on his way home when news of the serious nature of King Edward's illness first reached him, and he was at Suez when he received the sad tidings of His Majesty's death. He reached London on May 12, just in time for the funeral.

In that ceremony he took much the same part as he had in the *cortège* which followed Queen Victoria's coffin, riding just behind the gun-carriage and on the left of King George. A touching incident was noted when the new King and the Duke rode past the carriage in which sat the black-robed figure of the widowed Queen-Mother. Turning in their saddles, they both saluted her profoundly before they rode forward to join the procession. Nine Kings and thirty Royal Princes were present, including the German Emperor and the Kings of Spain, of Norway, and of Portugal. Four hundred thousand people had passed through Westminster Hall, where the late King had lain in state during the two previous days.

CHAPTER XXI

UNION IN SOUTH AFRICA
(1910; AGED SIXTY)

The Union of South Africa — The Duke leaves with the Duchess and Princess Patricia in the Balmoral Castle — Enthusiastic Reception — The Duke and the Sword-sling — The Opening of the First Union Parliament at Cape Town — "Union in the air" — "The Duke won all hearts" — Dignity and Accessibility — Other Great Functions — A Tour Up-country — The Tomb of Cecil Rhodes — Miners, Farmers, and Storekeepers — Presentations to the Duchess and Princess Patricia — Homage of the Basutos — Quaint Costumes — Natives' Fear of the Union — The Duke's Influence — Son of the Great White Queen — Sympathy and Understanding — A Country of War Graves — "Here lies a British Soldier" — "Pass, friend. All's well" — Departure from Durban — "South Africa is more than delighted with him" — In England again.

The months that followed the funeral of King Edward were uneventful. The Duke always took a great interest in Aldershot, and at this period he often attended some special parade or military operation of unusual interest. The Duchess and Princess Patricia sometimes accompanied him, and they spent long hours watching manoeuvres and military displays, lunching at Government House, and renewing the memories of the years when they were in residence.

Late in 1910 there came the ceremony of the opening of the first Parliament of the Union of South Africa. It had been arranged that the Prince of Wales should represent the Sovereign on that occasion, but his accession to the throne intervened, and the task devolved upon the Duke of Connaught. The Royal party travelled out in the *Balmoral Castle*, accompanied by a cruiser escort, and though mourning for King Edward precluded many of the usual functions, such as the banquets, balls, and similar entertainments common to Royal tours, the visit proved most impressive and of great historical interest. South Africans are not, as a rule, strikingly demonstrative, and this made their warm welcome of the Duke and Duchess even more impressive. The Royal party were received by enthusiastic crowds at every place they visited. Lord Gladstone was Governor-General, General Botha was Prime Minister, and Lord Methuen commanded the troops. A little incident in the first ceremonial procession through the streets of Cape Town proved that the Duke still retained the "gimlet eye" to which the soldier who had served under the Duke had once referred.[1] The head of Lord Methuen's General Staff was riding immediately in front of the Duke; the Duchess and Princess Patricia followed in a carriage. The sword-sling (technically called a carriage) of the General Staff officer was not in front of the gold tassel of his sash as it should have been. The Duke called to Lord Methuen, "Your staff have the carriage of the sword wrong."

Lord Methuen, who only heard the word "carriage," called out, "Officer of the escort, ride the other side of the carriage."

The sequel to the story was that the Duke met the Staff officer at luncheon, still with his sword-sling an inch or two out of place. He let the culprit have his luncheon in ignorance of the fact, but told him of his error afterward with an encouraging smile. That officer amended his ways for the future.

The Duke and Duchess arrived at the height of the South African summer, and the weather was oppressively hot for those unused to the climate, but the Royal party never shirked an engagement, and they often fulfilled three or four in one day. Under the most trying conditions they always contrived to look fresh, animated, and sincerely interested in their surroundings and in the people who were presented to them.

The opening of the Parliament was a deeply impressive ceremony, and the way in which the Duke played the part allotted to him elicited high praise from the South African Press, both British and Dutch. His delivery of the Royal Message was made in clear, ringing tones which could be heard in every corner of the Chamber. Only about eight years had passed since the Peace of Vereeniging, but "union was in the air," and the Duke's speech, a model of tact and lucidity, created a most favourable impression in the minds of its hearers.

Commenting on the occasion, *The Cape Times* said:

It is no mere conventional phrase in this instance to say that the Duke won all hearts. Public opinion is equally enthusiastic regarding

1 See p. 64.

the dignity of his bearing at State functions and appearances, his accessibility, and the keen interest he displays in conversations with everybody.

Accessibility was an attribute that won the Duke special favour in the eyes of South Africans from the back-veld. They had heard, and no doubt believed, much about British stiffness and reserve, and it was pleasant for them to find that a man who was not only British to the backbone, but Royal as well, was full of sympathy and always ready to listen to any matters of interest brought to his notice. There is no doubt that his presence in South Africa did a great deal to raise British prestige and to smooth matters for the Union.

Shortly after the opening of Parliament there was an official dinner at Government House, and the Duke made a fine speech which helped greatly in the reconciliation of South Africa and was highly appreciated by the many South African notabilities present at the dinner. The Press was unanimous in its approval, the comment of *The Cape Times* reflecting the general opinion:

> To the Duke of Connaught South Africa owes a deep debt of gratitude for his unfailing and marvellous kindness and tact. His speech was worthy in every respect of the great occasion. It is fair and sympathetic in its terms to all parties in South Africa. It notices the differences and possible difficulties with a tact and in a way which really could not have been better expressed.

By the express wish of the Duke his speech at the dinner was printed, and copies were presented to General Botha and to other South African leaders, an act of courtesy which gave great pleasure to the recipients.

Before he set out for the tour in the provinces the Duke opened the Selborne Dock at Simon's Town and reviewed the troops at Cape Town. He also laid the foundation-stone of the Cape University, and all the Royal party attended the most interesting Cape historical pageant, which was highly successful and pronounced by the Duke "most attractive." The appearance and bearing of the Duchess and Princess Patricia at this and all the functions and ceremonies won all hearts.

The tour lasted for five weeks, and was most exhaustive. The Duke saw every Province of the new Union, visiting Bloemfontein, Durban, Johannesburg, Pretoria, and also Rhodesia, where, in stiflingly hot weather, he waived all ceremony and received in their shirtsleeves the settlers who rode in for miles to meet his train. By the Duke's own special desire the tour became even more extensive than was originally planned, for if it came to his knowledge that the inhabitants of an outlying district had expressed a wish to see him he altered the route so that their wish might be gratified.

There were, of course, many formal ceremonies, receptions, presentations of addresses, and similar functions, but besides these the Duke arranged many interviews with personages whom he thought might be pleased at the opportunity, or when he had reason to believe that the country might benefit.

The Royal party visited Bulawayo, where they were particularly interested in the former kraal of Lobengula, King of the Matabele, and they also saw the wonderful Victoria Falls, which specially attracted Princess Patricia by their beauty. They made an expedition to the tomb of Cecil Rhodes in the Matoppos, the most grandly simple resting-place in the world, and spent a considerable time in the vicinity. From the summit of the World's View they admired the impressive grandeur of a prospect which, the Duke remarked, had never been equalled in all his travels. In accordance with his practice he talked freely with every one, knowing that he could not get below the surface by means of conventional interviews with heads of departments. With miners, farmers, and storekeepers he talked, and he encouraged them to talk to him. He thus learned, as he himself stated, more of the real South Africa from chance encounters than he would have ascertained from any history of the country.

The Royal party received many presents, and of course they distributed many. Consignments of the very varied gifts were dispatched to Bagshot Park, where they were carefully arranged by the Duchess on their return. The presents which perhaps pleased the ladies most were a wonderful jackal *kaross*, given to the Duchess, and a fan of black superfine ostrich feathers, offered to Princess Patricia.

At Bloemfontein the Duke received the homage of the Basuto chiefs. Besides being highly picturesque, this ceremony was one of great importance, since the Basutos, while they willingly accorded their allegiance to the British Crown, were doubtful about their relationship with the new Union of South Africa Government. There was a touch of comedy, as one and all appeared in European dress. They certainly did their best, but the results did not always match the solemnity of the occasion, although the Royal party succeeded in preserving their gravity. There were frock-coats topped by golfing-caps; there were Norfolk suits worn with immaculate top-hats; there were tennis trousers worn with dinner-jackets and surmounted by bowlers ; and one portly chief appeared attired handsomely in the uniform of a British naval officer, completed by a Glengarry bonnet.

The far-away Bechuanas also were afraid that their land was going to be confiscated, and, fearing what the new Union might mean for them, they had expressed their desire to remain under their King and his advisers.

The Duke took immense pains to set the natives' doubts at rest, as far as explanations and assurances could do so. He prepared his speeches in such a manner that the astute native chiefs could understand the Union and what it would mean to them, and it is difficult to overestimate the good that was wrought by the visit and the personal assurances of the son of the Great White Queen with whom they had made their treaties.

Letsie, the Paramount Chief of the Basutos, made a speech which was translated to the Duke, who made a reply that caused much pleasure. The chief presented His Royal Highness with a Basuto pony, and he was delighted to receive in return a fur coat, brought out specially from England. Before Letsie departed the Duke told the interpreter to tell the chief that he had been very pleased to see him, and, as the interpreter delivered the message, the Duke smiled kindly and gave Letsie a warm handclasp, causing much gratification at such a recognition of his status.

The Duke, speaking to all the chiefs, gave them his word, as the direct representative of King George, that no harm was meant to them or would indeed be allowed to befall them, and that the King cared for all his subjects impartially and would see that justice was meted out to all. The chiefs put many questions. These the Duke answered with great fullness, instructing the interpreter to repeat any sentence which he did not think they had quite understood and urging the chiefs to ask about any matters that were troubling them. The Duke's replies and his assurances satisfied their doubts, and before the meeting dispersed they gave their own Royal salute and then three British cheers. As a final tribute the aged Gaberone presented to the Duke two walking-sticks, which he had made with his own hands for

His Royal Highness. Each important chief was given a superb gold-mounted staff, which, as the Duke told them as he presented it, was specially given as a personal gift from the King. As may be imagined, these staffs were much treasured by the recipients, and used as a species of State wand on occasions of native ceremony.

Before the Duke's visit there had been some fear lest, owing to their ideas about the nature of the Union, there might be difficulties with the natives, and certain unprincipled people had been credited with attempts to stir up trouble which would have to be settled by the British troops before they left the country, but the Duke's explanations were so full and so carefully given that they completely satisfied the chiefs.

The general opinion among South Africans of the Duke's speeches can be gathered from another newspaper extract:

> The dominant note of the Duke's speeches everywhere — and their unusual verve and liveliness and simplicity were everywhere remarked as models of their kind — was his sympathy and understanding of the peculiar difficulties of each district.

Altogether, the tour was a triumphant success. Though the period of mourning for King Edward prevented the Royal party from taking part in many social engagements, yet the many interviews granted and the speeches made by the Duke did far more good than their appearance at any such functions would have achieved.

The ladies of the party were surprised at the shopping possibilities of places like Johannesburg, and the many really fine buildings scattered throughout the country, though they admired specially the typical South African farmsteads, with their Dutch gables and the stoeps on which the families gather in the cool of the evening.

The Duke took special note of the numerous war memorials to our men who fell in the South African campaign, which cover the length and breadth of the country. He praised specially the work of the Guild of Loyal Women — a band of prominent women residents who, soon after the war was over, had undertaken to look after all the graves of the fallen. This work, as the Royal party saw, had been carried out with the greatest care and thoroughness. The War Office had made a small grant of ten shillings toward the cost of erecting a cross over each grave if the relatives could not afford even that simple memorial, and the Government also gave free transport for such monuments as were sent out from England. The Duke saw many of them in his travels. The memorials varied in nature from marble monuments to iron crosses bearing the simple inscription "Here lies a British Soldier," and in remote districts there were until recently to be found placed at the head of graves little crosses of wood from biscuit-boxes, with the number and name of the dead man in nails hammered into the wood.

A story that perhaps touched the Duke most was one that was told him by an officer who had served throughout the campaign. After one engagement he had come upon a young subaltern doing his best with crude tools to chip letters on a block of stone, and on being questioned the lad said he was carving an epitaph for a dead comrade: "Pass, friend. All's well."

Over the hundreds of thousands of square miles of South African veld were strewn such memories of the sacrifice of life, of Briton and Boer alike, which had culminated after so few years in the administrative union of the two races by the ceremonies which the Duke, representing the Sovereign, had come to South Africa to perform. The Duke received the warmest of welcomes from undemonstrative races, which speaks much for his direct appeal to those who silently sum up a man at his true worth, regardless of his rank and standing. Some had expected Royal hauteur and official reserve. They found a man who talked to them as equals, doing his utmost to understand their difficulties, without minimizing them, and to realize their problems. In visiting South Africa the Duke proved himself a true ambassador of peace and goodwill, and of mutual understanding, without which permanent peace cannot be secured.

The Royal party left Durban on December 3, and *The Cape Times* summed up the impression that they had left behind them in a very few words:

> If the Duke says he is pleased with South Africa, South Africa is more than delighted with him.

At the end of January 1911 the Duke was entertained at a banquet at the Guildhall to welcome him back from his South African tour, and in a speech which he made on that occasion he gave some account of his experiences. While he did not underrate the difficulties, he expressed his confident belief in the future of the country and in that of the new Union. With his usual clarity and directness of speech, he inspired his hearers with his own spirit of hope and confidence in the country whose possibilities he described.

For some time after their return from the South African tour the Duke and Duchess remained in residence at Bagshot, where they took up the family life which they had enjoyed whenever the Duke's public and military duties permitted. Life there was made as simple as possible, though the entertainments that they gave were naturally in keeping with their rank. When they attended Court functions in London the toilettes of the Duchess and Princess Patrick were always greatly admired, the Princess's taste in dress and graceful charm making her noticeable amid the beauties of a London season. In the year in which he went to South Africa the Duke was made Master of Trinity House, of which he was already an Elder Brother. At this time he made use of several clubs, including the Savage Club, of which he became a highly esteemed member.

CHAPTER XXII

GOVERNOR-GENERAL OF CANADA
(1911-12; AGED SIXTY-ONE TO SIXTY-TWO)

Appointment as Governor-General of Canada — Coronation of King George — The Duke relieves Lord Grey in Canada — Reception in Quebec — "Vive Connaught!" — Parliamentary and Social Functions — Princess Patricia arrives — Conference at Ottawa — A Visit to New York — Social Life and Sport — Severe Illness of the Duchess — A Visit to England — Winter Sports — Popularity of Princess Patricia — The Duchess in Parliament — Old French Traditions — Kings and Convents — Princess Patricia's Romance.

Early in 1911 it was generally known that the Duke would succeed Lord Grey as Governor-General of Canada in the autumn, and so take up one of the most important of the many responsible positions that he has held throughout his career. In commenting on the appointment *The Times* said:

> The official announcement that the Duke of Connaught is going to Canada and that he will be accompanied by the Duchess gives great satisfaction. The Duke on his previous visits won golden opinions by his geniality and ardent interest in the country. The appointment means much to Ottawa, for undoubtedly the Connaught *régime* will attract the leisured classes of the Continent to the Canadian capital.

In the United Kingdom the greatest satisfaction was universally expressed at the appointment, and from its earliest mention Canada anticipated the appointment with the liveliest interest and the keenest anticipation. As *The Times* put it, " there was a feeble undercurrent of criticism." "A few anxious democrats . . . foresaw a rigid and arbitrary etiquette, the trappings of a Court, . . . offensive ceremonialism, and an era of social extravagance," so the Duke let it be known that there was no intention of establishing a Royal Court in Canada and that he would be a democratic Governor-General.

This prospect was in keeping with the Duke's simple outlook and real opinions, which have already been indicated by examples of his insistence upon the use of his military and not of his Royal rank in connexion with his work in the Army. The constant use of "your Royal Highness" in addressing him found small favour in his sight, and on one occasion an old Colonel who persisted in this practice on the parade-ground received a severe snub. "On the parade-ground," the Duke said, "I am 'sir,' and nothing else." Aware of this spirit, those who knew him were confident that his residence in Canada would be an unqualified success.

On June 22 King George V and his Consort, Queen Mary, were crowned in Westminster Abbey with all the ancient rites and ceremonials which traditionally are connected with the occasion. Under these it is prescribed that the Coronation Oath, dating back from the fourteenth century, shall be taken, and that the Coronation Chair, containing the old stone that has rested at Westminster since 1296, shall be used. To his nephew. King George, the Duke of Connaught rendered homage in the same form as he had to his brother. King Edward, in 1902. As on that occasion, he was responsible for superintending the military arrangements, and he paid special attention to the distinguished visitors from beyond the seas.

The Royal party left for Canada in the *Empress of Ireland*, and they arrived at Quebec on October 11, receiving there a loyal demonstration of welcome unprecedented in its enthusiasm. Amid the continuous cheering there were cries of "Vive le Duc!" and "Vive Connaught!" — greetings which left no shadow of doubt about the satisfaction of the Canadians of French descent at the sight of their new Governor-General.

Reports had already appeared in the Canadian Press giving details of the life led by the Royal party on board the *Empress of Ireland*, the interest they had shown in their surroundings, and the lack of any undue reserve in their relations with the other passengers, with whom they had mixed and talked freely. This no doubt helped materially to reassure a democratic people, and was largely the cause of so loyal and enthusiastic a welcome.

Reference has already been made to the Duke's love of horses. On this occasion he brought with him his own favourite charger and other horses to which he or the Duchess had been particularly attached.

There is a tradition, usually faithfully observed, that the new and the retiring Governor-Generals should pass each other on the high seas. The Duke and Lord Grey did not actually do this, but His Royal Highness passed the outgoing Governor near Rivière du Loup, their ships exchanging salutes as they passed.

The welcome conceded to the Duke and Duchess at Quebec was, as we have suggested, the more remarkable for the enthusiastic participation of so many of the people who were of French descent and, indeed, of French sympathies, and sometimes apt to speak as if France were their real mother and England but their foster-mother. As is well known, French is current both in conversation and in the written word, and is taught with English in the schools. Both languages are used in Parliamentary documents. The Duke and Duchess had last visited Quebec in 1890, on their way home from India, and Prince Arthur had been there in 1906.

The Duke's maternal grandfather, the Duke of Kent, was once in command of the Quebec garrison, living in Old Kent House, near the Falls of Montmorency. By the time of the Duke of Connaught's visit this house had been turned into an hotel. King George, as Prince of Wales, had visited the place in 1908 for the celebrations to a great pageant on the Plains of Abraham, where Wolfe fell, a review of troops, the dedication of the Battlefields (at which the Prince of Wales presided), a review of the Fleet, and thanksgiving services at both the Catholic and the Protestant churches. The Protestant Cathedral possesses a solid silver Communion service, presented by George III.

When the Duke of Connaught first landed in Canada *The Montreal Herald* published a leader welcoming him to the country:

> Your Royal Highness, welcome to Canada.
> Welcome for your own sake, welcome for your mother's sake and your nephew's, welcome for what by right of birth you represent; we welcome you as an old friend. And on entering on your duties as Governor-General you may have the consciousness that all that warm friendship for you personally can do towards giving you the confidence of the Canadian public is yours in abundant measure.

An official reception was held at Parliament Buildings, and when this was concluded the Duke drove round Quebec. As he did so a salute was fired from the frowning old citadel, and at night there was a wonderful display of fireworks, lasting for over half an hour.

On October 14 the Duke and Duchess attended an official luncheon, over which the Premier presided. This was held in an upper dining-room, and the whole of the *château* was lavishly decorated for the occasion, autumn leaves and palms being used in abundance. The Duke took in Mrs Borden, wife of the Premier. Mr (later Sir Robert) Borden took in the Duchess, and proposed the toast of the new Governor-General and his consort, which was honoured with great enthusiasm. The Duke read a message from King George, in which His Majesty sent the Canadian people a personal greeting and his assurance of abiding interest in the Dominion.

Soon afterward the Duke and Duchess attended a reception that was given by the Lieutenant-Governor of Quebec. This was a most brilliant affair, attended by representatives and descendants of all the greatest and oldest families in Canada. The Duke and Duchess shook hands with nearly 2000 people — a test of endurance which they succeeded in fulfilling without the slightest signs of weariness. After the reception a light supper was served in the smaller chamber, and their Royal Highnesses then prepared to depart, finding in the beautifully decorated grounds fully 10,000 people waiting to see them leave. As they passed on their way to the train they met with a further most enthusiastic reception from the crowds. They were escorted to their train by a guard of honour of the Royal Canadian Dragoons, who, in scarlet coats and shining helmets, made most picturesque figures as they passed on their black chargers.

The Royal train was in charge of specially picked men, and the conductor, as the Duke was interested to learn, was the same man (Reynolds) who had driven King George when, as Duke of Cornwall and York, he had visited Canada in 1902. After he had specially congratulated the Dragoons on the smartness of their turn-out the Duke and the Royal party entered the train and steamed out of the station amid tumultuous cheering.

It is the usual custom for the Governor-General to spend the winter and the Parliamentary season at Government House, Ottawa, and the spring and summer at the Citadel, Quebec, but the Duke and Duchess also toured all over the country, visiting each city and being everywhere received with the same cordiality. They visited Montreal, Toronto, and many other places, and charmed the people by the ease with which they adapted themselves to their democratic surroundings, which were evidently quite congenial to them, and by their tact and accessibility. Toward the end of the year they were joined by Princess Patricia, whom the Canadian people took immediately to their hearts.

She soon established in Canada as great a popularity as she had enjoyed in London and Ireland.

In November a Military Conference was held at Ottawa, and the Ministry of Militia gave a luncheon to those who attended the Conference, at which the Duke was present. In reply to the toast of his health the Duke said that he had no doubt that the Conference would desirably impress the country with the importance of the Militia, and that he hoped he and the delegates would see more of each other in the future.

In January 1912 the Duke visited New York, where he made a five-days tour. When he was boarding the car at the Grand Central Station on his departure he turned to the Ambassador, who was seeing him off, and spoke of the hospitality that had been shown to him in the United States.

"We were," he said, "very much impressed by the hospitality of the people. We were treated royally by the Press and public. The Duchess and myself are very grateful to the people of New York, and we shall look forward to another visit."

The Duke and the Ambassador shook hands with great heartiness, and both the Duchess and Princess Patricia embraced Mrs Bryce before the train drew out of the station to the accompaniment of loud cheers from the crowd assembled to see the Royal party off.

Shortly after their return from New York the Duke and Duchess took up their residence for a while at Strathcona House, Montreal. There they entertained largely, the Duchess giving most successful concerts as well as dances, receptions, and dinners, one of particular interest being given on the Duke's birthday on May 1. The Duchess and her daughter entered fully into the social life of Montreal, and took constant interest in schemes for the welfare of women and children and in all philanthropic institutions. The Duchess attended the meetings of the local Council of Women. Her speeches were always helpful, and she was always ready to advise on matters of importance.

Both the Duke and Duchess attended the Horse Show, which was held in May, and they displayed a lively interest in the entries. In June they presented a cup, to be known as the "Connaught Cup," for which the race took place at Blue Bonnets.

On June 15 there was a gymkhana in aid of the Royal Society for the Prevention of Cruelty to Animals. This the Duke attended informally. His sincere love for horses and for all animals has always led him to support the Society in the good work it has done in so many parts of the world, and during this visit he asked many questions about its work in Canada and in the other Dominions.

Up to this time both the Duke and Duchess had enjoyed really excellent health, which made the latter's serious illness in June of that year the more alarming. During the whole of the time that she had spent in Canada the Duchess had played her part as wife of the Governor-General with her usual activity and keen desire to fulfil her duties, and she had hardly ever missed a function of any kind. She had accompanied the Duke throughout all his tours, some of them of a very wearying nature, and it may be that her energy and her determination outstripped her physical strength, so that when illness came it was of a very serious nature. She developed peritonitis, and although an operation was not considered necessary at first she suffered severely.

Never given to making much of her own ailments, it is probable that the Duchess went about again before she was really fit to do so. When the Duke set out on an extensive trip to Halifax and the Maritime Provinces, extending his tour across the continent and through the Rockies to the West, she insisted on accompanying him, but the effort proved too much for her weakened constitution, and in January 1913 she again became seriously ill. She was then removed from Government House to Victoria Hospital. After some weeks' treatment she had recovered sufficiently to be taken by the Duke to England, but when she was at home the malady returned, and she was forced to undergo two serious operations. These impaired her health so seriously that it was considered doubtful whether she would ever be strong enough to return to Canada with the Duke. Later in the year she did return, and she was able to a certain extent to take up her former duties.

Previous reference has been made to the shyness of the Duchess at having to face public functions. This trait helped still further to increase her popularity in Canada, where she seemed to be more really at home than she had been in other countries. The Canadians liked the simplicity of her manner and the entire absence of 'frills' which has always characterized the Connaught family, and she gained the sincere goodwill of all who met her during those years in the Dominion.

The Royal party found nothing at all unfavourable in the climate of the Dominion, and they took part in all the winter pastimes for which

Canada is famous, particularly in the tobogganing parties by torchlight, which were a favourite amusement at Government House. Princess Louise had been specially fond of this pastime during the years when she and the Marquis of Lorne were in residence, and they had had a magnificent run made there.

The Duke and his family took part also in ice carnivals, skating parties, sleigh-drives, curling matches, and other winter recreations, which they enjoyed to the full. Princess Patricia, who, as may be imagined, was by this time idolized in Canada, entered into all these amusements with much zest. She was an expert skater. Often, too, with a party of young people, she would don snowshoes and go for long expeditions over the snow-clad country.

She soon accustomed herself to the cold, and when writing home to her friends she sometimes quoted the limerick ascribed to Kipling:

> There was a small boy of Quebec
> Who was buried in snow to his neck.
>   When asked "Are you friz?"
>   He replied "Yes, I is;
> But we don't call this cold in Quebec."

A photograph of her clad in furs was sold in thousands to the admiring Canadians. She accompanied the Duke and Duchess on many of their trips, and these she particularly enjoyed. Sometimes they camped out in vast primeval forests, sometimes they enjoyed fishing expeditions like those in which Princess Louise had revelled, and occasionally they visited Indian encampments. They travelled over the prairies to the Lakes, and naturally they visited Niagara Falls and spent some time in contemplating their grandeur.

The Canadians liked Princess Patricia's high spirits, lack of conventionality, and great interest in sport of all sorts. Like her mother, she was a good horsewoman and whip, and she was always ready for any adventure that offered itself. During one of their tours through the Rockies she rode on the cowcatcher of the engine, as Queen Mary did when she visited Canada as Duchess of Cornwall and York.

There are certain social traditions governing the life of the Governor-General's wife in Canada, and these the Duchess did nothing to break, though some features of her Canadian life must have seemed in strange contrast to what she was accustomed to in England. Rideau

Hall, the official residence at Ottawa, is a solidly comfortable residence not far from the Parliament Buildings, where the Duchess was allowed to listen to debates, staying even for an all-night sitting if she should wish to do so. A seat was provided for her next to the Speaker. The Duke, however, was not supposed to attend at all, presumably on the assumption that the Governor-General, by virtue of his office, must take no part in the political life of the country.

The Parliamentary season in Canada opens with a Cabinet dinner, and on the day following the Duchess used to accompany the Duke to the State opening of Parliament. She sat on the left of the throne in the Senate Chamber, rows of ladies in full evening dress being ranged on each side. The floor of the House was filled with Senators, and the Commons attended to hear the speech from the Throne, which is always read first in English and then in French.

In March a great Drawing-room was held in Parliament Buildings, when the Duke and Duchess stood by the throne with the Ministers grouped about them. First the wives of the Ministers came to curtsey to their Royal Highnesses, then the wives of the Senators, and then the rest of the ladies who attended.

When the Duke and Duchess entertained at Quebec, with its strong French element, the faith of most of the people was indicated by the presence of Roman Catholic Archbishops and other Church dignatories in full ecclesiastical robes, and as much French was spoken as English. As Governor-General the Duke when he was in Quebec held some of the privileges that had been handed down from the old Kings of France who once owned the city. One of these was the right to enter convent cloisters. If the Duchess accompanied him she would be allowed to enter, but if she were at any time to go alone she was only permitted to speak to the nuns through a grating!

Princess Patricia had a genuine affection for Canada for its own sake, and, as we have said, this feeling Canada warmly reciprocated, but she had another reason for becoming attached to the Dominion, since it was while her father was Governor-General that her romantic love affair had its beginning.

Commander Ramsay went to Canada with the Duke as his A.D.C., and from the first he and the young Princess saw a good deal of each other. The attraction was mutual and speedily ripened into deep affection, and the Princess determined to marry the man whom she loved or to remain single. There were difficulties in the way of the match. The Duke and Duchess both had the highest opinion of

Commander Ramsay as a man and an officer, but at that date it was rare for a Royal Princess to marry a commoner, no matter how deeply her affections might be engaged. Princess Patricia was, however, convinced that in the end the wedding would receive the Royal sanction, and she and Commander Ramsay resigned themselves to waiting.

In the Princess's own immediate circle the state of affairs was well known, and the Princess made no secret to her friends of her preference or of her intention to marry the man of her choice, so good wishes were showered upon her by all who were anxious for her real happiness. Many favoured the Commander's suit and attempted to remove the barriers, but for the young people there was a long period of waiting before the course of true love was to run smooth.

CHAPTER XXIII

FAMILY AFFAIRS AND THE OUTBREAK OF THE GREAT WAR
(1913-14; AGED SIXTY-THREE TO SIXTY-FOUR)

Marriage of Prince Arthur of Connaught to the Duchess of Fife — The Duke of Connaught's Visit to Newfoundland — Arrival of the Duchess and Princess Patricia at Ottawa — Start for a Western Tour — Accident on a Lake — The Duke recalled — Outbreak of the Great War — Canadian Enthusiasm and Loyalty — Activities of the Duke and of the Duchess — Mr T. P. O'Connor and Irish Loyalty — Death of Lord Roberts — Centenary of Peace with the United States — Tours and Inspections — The Duke's Old Chauffeur — "You had to pay for them, sir!"

While Princess Patricia had to wait for so long, the romance of her brother. Prince Arthur, developed without obstacles of any kind. In the summer of 1913 he became engaged to his cousin the Duchess of Fife, daughter of the Duke of Fife and Princess Louise, to whom the dukedom had passed on the death of her father without male issue.

Lady Alexandra Duff, as the Duchess was called before the death of her father, was very popular in Society, where she was known as one of the smartest of young Royalties, with a taste in dress which caused her toilettes to be widely and sometimes irritatingly copied. As children both she and her sister. Lady Maud Duff, had been great favourites with their grandfather. King Edward, and there are many charming photographs which show His Majesty with the two little girls.

The young Duchess of Fife was not known only in social circles. She was an excellent sportswoman. She could handle rod and line with expert skill, having been schooled in their use by her mother, who was devoted to angling.

The fact that Princess Louise suffered from ill-health for many years, and that her two daughters were her constant companions, enlarged their sympathies and widened their understanding. Before her marriage Lady Alexandra took much interest in her father's tenants. She often visited them, taking little delicacies to the sick and reading to the bedridden, and she was a great friend of the children on the estate.

Besides other accomplishments, she can speak French, German, and Italian, but book-learning, important as it is, was not considered enough, and the Duchess was also trained in housewifery, so that at the time of her marriage she could both cook and sew well and was more than competent to run her own establishment.

The sisters had always been great friends with their cousins. Princess Mary and her brothers. They played together as children. In later years they were constant companions, and Princess Mary and the young Duchess had an additional bond in their mutual interest in nursing.

When the date of the wedding was announced gifts began to pour in upon the young couple from all parts of the country, as the young Duchess was a general favourite and Prince Arthur was well on the way to becoming as popular as his father. Many of the gifts were very costly, but the one which Prince Arthur probably valued most was a cigarette-case that was given him by his bride inscribed "From Fife to Drum!"

The wedding was fixed for October 15, and just before that date the Duchess of Fife received a little note from a young maidservant, naively informing her that she also had arranged to be married on that date, and ending her letter, "Please, miss, would you mind?" The Duchess told some of her friends that, in spite of the strong counter-attraction, she could not see her way to object.

The wedding took place in the Chapel Royal, St James's. The ceremony was a quiet one, thoroughly English, and fewer foreign Royalties than usual were present. The Duke and Duchess of Connaught came home to attend. For the sake of convenience the King and Queen gave the wedding breakfast at Buckingham Palace, instead of this function being held at the Duke's country residence at Bagshot Park.

The young bride and her soldier bridegroom were loudly cheered on their way to and from the Chapel Royal, and the crowd also gave them a hearty send-off when they drove in a carriage and pair to the home of the bride's mother.

It had been arranged that the Duke should retire from the Governor-Generalship in the autumn of 1914, and throughout that summer he undertook many extensive farewell tours through the

Dominion. Early in July he visited Newfoundland, travelling in H.M.S. *Essex*. Before leaving Quebec he inspected the Boy Scouts, a movement in which he has always taken great interest and of which he is a wholehearted supporter. The Dufferin Terrace was lined with people anxious to give him an enthusiastic farewell, and the Duke departed to the accompaniment of much cheering.

He spent three weeks in Newfoundland, and it had been arranged that on his return his next visit should be to British Columbia. He proposed to arrive at Victoria on August 10, and, accompanied by the Duchess and Princess Patricia, to stay at Government House for a week. The intention was that during their visit the Duke should officiate at the inauguration of the University of British Columbia, and open the "Connaught" block of the Parliament Buildings, of which he had laid the foundation-stone. The Duke had contemplated going as far as Prince Rupert, though not to the Yukon.

The outbreak of war put an abrupt stop to this later tour, but the projected visit to Newfoundland was carried through. The Duchess and Princess Patricia were not with the Duke, but before his return they had arrived at Ottawa and had taken up their residence at Rideau Hall to prepare for the Western tour.

On July 8 the Duke arrived at St John's, in the Bay of Islands, where he received a warm and loyal welcome and was much interested in visiting the 'Old Colony.' Two days later he paid a lengthy visit to the fishing establishments at Blanc Sablon, Belle Isle, where he inspected closely the whole process of curing cod and received a hearty and unconventional welcome from the fishermen. One of them begged the Duke (to whom the idea appealed) to go fishing with them, and promised to show him something new in angling!

Soon afterward he paid a visit to the well-known Dr (now Sir Wilfred) Grenfell in Labrador, and made a tour of his hospitals. He asked the Doctor many questions about his work, and chatted with several of the patients. His Royal Highness also visited the Northcliffe wood-pulp mills, the largest in the world, which supply the raw material for many London newspapers and periodicals. He watched the pulping process, explored the mills, and conversed freely with some of the workers about their particular part in the labour.

The Duke returned to Ottawa on July 20 and began at once to prepare for the tour to British Columbia. With the Duchess and Princess Patricia he left on July 23, intending to be away for nearly two months. This was designed to be the last of their farewell tours, so they wanted to make it as extensive as possible.

At the Lake of the Woods, Kenora, a farewell regatta was arranged in honour of the Royal visitors. Over 400 motor-boats took part, and it was a very gay function. The Royal party were as usual taking a full share in the festivities when an accident occurred that might easily have had fatal results. The motor-boats in which they were travelling struck some floating logs with such force that large holes were knocked in them, and they began rapidly to sink. Luckily there were other boats near enough to go to the rescue in time, and the Duke and his party were rescued from their boats just as they were sinking. It was a narrow escape, but the Royal party, not wanting the mishap to interfere with the festivities, made light of the danger.

They continued their journey on the next day, but they had not gone far before word reached the Duke that, in view of the turn that events were taking, it would be better for him not to proceed. When the War did break out the people of the Dominion were in as great a ferment as their kinsmen in England. For a week before the actual declaration there was great excitement, and the wildest rumours flew round the cities, varying from a report of the assassination of King George to one of the suicide of the Kaiser. These persisted for some time even after war had actually broken out. From the first mention of hostilities there was not the slightest doubt of the intense loyalty and patriotism of the whole of Canada. *The Montreal Daily Mail* said:

As to Canada's attitude, there is no need for argument. Britain will be fighting for her life, and Canada is part of her life.

In every big town there were extraordinary outbursts of enthusiasm, both French and English joining in the various demonstrations. Processions constantly formed in the streets and marched through the towns singing patriotic songs and cheering wildly at the sight of any troops. When it was known that war was inevitable it was announced that Canada would mobilize at once, and on July 31 the Militia Council of Canada (with Colonel Sam Hughes as the Minister of Militia and Defence) made their preliminary arrangements for sending the first 20,000 or 25,000 men of the Canadian contingent to Europe, and wrote to the War Office announcing their intention. There were, however, other urgent problems besides the actual raising of troops, which, with patriotism at fever-heat, was an easy one. The Government was faced with the question of how to arrange for the safe transport of the troops to England, for it was known that German cruisers were abroad on the high seas, and it would have been a master-stroke on the part of the enemy to have sunk the transports.

The Cabinet was in constant session to consider this and other questions, and Ottawa was in a state of perpetual ferment. It was a busy and anxious time for the Duke after he hurried back from his Western tour. His special train left Banff at eleven o'clock for the capital, and once there he hastened to join the Cabinet, which sat all night waiting for the fateful declaration which was known to be inevitable. At seven o'clock (Canadian time) on the evening of August 4 the Colonial Secretary announced to the Governor-General that Great Britain had declared war on Germany.

When the news was spread throughout the city there were scenes of wild enthusiasm everywhere. Crowds marched up and down the streets, shouting and cheering, and a vast multitude assembled outside the Parliament Buildings to cheer the members of the Cabinet as they appeared. The arrival of the Duke was the signal for so mighty an outburst as to surprise even His Royal Highness, who was used to enthusiasm. He acknowledged the cheering again and again, but he looked grave and anxious. To one with his knowledge of soldiering the real meaning of war was too serious for it to be an object of evanescent enthusiasm. He was among the few who fully realized the terrible seriousness of the conflict that had just begun.

The Governor-General's Guards marched through the city in the evening, and practically the whole of the population turned out to cheer them as they passed through the streets.

The day after the declaration of war the Leader of the Opposition (Sir Wilfrid Laurier) was summoned to Rideau Hall to discuss with the Duke the part that Canada should play in the War. The conference was a long one. Later in the day the Duke on behalf of Canada sent the following message to the King:

> In the name of the Dominion of Canada I humbly thank Your Majesty for your gracious message of approval. Canada stands united from the Pacific to the Atlantic in her determination to uphold the honour and traditions of our Empire.

The outbreak of hostilities had provided the Duchess as well as the Duke with a new sphere of activity. One of her first actions was to call a mass-meeting of the women of Ottawa at Government House, in order to discuss ways in which to provide funds for a hospital-ship. The Duchess opened the meeting herself with a brief but pointed and appealing speech, in which she explained the plans for raising the money. The sum needed was 100,000 dollars, and Her Royal Highness headed the list with a donation of 1000 dollars. The women proved as patriotic as their menfolk, and before the meeting closed all arrangements for collecting the money had been made, but before it had been raised Sir Thomas (afterward Lord) Shaughnessy came forward with an offer to provide the ship. The women of Canada paid for her full equipment.

The emergency session of Parliament was opened on August 18, with little of the pomp and ceremony customary to State openings. The proceedings were suited to the solemn importance of the occasion. Many of the members were already in khaki. The Duke's escort of Princess Louise's Dragoons was in service uniform, as were the Governor-General's Foot Guards. The majority of the Duke's A.D.C.'s had already joined their regiments for active service, and he was attended only by Colonel Farquhar, who was to command Princess Patricia's Own Light Infantry.

The Duke delivered his speech "as representative of the King." Both the Premier and Sir Wilfrid Laurier delivered impressive speeches, in which they stressed the need for unity and for the laying aside of all political differences. After the speeches Sir Robert Borden gave notice of a Bill to provide a War fund of fifty million dollars, and the way in which this was received was fine proof of the temper of the House, which was reflected throughout the whole of the country.

The first Canadian contingent, a very fine body of men, of whom Canada was justly proud, was raised in record time.

Shortly after war broke out Canada sent a gift of a million bags of flour to the British people, each consignment bearing the simple inscription "Flour. Canada's Gift" — an act of generosity that was highly appreciated.

Early in August the Duke called together a representative body of leading Canadians in order to form an organization to render assistance to the wives and families of Canadians who volunteered for active service with the armies of the Empire or of the Allies. The Duke's appeal met with a generous response, and the organization, which was called the Canadian Patriotic Fund, succeeded from the moment of its inception. It did much to relieve distress among those for whom it had been formed. In February 1913 its scope was enlarged in order to include not only the families of soldiers, but also wounded soldiers themselves and the widows of those who had fallen. In this direction also a great deal of good was effected. The Duke was President and Chairman of the Executive Committee. He worked hard to ensure the success of the Fund, and so wide was the response that between the first appeal, which was made very soon after the commencement of the War, and December 1916, when the Duke left Canada,[1] there had been raised a sum of no less than 18,373,494.63 dollars, entirely in voluntary contributions. From the first the Duke and Duchess supported the Red Cross by every means in their power, using their personal influence to raise money for its service, attending every kind of meeting called in its aid, and sparing no effort to gain for it influential support.

As Commander-in-Chief as well as Governor-General, the Duke took a large share in helping to raise the Canadian Army to war-time strength. His all-round military experience was of very great help in the crisis, and in all his work he had the assistance of the leaders of the Canadian forces. The Canadian military organization worked with smoothness, and succeeded in putting the fine troops into the field with great speed. The large training-base was Valcartier Camp, where 30,000 men were rapidly collected for training under old soldiers. The Duke often visited the camp, and he praised heartily the fine body of men who were being trained there, as, indeed, he did the whole organization, which was really something of a marvel, with its rifle-ranges, great bathing-pools, and facilities for bridge-building and other engineering work. Everything had been well thought out and planned, and the whole organization reflected much credit upon every one who was responsible.

The Duke's well-known interest in the health of the men caused him to be particularly pleased with the medical inspection arrangements — not the least difficult of the many complicated matters requiring attention — and he also found much to praise in the way in which the transport of the men from all parts of Canada to Valcartier was managed.

1 The Duke's Governor-Generalship, which should have terminated in 1914, was continued until this date in consequence of the war.

During those first months of the War the Duke and all his staff — Military Secretary, Equerry, Comptroller, and A.D.C.'s — worked extremely hard, as the Duke was determined to use every resource which in any way could add to the efficiency of the forces that Canada was sending to the battlefields.

He helped to raise the second contingent, of 15,000 men, which Canada had promised the Home Government to have ready by January 191J, and he was always eager to inspect the reinforcements which were sent over steadily throughout the year. He was also Chief Scout for Canada, and often addressed meetings of Scouts on their work in the War. In Canada, as in all other countries where branches of the movement exist, the Scouts did most valuable work. They were useful in a hundred different ways — a fact which the Duke always emphasized on the many occasions on which he spoke on behalf of the movement.

On November 3, 1914, Mr T. P. O'Connor sent a message to the Duke in which he told His Royal Highness that, at the largest gathering of Irishmen ever held in Glasgow, there had been passed a resolution expressing the deepest loyalty to King and country. This pleased the Duke — the "Prince Pat" of former years — who has always retained happy memories of his time in Ireland, and in his answering cable he said:

> I much appreciate your telegram and wish your loyal and Irish movement every success. Sorry to miss seeing you here.

The death of the veteran Lord Roberts within sound of the guns in Flanders caused the Duke deep regret. He had, of course, known the Field-Marshal well. When in India he had seen a good deal of him, and the two soldiers understood and appreciated each other. He sent an official message of sympathy, addressed to the King:

> In my own name and that of the Canadian Government I desire to express our deepest sympathy with the British nation and Army at the loss they have sustained by the death of Field-Marshal Lord Roberts, whom we are so proud to remember was the Colonel of the Canadian Artillery.

The 9th of December marked the celebration of a hundred years of peace between America and Canada. Eight delegates from New York attended to take part in the Canadian Peace Centenary celebrations, although, owing to the fact that the country was at war, there was some question as to whether the original arrangements should be carried out. The Duke begged that the principal celebrations connected with the anniversary should take place, and this was done, with certain modifications suggested by the needs of the situation.

Besides the inspections at Ottawa and at the great camp, the Duke carried out in December a round of inspections at Quebec, Montreal, Kingston, and Toronto. At Montreal he delivered four addresses to the troops in one day, and spent a great deal of time in talking to the men, asking their names and the details of their service, and ending by calling for three cheers for the King. These were given with a will, and were followed by three spontaneous cheers for the Duke himself.

At St John's the French-Canadian Battalion received the Duke with a Royal salute. The Duke addressed the regiment in French, complimented them on their fine appearance, and said how pleased he was that they were going to fight for Britain and for France alike.

At Kingston the Duke stopped and spoke to Staff-Sergeant Birkett, who had formerly been in his service. After talking for a few minutes the sergeant reminded the Duke of an incident that had happened ten years earlier.

"Ten years ago, sir," he said, "I was your chauffeur in Ireland, and perhaps you will remember the day I took you in your car down the hill outside Dunlavin and ran into two sheep and killed them, and you had to pay for them, sir!"

The Duke seemed much entertained by the reminiscence, and shook the staff-sergeant warmly by the hand before passing down the ranks.

CHAPTER XXIV

CANADA IN THE GREAT WAR
(1914-16; AGED SIXTY-FOUR TO SIXTY-SIX)

Canada's War Effort — The Duke's Example — Princess Patricia — "Her Own" Canadian Regiment and its Achievements — The War Work of the Duke and Duchess — The Duke as a Soldier Governor-General — Inspections, Reviews, Parliamentary and Social Work — The Royal Memory for Faces — Widespread Popularity — The Canadian O.T.C. — McGill University — Destruction of the Parliament House at Ottawa by Fire — Its Quick Replacement — Departure from Canada — Farewell Visits and Speeches — The Duke's Canadian Regime — Tributes.

In describing the Duke of Connaught's activities as Governor-General of Canada in the Great War we feel that we shall have failed in our mission if we do not attempt, however inadequately, to place in its true setting the routine of parades, military inspections, organizing and appeal committees, and perpetual (sometimes, it may be, monotonous) work which was absolutely necessary to disseminate throughout a great nation the true significance of the tremendous struggle upon which Great Britain had embarked. Enthusiastic support was accorded by the whole Empire, which, according to German national psychologists, would break away from the United Kingdom if called upon to face the terrific sacrifice entailed both upon the fighting forces and upon the nations behind them. Nevertheless, the people of Great Britain were accustomed to short wars in which business could be carried on "as usual," and there was no realization, even among the newly created General Staff,[1] of the serious prospects to be faced by every man, woman, and child before victory could be secured.

1 See the writings of Field-Marshal Sir William Robertson (From Private to Field-Marshal, Soldiers and Statesmen, etc.), and of other military authorities behind the scenes at the time.

Canada's military contribution, starting with a permanent force of only 3000, reached a total of nearly 629,000 for the Army alone before the conclusion of hostilities, of which number over 590,000 enlisted on Canadian soil in the Canadian Expeditionary Force. Over 422,000 were sent overseas from Canada. There were more than 210,000 Canadian casualties in France, of whom nearly 52,000 were killed in action. Only 3700 were taken prisoner, and only 6 were returned as 'missing.'

There is no doubt that so keen a soldier as the Duke of Connaught craved for active employment at the Front, as did all the senior officers in the Army. There is a story of a Yeomanry officer in England in the early days of the War who was pining, protesting, and complaining because he and his men were employed upon easy work, close to their homes, when they wanted to serve in wider and more glorious fields. He was reminded by the authorities of the case of Naaman the Syrian, who resented the easy simplicity of a bath in the Jordan when he would have preferred ceremonial ablution in the great rivers Abana and Pharpar. The officer carried on without further complaint, and others did their allotted duty and took comfort from the story. In a war of masses the individual, as the phrase went, did not count: each had to do his particular task without question, and in this, nobly supported by the Duchess and Princess Patricia, the Duke set a fine example to others.

Each Canadian contingent was reviewed by the Duke before it sailed, usually at the great Valcartier Camp. At the first of these inspections, where 23,000 men paraded. Sir Robert Borden, Colonel Hughes, the Minister of Militia and Defence, Sir Wilfrid Laurier, and other prominent Canadians were present when the Duke complimented the officers on the smartness of the troops and expressed himself as well satisfied with their efficiency and general appearance. The Duke remained at the camp over the week-end, in order to see as much of the men's movements as possible, but unfortunately the weather was very wet, so the inspection was not as complete as he had hoped to make it. At later inspections the Duke said that the men had shown improvement every day, and that the parades reflected great credit on all ranks, as well as on the authorities. At the last review before the first contingent sailed the Duchess and Princess Patricia accompanied the Duke. The Princess brought her camera, with which she had become very expert, and took numerous snapshots of the men to add to her collection.

The Princess was her mother's most able and enthusiastic assistant at this time in all the numerous War activities. She attended Red Cross meetings, assisted in countless efforts for the funds of War charities of every description, and on one occasion contributed some of her paintings to be sold for the benefit of a Work Bureau which the Duchess opened. She took stalls at bazaars, and spared no effort to render every service possible. In November 1914 she opened a new ward, play-room, and sun-room at St Luke's Hospital, Montreal, which had been given to that institution by the May Court Club. She was met at the hospital by Miss Edith McPherson, the May Queen, as the elected head of the Club for each year was called, and after declaring the new ward open in an appropriate speech the Princess made a tour of the hospital, chatting with many of the patients. On the following day the Duke and Duchess of Connaught opened a new wing in the same hospital, and they also made a tour of the building.

Untiringly as Princess Patricia carried on her unobtrusive work in those first War years in Canada, it is probable that her name is most closely associated with the raising of "her own" Canadian regiment. "Princess Patricia's Own Canadian Light Infantry," to give this fine regiment its full title, was raised in sixteen days from the date when due authority was given. The men who joined were nearly all veterans of other wars, most of them with medals to show, and by the time the regiment was complete it was said that its ranks held a representative from every regiment in the British Army and that a finer lot of men have never been seen in any single corps.

"Princess Pat's," as they soon came to be called, a thousand strong, were trained in Lansdowne Park, under the command of Colonel F. D. Farquhar and equipped by Major A. Hamilton Gault, of Montreal, who accompanied the regiment to Europe as second-in-command. On August 23, 1914, the regiment paraded at Ottawa before the Duke, the Duchess, and the Princess, who at this parade presented them with the Colours which she had herself made for them, red on one side and blue on the other, with the monogram "P.O." worked in gold.

A huge crowd assembled at the station to see the men off. All the Royal party were present, and when Princess Patricia said farewell to her own regiment she made no effort to hide the tears in her eyes. "Princess Pat's" sailed in the *Megantic* with the first of the Canadian contingents. They were inspected by King George on Salisbury Plain on November 14, and they went to the Front on December 20, the date of the defence of Givenchy, where the first French offensive of 1914-15 was being launched. Once "over there," General French inspected them on New Year's Day, and on the night of January 7, 1915, they were under fire for the first time.

Throughout the whole of their service this regiment gave the Princess every reason to be proud that it should bear her name. They never lost a position or failed to reach an objective, and the personal gallantry of the men was of a very high standard. They received three V.C.'s, besides many other distinctions, and later they became a regular unit in the Canadian Army. They suffered severe casualties. The commanding officer. Colonel Farquhar, formerly on the Duke's staff, was killed in March 1915, and by June of that year only 300 men remained out of the original 1000. *The Times*, speaking of the regiment, said:

> The Canadian regiment to which Princess Patricia has given her name has worthily upheld that name, and will be held in honour for the glories it did in the War for many generations.

After "Princess Pat's" had lost heavily in action "Eye-witness," the officially appointed correspondent, wrote:

> Sunday, August 23, 1914, was a grey, gloomy day when thousands assembled in Lansdowne Park to see the Princess give the Colours she had worked to her regiment. She told them she would follow their fortunes and wished that they might all come back safely. Even the wishes of a gracious and beautiful Princess could not safeguard the lives of the splendid men who laid them down upon the battlefields of Flanders.

The doings of the regiment attracted great attention throughout the whole of the Dominion. In Montreal they were known as "Princess Pat's Pets," and the Canadian Press recorded their movements at great length to a public justly proud of their gallantry.

At Christmas-time the Duchess of Connaught sent to every officer and man in the Canadian Overseas Contingent a box of maple sugar, the favourite Canadian sweetmeat, containing a card bearing the words "Good luck and best wishes for Christmas 1915 from Louise Margaret, Duchess of Connaught." In Canada "the Connaughts" gave a large Christmas-tree to the school-children at Ottawa, and they also attended a party at which another tree was given by the May Court Club.

A Canadian sculptor had executed a statue of King Edward as a memorial to that monarch. This the Duke had unveiled at Montreal in October 1914, afterward writing his appreciation of the work:

> I want to say how pleased I was at all the arrangements in connexion with the King Edward VII memorial. I think the statue is a very good likeness and excellent in every way.

The Duke's readiness to show appreciation of good work of all descriptions, and his anxiety to give praise where praise was due, made him as popular in his military capacity as he was as Governor-General. All ranks knew that their efforts were noted and that the Duke saw to it that merit was always praised and bad conduct censured.

In its issue for March 24, 1915, *The Montreal Daily Mail* paid due tribute to the Duke's services in his dual capacity:

> Since the War began His Royal Highness has travelled many miles and undergone unusual exertions of a trying nature with a cheerfulness and a competency that has made a most favourable impression upon the public of Canada.
>
> What compels admiration is the manner in which the Royal Governor-General has placed himself at the service of the country. No one could better have performed the functions of such an office as His Royal Highness holds, in the time of national and imperial crisis.
>
> His military bearing and active movements are impressive; the manner in which the Canadian Royal Governor-General has risen to his opportunities in this time of trouble has already created a tradition that will long be cherished.

It was on this date that the Duke carried out one of his most important inspections at Montreal. Three thousand Montreal soldiers were timed to parade at three o'clock, but long before that the great field in which the inspection was to take place was crowded with spectators, anxious to see their relations and friends in uniform. As the hour for the ceremony approached the concourse numbered at least 25,000; yet despite this vast crowd the Duke managed to enter the grounds without being recognized until he was half-way across the field. Then, when the crowd identified the soldierly figure in Field-Marshal's uniform, it broke into a roar of welcome, and throughout the whole of the ceremony this cheering was repeated each time the Duke came anywhere near the crowd. During the parade the Duke constantly stopped to talk to men in the ranks whom he recognized. He never passed a man whom he had met elsewhere, and sometimes he even reminded the men of incidents which they had themselves forgotten. At the conclusion of the inspection the soldiers gave three cheers for His Royal Highness, and then, as he was leaving the ground, a spectator called for three more, which were given heartily by soldiers and civilians alike.

Later in the same day the Duke inspected the Red Cross headquarters, and in the evening he was the guest of the officers of the 3rd and the 24th Battalions of the Victoria Rifles at a banquet which was given to mark the fact that he was Honorary Colonel of the regiment. The allied units were the recipients of a life-size portrait of the Duke, and in return they presented him with a silver bowl. At the end of the entertainment the whole party sang *For he's a Jolly Good Fellow* and *Will ye no' come back again?*

Any Canadians who were under the delusion that the office of Governor-General was something of a sinecure, if such there had been, must have been speedily undeceived by the ceaseless activity of His Royal Highness, who worked even harder in those years than he had ever done before in his extremely active career. Apart from his military duties, which at that time were naturally onerous, his presence was in constant demand at every possible kind of social function connected with the War, and if the object were in any way meritorious the Duke never refused. It was no unusual thing for him to attend two important conferences in the morning, take a parade or military duty of some kind in the afternoon, and attend a formal dinner in the evening, and this would be the routine on three or four days in the week.

The Duchess was equally active. Besides her work on committees and at various functions in connexion with the many War charities in which she interested herself, he did a large amount of needlework and knitting. Often both she and Princess Patricia contributed articles which they themselves had made to various causes, hand-knitted socks to 'sock showers,' comforters and woollen helmets to be sent out to the troops, and little garments for War orphans.

The death of Colonel Farquhar in action was deeply regretted by the Duke. The gallant officer had been with him in Canada before going over with Princess Pat's Regiment, and the Royal party all attended the memorial service that was held in Ottawa in memory of the Colonel.

In March the Duke opened the Canadian Academy of Arts, which was open for the whole of the week, the proceeds going to the Belgian Relief and Red Cross Funds.

Parliament sat constantly through that first year of the War. The Duke attended many of the sittings, and he was present, accompanied by the Duchess and Princess Patricia, in the Senate Chamber when the spring session closed. In April there was yet another great inspection of troops at Montreal. Men drawn from the workshops, from the lumber-mills, and from office desks were all ranged up ready for service in the field, which they gave ungrudgingly in the cause which the Canadian nation had made its own.

As on former occasions, the Duke spoke to many of the men in the ranks, surprising and pleasing them by recalling faces which he had not seen for several years, and then only at some temporary meeting. In one of the batteries he picked out a gunner who had been presented to him when he was in the Sudan. The man had been a civil engineer on some bridge-construction works in which His Royal Highness had been interested, but he had never seen him since. He recognized the gunner at once, and stayed chatting with him for several minutes.

It is only by recalling that in the course of a year the Duke carried out many inspections of many thousand troops that this feat of memory can be estimated justly. It really meant more than an excellent memory. One of the secrets of the Duke's widespread popularity, both in his civil and in his military capacities, was his sincere interest in the people whom he met, irrespective of their rank. People made an impression upon him because he was genuinely interested in them, and his wide sympathies caused him to remember what most men would forget.

Later in the day of this review the Duke and the Duchess visited the new Convalescent Home provided by the Khaki League, and the Duke also inspected the nurses who were going overseas. After his inspection he paid a fitting tribute to the nursing organizations of whose members so many had volunteered for duty at the Front. In his military capacity he had seen a good deal of the work done by such women, and he never lost an opportunity of praising them or of doing justice to the value of their services. In this he was followed by the Duchess, whose own Red Cross work had given her opportunities of appraising the value of an efficient and inspired nursing sisterhood.

On April 23 (St George's Day) there was an interesting event. The Duke, wearing his robes as Doctor of Laws over his Field-Marshal's uniform, presented diplomas to some thirty students, all of whom were in khaki and all about to go on active service. The Duchess, also in her LL.D. gown, and Princess Patricia were present at what was in some ways rather a pathetic ceremony, in view of the probability that some who had qualified in the halls of learning would fail to gather the fruits of their application.

On the 30th a solemn and moving memorial service was held on Parliament Hill for the men of Canada who had already fallen, and the Duke and Duchess, with the Princess, attended. There was a vast crowd at the service, the majority being relatives of the men who had fallen, and the ladies were visibly affected before its conclusion.

The Duke carried out a particularly interesting inspection during this year when he saw the McGill University section of the Canadian Officers' Training Corps. The assembled crowd gave him as usual a rousing reception. The occasion was charged with emotion. Some of these men were going out to fill the gaps in Princess Pat's Regiment. Reference has already been made to the losses which the regiment had suffered. The Duke addressed the assembly of 700 with great feeling. He said:

> I wish specially to say a word to the Third University Company. They will shortly be going over to reinforce Princess Patricia's Regiment, one that has been through great things for this country and the Empire.

Accounts of the valour of the Canadian troops in the various battles in which they had taken part were constantly being received in the Dominion. They fought in the second battle of Ypres, and they were present during the first German gas-attack, in which they suffered severely. Their steady bearing and avoidance of panic on that historic occasion probably prevented a great disaster, and the pride of the Canadian people in this and in their other achievements did something to assuage the grief at the heavy bereavements.

Princess Patricia kept a scrap-book in which she pasted every item of information that concerned her own regiment, and this is still one of her most treasured possessions. She naturally took the greatest personal interest in all the men, and she often knitted socks and garments to be sent out in the parcels dispatched by the different societies.

Canada continued to send reinforcements, each batch of men as fine as those preceding them, and all meriting this description which was given by a British officer: "In this battle the Canadians fought like very devils. They are great, hard-looking chaps who have proved themselves a match for the Germans."

The Duke's love for animals has several times been mentioned. He often inspected remounts, impressing all who were present by his wide knowledge of horses and their needs, which he did his best to see fulfilled, though at the same time he doubted the value of cavalry in the situation which obtained on the Western Front in France and Flanders, and looked forward to the day when, even for transport, horses would be superseded by mechanical vehicles.

On February 3, 1916, the fine Parliament House at Ottawa was destroyed by fire. Fortunately the Senate House and the Library escaped, but the damage that was done was considerable. The Duke wrote to Sir Robert Borden, the Premier:

> I desire to express through you my warm sympathy to both Houses of Parliament in the terrible calamity of last night, by which those historic buildings were almost destroyed by fire. I know how universal will be the regret felt not only in the Dominion itself, but throughout the Empire. I deplore the loss of life which has, I fear, occurred, and desire to express my deep sympathy with the relatives of those who have so unfortunately perished.

Plans were immediately forthcoming for rebuilding the edifice, and the Duke laid the foundation-stone of the new building in September, using the cornerstone that King Edward, as Prince of Wales, had laid on September 1, 1860. With their characteristic energy, the Canadian people soon had their Parliament Buildings restored.

Arrangements had been made for the Duke to relinquish his Governorship in October 1916, so in June he and the Duchess proceeded on a tour to the camps in the West. There they attended many inspections, reviews, and similar military ceremonies. It was an extensive and rather an arduous tour, and no doubt it helped to exhaust the strength of the Duchess, since both she and the Duke were determined to crowd as much as possible into their programme. A farewell visit was paid to Toronto, and the Duke spent a day among 25,000 troops at Camp Borden. They were greeted wherever they went with the greatest enthusiasm, tempered only by the knowledge that this was to be the last tour of the Royal couple whom Canada had learned to know and to revere. There is no doubt that their Royal Highnesses made their farewells with deep regret. The experience after a few weeks in South Africa was repeated after five long years in Canada, and it was said that, if the Duke was pleased with Canada, the feeling was reciprocated with enthusiasm.

Though war conditions precluded many functions that would otherwise have taken place, many farewell receptions, dinners, and entertainments were given in honour of their Royal Highnesses, and the Duke made various speeches in which he spoke of the happiness which he and his family had known during their residence in Canada and with what regrets he ended his tenure of office.

Between March and October 1913 he had been obliged to leave Canada for England on account of the serious illness of the Duchess, Sir Charles Fitzpatrick acting as Administrator in his absence. That his thoughts were with the Canadians was proved by his announcement in London in May of that year (when he was appointed by the King President of the Boy Scouts Association) that Canada already had 30,000 Boy Scouts. The announcement in June that he would be able to return to Canada in October accompanied by the Duchess was received there with great enthusiasm. So was his consent to remain in Canada when war broke out, and he agreed to stay on indefinitely when Prince Alexander of Teck, who was to have succeeded him, went to the Front with his regiment. His speech on September 11, 1914, at the Toronto Exhibition is still remembered:

> I bid the people of Canada be of good cheer. This is a time for courage and confident belief in the resources of the Dominion, that they are equal to any situation which we may be called upon to meet.

In 1915 Government House at Ottawa had been a very quiet centre, since many officers who had been with the Duke had been killed or wounded. His duties were constant and very onerous. In an annual report on Canadian affairs for the year we read that

As a British Field-Marshal, experienced in the preparations and practices of war in many countries, the Duke of Connaught was an eminently useful factor in the military life of the moment. As an uncle of His Majesty the King and more than *persona grata* with the rulers and leaders of the Allies, he was an important link in the relations of Canada with the Empire and the nations at war. As personally one of the most popular of Governor-Generals, with no critics on the platform or in the Press, he is an ideal Head of the State and a very busy man.

In *The Toronto Globe* we read:

No other Field- Marshal in the British Army has a greater claim to be regarded as a thoroughly trained veteran, or a capable military adviser. Since the War broke out, he has given most of his thought and time to the task of making the Canadian Contingent as perfect as possible, for the severe strain to which they are subjected. To the public, who gets occasional glimpses of him in the course of his duties, he is very much the ' British officer,' quietly active, habitually reticent, invariably gentlemanly, perennially vigilant, cordially sympathetic and tactfully modest and charming.

The year 1916 had been equally taken up with military duties, reviews, inspections, visits to hospitals, receptions to soldiers, committee-meetings of all kinds connected with war arrangements, in addition to many matters of civic importance such as town-planning, which were not disregarded. The announcement in June that the Duke would be leaving in October had raised a chorus of regret, with the warmest expressions of affection for him and his family. The regret was universal, as can be gathered from organs of the Press credited with strong Radical sympathies, such as *The Toronto Telegraph*:

He combines all the qualities of the ideal Governor-General; pity 'tis he is not to be with us longer.

The Winnipeg Tree Press paid a sincere personal compliment:

The success which attended the Duke of Connaught's occupation of Rideau Hall ought not to be regarded as a precedent. The next Royal Viceroy might be as great a failure as the Duke was a success.

After five years of devoted service the Duke sailed for England on October 11, leaving as his last message:

> In bidding farewell I pray that God may ever bless Canada and its people.

The Duke's Canadian regime had a good effect in many directions. It demonstrated to a democratic country that the scion of a Royal House could understand and sympathize personally with all its problems. It thus bound the Dominion more closely to the United Kingdom through the medium of loyalty to the same Sovereign. It also proved that a Prince of the blood could be a most efficient soldier as well as a wise, just, and far-sighted administrator. It did more than that, in so far as, by the constant expression of such sentiments in the Duke's speeches, it assured the Canadian people of the interest taken by the people of the United Kingdom in the other nations of the British Commonwealth, for which there is no precedent in history.

On the personal popularity of the whole of the Connaught family there is no need to enlarge further. The Duke's geniality, his serenity of temper, often under very trying circumstances, his strict sense of justice, his love of fair play, and his entire absence of the social reserve which some Canadians had expected, all these attributes contributed to make him a general favourite wherever he went.

The Duchess had created an impression no less favourable. By her simplicity, her gracious sympathy with all sorts and conditions of humanity, by her genuine desire to be of service to those about her, she set an example which was particularly helpful as coming from a Royal Princess. Shy and retiring by nature, Her Royal Highness may have found particularly congenial the less ceremonious atmosphere of the Canadian circles in which she moved. The people loved her, and she repaid their affection by sparing no effort to serve them and their country. With her invariable tact and good feeling, she declined a farewell gift from the women of Canada (a similar gift had always been received by her predecessors). She said that in war-time she should very much prefer that the money be put to other purposes, and begged, in a message of much feeling, that nothing might be given to her. As a further indication of the place gained in Canadian hearts by the personal charms of Princess Patricia, it is only necessary to add that in 1916 the sale of her miniature raised a large sum for Red Cross purposes.

The years which "the Connaughts" spent in Canada marked a great epoch in Empire development. It was said by Mr Gladstone, nearly seventy years ago, that "no community which is not charged with the ordinary business of its own defence is really or can be, in the full sense of the word, a free community." During those great years of sacrifice to a common cause the free, self-governing Canadian nation developed a still stronger spirit of nationality, but this was combined with a more widespread loyalty and personal affection for the Sovereign and the members of the Royal Family.

CHAPTER XXV

BEREAVEMENT
(1917-20; AGED SIXTY-SEVEN TO SEVENTY)

Illness and Death of the Duchess of Connaught — Her Character — The Duke at the Front — Prince Arthur's Mission to Japan — Princess Patricia's Marriage — Commander the Hon. A.R.M. Ramsay — Birth of their Son — His Upbringing — The Duke as a Grandfather — He goes to the South of France — Interest in his Son's Public Work — Clubs for "British Boys Unlimited" — Care for the Veteran and for the Serving Soldier — Pleasure derived from Army Progress.

In the spring of the year following his return from Canada the Duke suffered a great bereavement from which he has never wholly recovered. The illness of the Duchess in 1912 had been very severe. The effect had been to weaken her heart, and the untiring zeal with which she had laboured in Canada, strenuously endeavouring to do her utmost to fulfil her duties as wife of the Governor-General, had greatly increased the strain.

Always making light of illness, and disguising as far as possible all fatigue and weakness, she had not given herself the chances of full recovery that anyone less conscientious would have taken. In no way self-centred, but devoted to the service of others, she was apt to resent indisposition. She strove against it with all her might, and only a strong and brave spirit enabled her to carry on for so long a period. The Duchess was fairly well during the first few months after the return to England, but on February 13, 1917, she was taken ill with influenza and bronchitis. During a slow recovery from the effects she unfortunately contracted measles and then broncho-pneumonia, which brought too great a strain upon her weakened heart, and, in spite of all that medical skill could do, she passed away on March 14.

Herself the daughter of a soldier, the Duchess had proved herself an ideal wife and a most devoted helpmeet to her husband in every capacity. Throughout the whole of their life together she had been of

267

the greatest assistance to the Duke in his career. Never was the saying more true that "a happy marriage halves the sorrows and doubles the joys in the life of a man."

The difference in their temperaments made them particularly suited to each other. Though constitutionally shy, the Duchess possessed a keen sense of humour, which enabled her to find amusement under conditions which others might have found dull and wearisome. An excellent judge of character, she was invariably gracious to all about her, and while quick to detect insincerity or flattery, she could appreciate good qualities wherever they were to be found. It may be that she lacked some of her husband's serenity of temperament and placidity of outlook, but these attributes she supplemented by others, and as a shrewd observer of events her opinions were of the utmost value to him.

It is hardly needful to mention the devotion of the Duchess as a mother. One of the great griefs of her earlier married life had been the separation from her children for such long periods during the course of the Duke's service in India, whether the break in the family life was enjoined by the age of the children, by the climate at certain times of the year, or by the intervention of Queen Victoria.

The Duchess's love for her children had not led her by any means to spoil them. They had been brought up very simply. Prince Arthur was given the usual education of an English schoolboy, and she had not opposed his beginning that education at a boarding-school at the age of ten, while the Princesses had both been trained in housewifely duties under her own personal supervision.

By no conventional phrases can the Duke's loss and suffering be described, coming as it did at a time of lowered vitality from which the whole nation was beginning to suffer under the strain of the great world-conflict.

The sadness of the occasion was heightened by the fact that, owing to war conditions, her eldest daughter, the Crown Princess of Sweden, could not be with her mother at the last — a matter which grieved Princess Margaret deeply, for the family had always been a united one. This, the first occasion on which death had caused a gap in the home circle, was a deep and abiding sorrow to all its members.

On her deathbed the constant thoughts of the Duchess were with her children, and she made it known as her last wish that all obstacles to the engagement between Princess Patricia and Commander Ramsay should be removed and that the young couple should be allowed to marry. A promise was given that her wish would be granted and observed.

The Duke's deep personal sorrow, combined with the anxieties of that fateful period when the issue hung in the balance, told severely on his health. He was obliged to winter abroad, where he slowly recovered his strength, but the effects of his loss were plainly visible, and an intimate friend in writing of him at that time said that he seemed like only half a person, so much of his vitality appeared to have been sapped. The devotion of his daughter, Princess Patricia, provided great consolation, but with them, as with nearly every family in the land, there remained the constant dread of the long casualty lists of those War years. Prince Arthur was serving on the Western Front, and numerous friends were with the fighting forces.

Within four days of the Duke's arrival in England he inspected the Reserve Battalion of the Grenadier Guards at Chelsea, and two days afterward the Guards Depot at Caterham. Then he left for France in order to visit our Front, and especially the Guards Division, whom, as senior Colonel of the Brigade of Guards, he inspected. The Duke spent some days in France, visiting various corps, etc.

This visit was repeated on several occasions during the next two years, and His Royal Highness visited all the Army fronts, as well as the Canadian Corps, the Guards Division, several battalions of the Rifle Brigade, the Royal Dublin Fusiliers, the various ammunition depots. Veterinary Hospitals, and the Ordnance Workshops at Havre.

His Royal Highness also twice visited the Italian Front, staying as the King of Italy's guest at his Headquarters once, and another time at our own Headquarters with Lord Cavan.

In January 1918 His Royal Highness left for Egypt, in order to present decorations to the Egyptian troops, as well as to the Australians and New Zealanders, on behalf of the King, as it would not be possible for these troops to receive their decorations from His Majesty. The Duke carried out investitures in Cairo, and then proceeded to Khartoum, where another investiture was held. An investiture was held also in Palestine.

The Duke inspected various Divisions, both on the Canal and in Palestine, and was present with Lord Allenby at the crossing of the Jordan by the Australian troops.

At the end of March the Duke left Cairo for Greece, in order to decorate the King with the G.C.B. From Greece he proceeded to Italy, visiting our Front, and he stayed there till April 13. He then returned to England through France, visiting Sir Douglas Haig at his Headquarters.

On June 25 His Royal Highness again left for France, in order to present decorations to the French troops, visiting various French headquarters, as well as decorating French officers and men attached to the British forces.

On completion of this duty the Duke proceeded to the Headquarters of the Belgian Army, and held an investiture. In addition to these visits abroad, at the request of the War Office he inspected Officers' Training Corps of the English Universities and public schools, as well as a large number of volunteer battalions.

The Duke visited an enormous number of military hospitals all over England, and he accompanied the King on his various visits to Aldershot.

In 1918 the Duke derived much pleasure from the selection of Prince Arthur to proceed upon a special mission to Japan and from his receiving the G.C.M.G. in September.

At the end of 1918 the engagement of Princess Patricia to Commander Ramsay was announced. The period of mourning for the Duchess had at first delayed the formal consent being given, and afterward the Princess had not wished to leave her father while he was still broken in health and before time had softened the acuteness of his suffering. The engagement was thus publicly announced in the Press:

> The King and Queen have received the gratifying intelligence of the betrothal of Her Royal Highness Princess Victoria Patricia of Connaught, their Majesties' Cousin, to Commander the Hon. Alexander Ramsay, R.N., to which union the King has gladly given his consent.
>
> Nothing could possibly be more popular with the English people than the betrothal which is announced this morning of Princess Patricia to a naval officer of her own race. A love-match is always popular, and in this case the bride is one of the best known and most admired of Royal ladies, wherever throughout the Empire she has supported her gallant father. The bridegroom is of the Service which is dearest of all to British hearts.

The Hon. A.R.M. Ramsay is the third son of the thirteenth Earl of Dalhousie and brother of the present peer. He entered the Navy in

1894, and he was A.D.C. to the Duke of Connaught in Canada until war broke out, when he took part in the Gallipoli campaign, in which he earned the D.S.O., and in other operations. To the general public he was the embodiment of their ideal of a naval officer; thus the engagement was immensely popular on account both of the bride and of the bridegroom. Somehow or other the story of their constancy and of the hopeless nature of their engagement at first had become known, and the public were delighted with so genuine a romance.

Princess Patricia was radiant with happiness that enhanced her well-known grace and beauty. We have noted some of her activities as her mother's able assistant in various parts of the Empire and her devotion to her father in his loneliness. A brilliant figure in her social surroundings, an artist of considerable skill with the brush, the possessor of a fine and well-trained voice, she had travelled widely, and so gained an insight into varying phases of life. Those experiences had deepened and broadened her sympathies and outlook, and added wit and interest to her conversation, but she had retained throughout a true sense of values. Her tastes being like those of her family, simple, she gave up her Royal status at her own request on her marriage, becoming the Lady Patricia, the title she would have held as the daughter of a Duke who was not a member of the Royal Family.

The marriage was celebrated in Westminster Abbey on February 27, 1919. Though hostilities had ceased, the War was not technically over, so it was largely a khaki wedding. Many of the guests were still in Army uniform, and the blue of brother officers of the bridegroom was well in evidence. More simple than many Royal weddings, and with fewer guests, it was a beautiful ceremony, and it made a very strong appeal to the popular imagination.

By the Princess's special wish the Guard of Honour was composed of men of "her own" Canadian regiment. The Colours which she had worked when the regiment had been formed were carried, and the Guard looked very proud of the honour as the graceful bride walked smiling between their ranks.

She wore an exquisite Venetian gown with a priceless lace veil. This, according to the custom of Royal brides, she wore thrown back from her face, and a narrow circlet of myrtle-leaves rested in her hair. Commander Ramsay wore uniform, and as they stood before the altar it was noticed that bride and bridegroom were almost exactly of the same height, Princess Patricia being very tall. The Princess had followed her sister Margaret's example, and had chosen blue for the dresses of her bridesmaids. The Duke, who gave his daughter away, wore his Field-Marshal's uniform. The King and Queen were present.

His Majesty in naval uniform as a compliment to the bridegroom, and many relatives and friends attended. There were but few foreign Royalties, for dynasties had been destroyed in the furnace of war from which the Royal House of Windsor had emerged tempered and strengthened. The Princess, a little paler than usual, was perfectly composed. Radiant in white and silver, she rendered her responses in firm, clear tones that could be heard by the whole of the congregation.

London was thronged with demobilized men from all parts of the Empire at the time, as well as by a population increased by War workers, and a tremendous greeting was given by the crowds both to the Royal Princess on her way to the Abbey with her father and to Commander and Lady Patricia Ramsay after the ceremony. The bridegroom's hand hardly left the salute, while the bride smiled and bowed again and again in answer to the cheers and shouts of greeting that came to her from every side. The Duke of Connaught received an ovation. For him the joy and promise of the occasion were tempered by sadness at the parting from so loyal and devoted a daughter, for it marked the breaking up of a family life and the happiness therein which had lasted for so many long and eventful years.

A vast number of wedding-gifts were received from all parts of the Empire and from people of all ranks. The Princess had many from friends that she had made in Canada and from people who had grateful reason to remember the Duke's *régime* there. Ireland too remembered the charming "Princess Patsy," who had so successfully 'put the comether on them' when the Duke held the command. Among the presents there was very little jewellery, because the Princess had expressed a wish that only relatives or very intimate friends should give jewels.

In July Commander Ramsay was appointed British Naval Attaché at Paris. Some time later he assumed the command of H.M.S. *Dunedin*, and has since followed his vocation in various ships.

On December 21 a son and heir was born and christened Alexander Arthur Alfonso David. He soon became a very great favourite with his grandfather, the Duke, with whom he spent much time when he was little, and did much to form a new interest to relieve his loneliness. Lady Patricia also has spent as much time as she could with her father since her marriage. A perfect understanding exists between father and daughter. Her husband's career has, of course, caused him to be stationed at various foreign ports, and whenever possible Lady Patricia has accompanied him. These various places have provided her with subjects for some of her most successful pictures. She is a devoted mother, and she has personally superintended the upbringing of her son, who has contrived to resemble both his father and mother.

The Duke played games with his grandson as a child, and he once had an amusing tale to tell of "Sandy's" powers of observation and mimicry. Deciding to play at ' Doctors,' the boy borrowed the Duke's stick and silk hat, and went out of the room. He marched in again solemnly, pushed a small forefinger on his grandfather's chest, and said, all in one breath, "Have-you-a-temperament-three-guineas-please-good-morning!" Then, with his large hat still swaying on his head, he marched out.

Sandy and his elder cousin, the young Earl of Macduff, Prince Arthur's son, are great friends. They often played together some of the Scout games. These were learned first by the elder boy and then by the younger when, very proud of the turn-out when first it was received, he became a Boy Scout himself. About the music of the bagpipes their tastes were not as much in accord as they were over the attractions of Scouting. The Duke of Fife's family were always particularly fond of them, and Prince Arthur of Connaught (who is Colonel-in-Chief of the Scots Greys) has told of the impression that was made upon him by hearing two hundred pipers play *The Blue Bonnets are over the Border* at the crossing of the Rhine, so the young Earl inherits an affection for the pipes from both sides of his family.

The bonds of affection between the Duke and his son and daughters drew them still closer to him after the loss of their mother. For some time after her death one of them was usually staying with him when he was not paying a visit to them. He is devoted to his grandchildren. He has always kept up a correspondence with the children of Princess Margaret, and it was to him that Lady Patricia's son penned his first epistle as a child.

Owing to impaired health, the Duke spent the colder months of 1919 in a villa which he rented in the South of France, and although for a time he abandoned some of his former activities, he still took an interest in every scheme that was in any way connected with the Army, and he was, and is always, willing to extend his patronage to movements likely to assist in military progress. In 1929 he became Patron of the Society of Army Historical Research, thereby giving a great impetus to an important movement.

273

In such matters Prince Arthur resembles his father. He is always ready to lend his influence to any good cause or to speak on behalf of any welfare scheme. The Duke, who has long realized the importance of athletics and of healthy games to the growing boy and the need for open spaces for him to play in, has been much pleased by his son's association with the National Union of Boys' Clubs. He has made every endeavour to endorse the statements in a speech of Prince Arthur's on behalf of the London Federation of Boys' Clubs. The Federation, he said, was formed fifty years ago, and its work has spread to every large city. For every five working boys between the ages of fourteen and eighteen only one is at present touched by an organization such as theirs. In London alone it was estimated that 100,000 boys were 'drifting' in their leisure hours. Progress has been slow and fluctuating because until lately there has been no central headquarters to co-ordinate, inspire, and expand the movement. It is necessary to combine and to play toward the same goal on behalf of these lads, and the more players on the field the better. Never in the history of the nation has there been so great a need for wholesome influences to counteract the demoralizing effect of unemployment upon young minds and bodies. What is wanted most is to bring into the movement that indefinable something that is called the public-school spirit. The appeal was not for charity, but to give working boys the chance to which they are entitled, and no investment could be better than one in a great company, "British Boys Unlimited."

The Duke has taken, and does take, as much interest in the old as in the young, and supports any scheme to benefit the aged, particularly the old soldier. He has been a keen student of all kinds of pension plans that apply to the disabled, and has been a frequent visitor to the pensioners at Chelsea. They all know him, and he has had many lengthy talks with that interesting community of veterans.

The improved moral of the Army, of both officers and men, to which the Duke has done so much to contribute, has given him great encouragement. He hopes to see the time when an Army officer will be able to live on his pay, because he fears that a really keen type of prospective leaders of men will otherwise be excluded from adopting a military career. To his interest in the young soldier, in Army rations and cooking, in diet and hygiene generally, and in the provision of counter-attractions to excessive drinking we have constantly referred in previous pages. To the Duke and to other similar reformers we can attribute the great advance made in all such matters until in these days service in the Army attracts some of the pick of the population. The realization of the change, and perhaps of the part which he had taken in bringing it about, did, we hope, help one whose life has been devoted to others to face the first three years of his own great sorrow.

CHAPTER XXVI

FURTHER BEREAVEMENT AND PUBLIC SERVICE
(1920-21; AGED SEVENTY)

The Duke's Saddest Birthday — Death of Princess Margaret — Appreciation of her Character — The Duke and his Loss — He opens, with Lady Patricia, the Duchess of Connaught Memorial Hostel — Its Objects and their Achievement — Transferred to the University of London — Prince Arthur in the Great War — He retires from the Army — Becomes Governor-General of the Union of South Africa — The Duke in Retirement — A New Call to Duty — Preparation for a Visit to India — He presents a Nursing Home to Bagshot in Memory of the Duchess.

We have traced the life-story of His Royal Highness the Duke of Connaught until the New Year of 1920, when he had slowly regained his strength during the years that had followed his irreparable loss in 1917, and when with that renewed strength the power and will to resume his public activities was returning. We took note of the comfort that he had derived from the constant sympathy and occasional company of his children and of his young grandsons, but on May 1, 1920, his seventieth birthday, he was destined to face without warning yet another severe blow. His elder daughter, Margaret, Crown Princess of Sweden, the "Daisy" of earlier years, passed away suddenly after a short illness, and the tragedy was even more poignant in that it was wholly unexpected. The Princess had always enjoyed good health, and she had led an active and busy life, caring constantly for her four children and fulfilling her State duties with interest and enthusiasm. The news of her death came as a profound shock to her family. The trouble began with a formation of matter behind one of the eyes. It was hoped that this could be put right and that it need have no serious consequences, but erysipelas and blood-poisoning set in, and she died after a very short illness.

Endowed with an exceptionally sweet and gracious nature, the Crown Princess had speedily endeared herself in her adopted country, while by her sympathy and qualities of heart and mind she had made for herself many devoted friends in her immediate circle. Talented, like her sister, Princess Patricia, she painted well (a gift both sisters doubtless inherited from their mother, who never travelled far without her sketch-book), and she had also shown considerable literary skill. Not long before her death she had published a charming little book describing the gardens which she had made at her Swedish homes. Sweden's position as a neutral country during the War had given her opportunities for performing devoted work on behalf of unfortunate prisoners of war. She had laboured unceasingly to do all that she possibly could for them, sparing no effort to assist in any plan she thought might be for their benefit.

The Princess was a devoted mother, and the home life of the family of the Swedish Crown Prince was always marked by the most intimate affection. Loyalty in friendship was one of her strongest characteristics. She never studied her own interests if an opportunity presented itself to serve anyone who was dear to her. A tribute paid to her memory by Princess Henry of Pless only echoes what all her friends thought about her.

> From the beginning to the end of the War the late Crown Princess of Sweden was more kind to me than I have any words to say. Such a friend! Time, trouble, risk: at need all these were as nothing. What a loss her death was to her family, to her friends, to Sweden!

The lowered vitality and constant anxiety of the War years had thus claimed the sacrifice of another life devoted to the service of others, leaving an empty blank in many hearts. Upon the Duke, her father, the blow fell as heavily as it did upon her husband and children. It drove him for the time being back to a life of retirement, and it prevented him from fulfilling, in May, an engagement to open, in company with Lady Patricia, the Duchess of Connaught Memorial Hostel — a ceremony which did not take place until June 25.

From its beginning the Duke has taken great personal interest in the Hostel, which owed its existence to a fund which the women of Canada subscribed during the course of the War and handed to the Duchess of Connaught in her capacity of wife of the Governor-General to distribute as she thought best. At the suggestion of Her Royal Highness, the money became the nucleus of a fund for the benefit of Canadian prisoners of war. By the end of the War the fund had increased to the large total of nearly £18,000, which included a donation of £5000 from the Maple Leaf Club at the instigation of Lady Drummond. In course of time the fund was no longer needed for its original purpose. The Dominion Government was occupied with the problems of demobilizing and repatriating the members of the Canadian Forces, and many men who were born in England preferred to remain in the country. These, providing they had independent means or were capable of supporting themselves, were demobilized in England, but, owing to the great increase in unemployment and to the general state of chaos in many trades which were the immediate result of the War, many of the men were unable to obtain the work that they had anticipated. In addition to these a certain proportion of the men already demobilized were ill or suffering from the effects of wounds and unable to obtain even board and lodging.

Many cases of this kind were known at the Canadian Red Cross Headquarters in London. Lady Perley and Lady Drummond, together with the officials in charge of the office in Parliament Mansions which had been set up, with financial help from the High Commissioner, for the temporary relief of such cases, considered the problem, and at last it was decided to bring the matter to the notice of the Duke and Lady Patricia. It was believed, in view of their well-known interest in all things Canadian, that they would make some helpful suggestion.

The response of the Duke and his daughter was immediate. They suggested at once that the money remaining in the funds for the Canadian prisoners of war should be used to erect a Hostel where Canadian ex-Service men temporarily stranded could live comfortably and cheaply.

In addition to the large sum available for the erection and maintenance of the Hostel there was also in hand £200 from the balance of money from the Imperial Order of Daughters of the Empire Fund, and this sum Lady Perley handed over to help in cases of real hardship. This money was used largely as loans, so that when paid back it could be used again and again. A great deal of good was thus effected, the men helped being the self-respecting kind who would have refused any suspicion of charity but were glad to be able to borrow money which they intended to repay.

When the plans for the Hostel were made the Duke consented to be Patron, and Lady Patricia President. The Trustees were the Rev. the Hon. E. Lyttelton, D.D., Major-General J. H. MacBrien, C.B., C.M.G., D.S.O., and R.B. Barron, Esq., who was also the chairman of a committee of which the members were Lady Drummond, Lady Perley, Mrs Geoffrey Myatt, and the Trustees.

Lady Patricia took much interest in all matters connected with the Hostel from the beginning. She was delighted when the Committee announced that suitable premises had been found at 13 and 14 Bedford Place, W.C.1, on a ten years' lease, and she made several suggestions herself about altering and redecorating the premises, the installation of central heating, with due regard to Canadian preferences, and the provision of a constant supply of hot water. Besides a lounge, dining-hall, and reading-room, there was a 'Silence' room for use by men who were studying for examinations and by the Rhodes Scholars from the universities who should spend their vacations at the Hostel.

At the formal opening by the Duke and Lady Patricia a large and distinguished company attended, including Sir George Perley (High Commissioner for Canada) and Lady Perley, Lady Drummond, the late Viscount Milner, Lord Aberdeen, Sir George and Lady McLaren Brown, Sir Frederick Milner, Colonel Walter Long, the Agents-General for Nova Scotia, British Columbia, Ontario, and Quebec, Alderman Ryding, of Toronto, the Trustees and Committee of the Hostel, and many prominent Canadians who were in London at the time.

The Duke spoke of the great interest which the Duchess had taken in everything connected with Canada, and he added that it had always been her wish to do something for Canadian men living in London. Knowing this, it had given him great pleasure to place the money at the disposal of the management of the Hostel.

The work that was carried out by the Hostel was wide and varied and of great service to the men for whom it had been opened, which gave great satisfaction to the Duke and Lady Patricia. The men who used it first were Canadians on their way to France to visit War graves, and they found the Hostel of immense value on their way to and from their sad mission. Next there came the men who had to make repeated journeys to London to have their artificial limbs fitted, and it is easy to realize the comfort that it was to incapacitated men to be sure of comfortable, convenient, and inexpensive lodgings. Those who had experienced difficulty in getting their pension-claims through found both accommodation and assistance until their claims were allowed.

As time went on the Hostel was useful to smaller numbers, and by the end of 1922 it was used chiefly by students who had been in London for their final examinations. Though some stayed for weeks at a time, there were frequent vacancies, so it was decided that, should there be no Canadian applicants, overseas men generally should be given accommodation if they so desired.

A feature connected with the Hostel which pleased the Duke very much was the number of letters that he received from the men who had stayed there, not only expressing appreciation of the hospitality received, but also saying that the genuine feeling of brotherhood engendered at the Hostel lasted long after their departure and had a powerful influence on the younger men in directing their lives. Parents often wrote much to the same effect to tell the management how much the Hostel had done to provide the right kind of atmosphere for their sons during the time they spent in London. The whole work was most successful during the eight and a half years when the Hostel was open. It may be noted that 63,252 beds were occupied and a similar number of breakfasts served. There were no serious difficulties, a fact which reflects great credit upon all who strove so devotedly to ensure the success of the good work that was undertaken.

In 1925 the ground rent was raised from £200 to £500, and to make up the amount required the Imperial Order of Daughters of the Empire generously subscribed over £452.

By 1928 the work for which the Hostel had been opened had been completed, and the Committee recommended the Duke and Lady Patricia to give permission for the Hostel, just as it stood, together with the investments for its upkeep, to be transferred to the University of London for the benefit of students, giving preference to Canadians. To this proposal agreement was given. Throughout the whole period the Duke and Lady Patricia had been frequent visitors. They took a keen interest in everything connected with the place, and they always made a point of going into the lounge, where they talked to the men, asking them about their War service and about their homes overseas. Many of them had seen the Duke during his Governor-Generalship, and some had been in battalions which he had inspected. He never failed to remember these occasions, while Lady Patricia was naturally specially interested when she met a man from her own regiment. When she visited the Hostel she always looked out for the familiar badge. Princess Louise, Duchess of Argyll, who had been so closely connected with Canada during her husband's tenure of the Governor-Generalship, also took a great interest in the Hostel. She contributed books and pictures at the time of the opening and became a frequent visitor.

We have hitherto referred only incidentally to Prince Arthur of Connaught's services in the Great War. Like his father in the Egyptian War of 1882, he "took his chance like anyone else." He went out with the original "Old Contemptibles" on the Headquarters Staff as A.D.C. to Sir John French, and served in similar Staff appointments until September 1916, when he went to his regiment and served with it until March 1917. He was then transferred to the General Staff of the Canadian Army Corps, retaining that appointment until January 1919, when hostilities had ceased, with a brief interval between May and August 1918, when he proceeded upon his mission to Japan. He was twice mentioned in dispatches, became a Brevet-Lieutenant-Colonel in June 1919, an Honorary Major-General in October 1920, and retired from the Army in March 1922, joining the Reserve of Officers with the rank of Colonel, the Companionship of the Bath, and many War decorations earned in the field. In 1920 he was selected to fill the high post of Governor-General of the Union of South Africa, an appointment which was welcomed by all who knew of the excellent impression made by his father ten years before in the momentous days of the establishment of the Union. Such memories ensured for the Prince a hearty welcome by South Africans of both races. As may be imagined, the Duke derived much satisfaction from Prince Arthur's appointment, and was able to give him valuable advice and shrewd estimates of South African character which proved of great service.

Though the strain of bereavement and somewhat impaired health compelled the Duke to live much in retirement at this period, he was as ready as he always had been to undertake services in the interest of his country, even when they entailed journeys and labour from which age alone might well have excused him, and only a short time was to pass before, at his own express wish, another great Empire mission fell to his lot. The Montagu-Chelmsford reforms in Indian administration and government were beginning to take shape at the time, and the special occasion was the inauguration of the important Provincial Legislative Councils for Madras, Bengal, and Bombay. The Duke went to India for the purpose as the direct representative of the King-Emperor.

Matters were not working very smoothly at the time. Agitators were trying to stir up trouble among the ignorant classes, and the Duke, whose lifelong ambition had always been to do good service for his country, felt that the knowledge of the Indian mind which he had gained during his long residence in the country might be useful at the moment. For that reason he was willing to forgo his peaceful life, to put aside his own comfort, and to undertake the mission. Knowledge of the status of Royal Princes in the eyes of the peoples of India provided another incentive to the Duke, who must have felt also that the fact that he was known to so many in India would strengthen his hands. His well-known modesty and simplicity of outlook did not, perhaps, allow him to attach full importance to that personal factor, but he did realize that his knowledge of the people, with their strongly defined castes, their different religions, and their various races, might once more be useful to his country. He accordingly prepared to embark, in his seventy-first year, upon yet another voyage to India.

The old house at Bagshot to which the Duke took his bride fifty years ago was still his home, as it is to the present day, and he stayed there for some time before setting forth upon his Indian tour. All the family had been much attached to their country house, and the Duchess had often expressed her affection for the home of her early married life, where Princess Margaret had been born and all three children had been brought up. She had shared with the Duke a great interest in the neighbourhood and in the welfare of its inhabitants, and soon after she had passed away he had decided that the village of Bagshot should contain a memorial of a description that the Duchess, with her constant desire to help others, would herself have approved.

Just before he left for India His Royal Highness told the people of Bagshot that he wished to present the place with a nursing home in memory of the Duchess, who had spent so much of her life among them. He told them that he had already bought a house, which was being fitted up with everything that would make it useful for its purpose. He added that it would in all probability be ready for use in the spring. This is only mentioned as affording another instance of the Duke's unfailing thought for all about him even when suffering himself. By his example he has bequeathed the same quality to his children, and thus caused them to earn the high esteem with which they are regarded in all parts of the Empire which they have visited.

CHAPTER XXVII

A LAST GREAT MISSION TO INDIA
(1921; AGED SEVENTY-ONE)
THE DUKE AS FREEMASON
(1874-1921)

The Duke leaves for India — Agitators in India — Incident on Landing — The Duke's Speeches — "Rip Van Winkle" — Objects of his Mission — Its Great Success — "A memorable climax to a long career of splendid and devoted service."

The Duke as Freemason — His High Offices — The Royal Family and the Craft — The Duke's Initiation — Senior Grand Warden — Grand Master of England — Freemasons in the Great War and After — "Freemasonry is something real and vital."

The Duke's *régime* as Commander-in-Chief in Bombay had not been forgotten by the Indian people, and when it was known that he was to visit the country once again a great welcome was prepared for him. There was the usual agitation engendered by those whom hostile propagandists persuade that violence can accelerate, instead of delaying, reforms in the slow-moving East; meetings were held protesting against British rule and British everything, and determined attempts were made to induce the people to boycott the Royal visitor. Although the authorities thought fit to take certain special precautions, this propaganda met with very little success. Thirty years had passed since the Duke had held the command, but the effects of his residence still remained. Many remembered him personally, and were only too anxious to welcome back a man who had fulfilled his administrative duties so ably and with so sympathetic and broadminded an outlook.

The Duke left England on December 18, 1920, on board H.M.S. *Malaya*, accompanied by Lord Cromer. During the voyage he mixed freely with the crew, exchanging reminiscences with the officers and endearing himself to all with whom he came in contact by the hearty interest that he took in all forms of ship's sports. He landed at Madras on January i10. It had been arranged that the cruiser *Caroline* should go out to meet the *Malaya*, in order to bring the Duke to land, but there was such a swell at the time that the plan had to be abandoned and he was transhipped in a tug. The swell was so heavy that the Duke and his suite had to make a dash for safety and run along the gangway plank from the *Malaya* to the tug, an occurrence that highly amused the Duke, who was quite devoid of the form of pomposity which would have found in such a happening an outrage to dignity. He landed in the uniform of a Captain in the Royal Naval Reserve, and the welcome that he received surprised even those who were prepared for a certain amount of enthusiasm. Vast crowds had assembled, cheering and waving flags, and his journey partook of the nature of a triumphal progress.

The Duke's speeches, of which he made many, were models of lucidity and helpfulness. They had a pronounced effect all throughout India, where they were widely reported and most favourably commented upon in all circles. He had kept touch with Indian affairs, and fully realized the vast changes that had taken place in the Indian Empire since he had been in residence there. He did not make the mistake of appearing to recognize no differences, and the feature of his speeches that attracted most attention was his full recognition of the difference in outlook, of the many political changes that had taken place in the last decade, and of the problems which those changes had brought inevitably in their train. Ever since he had relinquished his Indian command in 1890 the Duke had been a keen student of the problems of the country, and in many instances he had made a shrewd forecast of events. He was thus well fitted to understand and to appreciate the many changes that had taken place. His knowledge of the native mind led him not to despair, but to hope, a hope based not upon a foolish and groundless optimism, but upon knowledge and experience. In one of his most widely quoted speeches the Duke said:

> Do not imagine that I come back to you like Rip Van Winkle, expecting to find things as I left them and surprised and shocked that they are not. A new spirit is abroad in India, a strong spirit of progress. Through the clouds the bright dawn of morning is shining on the land, and if patriotism guides the leaders, nothing can debar India from her great destiny.

Do not peer into the troubled waters in the wake of your ship. Lengthen the focus of your glasses and look ahead.

The Duke held many conferences during his visit with those in authority. His knowledge of the problems and of the difficulties of administration, and his sincere sympathy with both rulers and ruled, made the happiest impression upon all with whom he thus came in contact.

The reforms in Indian administration and government had been embodied in an Act of Parliament in 1919, and the Duke's object was to open the Provincial Legislative Councils in January 1921. The All-India Legislative Assembly and the newly constituted Chamber of Princes, to which we have previously referred, were opened in February. The King-Emperor could have had no finer ambassador to the Indian peoples at so critical a stage in their development. The Duke conveyed the special greetings of the Sovereign to the Princes of the Indian States and to all his subjects in India on their reaching a new epoch inaugurated by the Act of 1919, which was designed to gratify a growing desire among those subjects to make a definite step on the road to self-government.

His Royal Highness made a State entrance into Calcutta, and in spite of strenuous efforts that were made by extremists to disturb the peace, this was highly successful. He received a most enthusiastic welcome. Crowds lined the route, and the cheering was continuous. Altogether, the visit was a conspicuous success, and it did a great deal of good. *The Times* expressed the general opinion when commenting upon the Duke's visit:

> The Duke of Connaught in his present mission to India is more than the representative of the Crown. He also represents in a very real manner the British people, and he was expressing the sincere truth when he said at Madras that on her onward march India could count upon the warm support and sympathy and goodwill of Great Britain.

And, as was most fittingly said on another occasion, "This great mission was a memorable climax to a long career of splendid and devoted service to King and country."

. . . .

At this stage in the account of the Duke's life a favourable opportunity is offered to recall his high positions and lifelong activities in connexion with Freemasonry. To these we have already referred, but only incidentally, thinking that it would be better to reserve the complete story, keeping it apart from the recital of his career as a soldier and administrator.

The full titles of the Duke of Connaught in Freemasonry are Most Worshipful Grand Master of England, Most Excellent First Grand Principal of England in Royal Arch Masonry, Past Grand Superintendent of Bombay in Royal Arch Masonry, Grand Master of England in Mark Masonry, Past Provincial Grand Master of Sussex in Mark Masonry, Grand Master and Knight Grand Cross of the United Religious and Military Orders of the Temple and Knights of Malta in England and Wales, and Grand Master and Sovereign Grand Inspector General of the Supreme Council of the 33rd Degree of the Ancient and Accepted Rites for England and Wales and Dependencies of the British Crown.

Active support of, and participation in, Freemasonry has for a long time been a tradition in the Royal Family. From the time when the great Union of the Freemasons of England took place at Freemasons' Hall in 1813 the Duke of Sussex, the Duke of Connaught's great-uncle, was Grand Master of England until his death in 1843. As Prince of Wales King Edward VII became Grand Master of England in 1875, stepping into the breach when Lord de Grey became a Roman Catholic and resigned the Grand Mastership, and he held the post until 1901, when the Duke of Connaught succeeded him. The Prince of Wales and the Duke of York are both Freemasons, and Prince Arthur of Connaught was initiated in the Royal Alpha Lodge, No. 16, London, in 1911, the ceremony being rendered in the presence of the Duke by Lord Ampthill, Provincial Grand Master.

Besides the Masonic activities of the Duke of Connaught that are indicated by the titles recited above, he is Patron of three great Royal Masonic Institutions and Permanent Master of the Royal Alpha Lodge, the Navy Lodge, the Old Wellingtonian Lodge, the London Irish Rifles Lodge, the Aldershot Army and Navy Lodge, the Royal Colonial Institute (now Royal Empire Society) Lodge, and many others.

The Duke was initiated into Freemasonry on March 24, 1874, shortly before his twenty-fourth birthday, in the Prince of Wales's Lodge, No. 259. He became Senior Grand Warden in 1877. In 1886 he was appointed Provincial Grand Master of Sussex, and District

Grand Master of Bombay in 1887. In 1901 King Edward VII became Protector of the Order on his accession to the throne. The Duke of Connaught was then elected Grand Master of England in his place, and he was installed in that office in the Albert Hall on July 17, 1901. Here we can take note of the high place that is taken in the world by the United Grand Lodge of England. It is said to be recognized as the premier Grand Lodge of the world and to receive the respect due to its august sovereign jurisdiction. In the same year the Duke became First Grand Principal in Royal Arch Masonry.

At the outbreak of the Great War there were 3181 Lodges on the Roll of Grand Lodge, and of these 1360 suffered losses in the War, the total number of deaths being 3089 subscribing members, as well as many Others not on the roll of a particular Lodge. A special Grand Lodge was held on June 23, 1917, to celebrate the bicentenary of the "First Assembling of the Grand Lodge of England, which took place on the Festival of Saint John-in-Summer, 1717." At this meeting the officers of the Lodge of Antiquity, No. 2, Royal Somerset House and Inverness, No. 4, Fortitude and Old Cumberland, No. 12 — the three surviving Lodges of the four which founded the Grand Lodge of England in 1717 — were invested with their present distinctive collars, which have a stripe of Garter blue one-third of its width in the centre of the light blue collar.

In 1919 another special Grand Lodge was held to celebrate peace, and attended by a vast number of the Brethren. The Most Worshipful Grand Master (the Duke of Connaught) then made, in connexion with the close of the Great War, his first appeal to the Craft. He asked for funds to provide a Masonic Peace Memorial worthy of the Craft, and the Masonic Million Memorial Fund was thus inaugurated. A strong committee was formed by Grand Lodge (with the Duke at its head) to promote this scheme.

Lodges subscribing not less than ten guineas per member were to become "Hall Stone Lodges" and receive a special medal, which their Masters for the time being are entitled to wear. By 1926 the Lodges that had qualified in this way numbered nearly a thousand. A special medal is also given to individual Brethren who subscribe not less than ten guineas to the fund. On December 7, 1921, Hall Stone Medals were first presented in Grand Lodge to the London representatives. On August 8, 1925, a special festival in aid of this fund was held at Olympia, under the Presidency of the Grand Master. It was attended also by the Duke of York and by Prince Arthur of Connaught, together with some 7000 Brethren who had become Stewards for the occasion. At this wonderful gathering the Grand Master announced promised contributions to the fund amounting to over £826,014. The Memorial will take the form of a new headquarters of the Craft in London, on the site of and adjoining the present buildings in Great Queen Street. The plans show a very magnificent building of great dignity.

Turning now to the War, and to other work performed by members of the Craft under the Duke of Connaught's supreme guidance, in August 1916 the Freemasons' War Hospital was opened at Fulham Road, Chelsea, and in May 1918 the Freemasons' War Hospital No. 2 was opened at the Bishop of London's palace at Fulham. After the War was over the War Hospital at 237 Fulham Road was retained, and on June 29, 1920, the Freemasons' Hospital and Nursing Home was formally opened by the Duke of Connaught. It accommodates at present about forty-two in-patients, who must be Freemasons or their relations or dependants, and who pay fees calculated in proportion to their means. There is a waiting list, and the extension of the scheme has become a growing necessity. There are now 1551 Founding Lodges, and the Endowment Fund has reached over £150,000. The hospital has a great reputation for efficiency. There is a Samaritan Fund to defray the small fees required in cases of real necessity.

The Freemasons have a Board of Benevolence, which meets monthly to deal with applications and to dispense the Charitable Fund. In a typical year (1923) this amounted to about £48,000, and out of it the Board made 302 grants and a number of smaller donations, amounting to £17,700 and £10,295. The capital Fund of Benevolence stands at about a quarter of a million.

The Craft educates the children of poor Brethren, relieves the necessities of Freemasons and their widows, provides pensions, and gives annuities in deserving cases. In connexion with the Duke's interest therein we can conclude with a quotation:

Why have Kings and Princes, the Nobility, Judges and Statesmen, Soldiers and Sailors, Clergy and Doctors, and men in every walk of life sought to enter the portals of Freemasonry? It cannot be for mere social pleasure. . . . Neither can it be to give vent to charitable feelings. . . . Some other reason must be sought which gives it that irresistible attraction to the best of the nation. Is not that reason to be found in the principles and tenets which are inculcated in the teachings of the Craft ? Right down the era of Grand Lodge, Brotherly Love, Relief and

Truth have been the watchwords of Freemasonry ; and its moral precepts are well calculated to assist in that character-building which is the striving of all honest and upright men.

Freemasonry ... is something real and vital, something to be lived and practised, so as to become part of one's very being. By its faithful practice the world may be shown, in no uncertain manner, that Freemasonry is always on the side of what is good and beautiful. . . . Great indeed might be its possibilities for good.[1]

The Duke of Connaught has practised it faithfully for fifty-five years.

1 *From The Birth and Growth of the Grand Lodge of England,* by G. W. Daynes (The Masonic Record, Ltd., 1920).

CHAPTER XXVIII

REST AFTER LONG LABOUR
(1921-29; AGED SEVENTY-ONE TO SEVENTY-NINE)

Frequent Public Appearances — Boy Scouts and Girl Guides — The Disbandment of the Irish Battalions — The Wembley Exhibition and the Royal Memory for Faces — Stories of the Grandchildren — The Officers' Training Corps — Confidence in the Future — The Duke on "Physical Degeneracy of the Race" — A Snub for a Pessimist — The Duke on Womankind — "A Battalion of Amazons" — The Duke's Reading — Dislike of Malicious Tittle-tattle — His Political Outlook — No Place like England — Inspection of the Grenadier Guards — Memories of the Horse Guards Parade — *Au Revoir.*

The Duke spent the summer of 1921 in England after his return from India. In October he was given the Freedom of Portsmouth. The visit to India was the Duke's last great public mission, and afterward he returned to the seclusion into which he had retired after the crushing blows dealt him by the deaths of the Duchess and Princess Margaret. Nevertheless, he made frequent public appearances and spoke at meetings in support of any cause which he considered desirable, such as those connected with the Boy Scout movement, in which he always took much interest. He also approved highly of the Girl Guides. He sympathized with Princess Mary's connexion with them, and he often questioned her about the activities of her own particular troop.

The disbandment of the regiments recruited in Southern Ireland followed in 1922, and at the moving ceremony at Windsor when the King received back the Colours crowded with battle honours the Duke was present — for the last time — as Colonel of his regiment, the Royal Dublin Fusiliers.

In 1924 the Duke opened the Great Imperial Scout Jamboree at Wembley, and, it may be said here, in the summer of 1929 he declared open the coming-of-age Jamboree. The Duke was a frequent visitor to the British Empire Exhibition, and during his visits he made a thorough tour of the displays, of which those that interested him most were the Indian and Canadian exhibits. He spent a considerable time over them, and at the Canadian section he had an amusing experience. He was talking to one of the assistants, who, unaware of the Duke's identity, was expatiating to him on the beauties of Canada. "I was on a lumber camp there," he said, encouraged by the Duke's sympathetic interest. "Fine it was, but it's never any use describing it to anyone. You have to see it yourself."

"I did see it," said the Duke, "and I saw you too, when I was making a tour there in 1913." Then he astonished the man by recalling in detail the incidents of his visit to the lumber camp during one of the many tours that he made through the Dominion.

The Duke made many purchases at Wembley, including a pair of moccasins for his smallest grandson. The young man received them with a disappointing lack of enthusiasm, and when he was asked the reason he announced that he preferred "my legs wound up," which was his method of describing puttees.

The Duke continues his interest and activities in connexion with Freemasonry, and photographs of him in his dress as Grand Master have always been of great interest to his small grandsons. One of them announced once his intention of joining "Grandpa's regiment where he wears the gold apron!" The Duke's children and grandchildren are constantly with him, and the Crown Prince of Sweden came over on a visit in 1924.

As may be expected, His Royal Highness is keenly interested in the Officers' Training Corps, which he regards as representing a very fine movement. He is always willing to inspect detachments at the different schools, where he talks to the members and often entertains them with reminiscences of his life in the Service. He promises those who mean to join the Army a far better time than they would have had in the days of his own youth. Once, when he was inspecting the O.T.C. at Harrow, he said, "I do not know where we should have got the necessary officers in the War had it not been for the O.T.C."

The Duke has an inexhaustible fund of most interesting reminiscences of life in the Army and the great improvement that he has witnessed in his lifetime. The increase in the comfort of the men's uniforms which he advocated long ago has been a source of much gratification to him. He was a strong advocate of Service dress which, since the War, has been copied so widely abroad, and as the word 'khaki' has come into current use as representing a colour which was a product of the Anglo-Boer War, it is interesting to recall that the word in Hindustani comes originally from the Persian *khak*, meaning dust. The Duke was one of the first to consider it in every way a great improvement on the old red coats.

Another improvement upon which the Duke constantly discourses is the reform in the comfort and equipment of training camps. During the latter part of the War period he was familiar with most of them at and near Aldershot, at Shorncliffe, Shoreham, Frensham, Frimley, Epsom, Hornchurch, Colchester, Grantham, and York. He was delighted by the great change, always for the better, that had taken place in the arrangements for the comfort and welfare of the troops, and at changes that are still in progress which tend to attract to the Army a really fine type of young manhood. This type, as the Duke has always maintained, is the one that the Army really requires.

Despite having spent a lifetime devoted to the service of Mars, the Duke, like most soldiers who have personal experience of warfare, is a sincere advocate of peace, provided that it can be peace with honour. He always takes a keen interest in the activities of the League of Nations, and he derives great hope from this and from similar movements. He also follows with interest the development of aviation, but he naturally dislikes the idea of aerial warfare, though fully alive to its possibilities. If wars there must be he would prefer the chivalry and the glamour of the past, the settlement of the issue by men rather than by the soulless machine, which to him is abhorrent.

Of the future both of his country and his countrymen the Duke is confident. He has seen too much of the march of events during his seventy-nine years to be anything but hopeful, just as he has seen too much of the average Englishman under every possible condition, both of war and of peace, to have any doubt that he is as sound at heart as he ever was, and still just as much to be depended upon to keep his head and to play the game in times of crisis. For assertions about the physical degeneracy of the race he has nothing but amused contempt. To one old croaker who persisted in such assertions he said, "Take six young men selected haphazard, and also six suits of ancient armour, the kind worn when 'Men were men,' as you tell me that they were. If you can get the former into the latter, come back and talk to me again, and I will give your words some credence."

Another matter in which the Duke adopts the modern outlook is in his appreciation of enlarging the sphere of womankind. He has always been ready to applaud women's achievements in art, science, the professions, and sport. Sometimes he has gone farther than that, and he has remarked with a touch of humour that if he had been born a hundred years later he might have had the good fortune to command a battalion of Amazons.

His Royal Highness reads a great deal in these days of retirement after long years of labour, principally books of biography and travels. He has never been a great novel-reader, but he enjoys reminiscences, provided that they are free from the malicious tittle-tattle that spices so liberally some volumes of that sort. He has received many offers to publish his autobiography, but so far he has steadfastly refused to do so, though such a record would be of unique interest. His birth, his upbringing, and his career naturally incline him to Conservatism in politics, but neither in that nor in anything else is he a bigot. He understands and sympathizes with the ideals of democracy as much as his great-nephew the Prince of Wales does. (The Duke, by the way, has watched the Prince's career with the greatest interest. They have always been on excellent terms.) Long contact with the men in the ranks, whose welfare has always been his foremost consideration, has convinced him of the solid worth of "the man in the street" and of his just claims to fair play.

Though forced to spend much of his time nowadays at his villa at Cap Ferrat on account of his health, the Duke still, like the true Britisher that he is, thinks that there is no place in the world like England. He still says, as he did in those far-away days when he refused a throne, "England is good enough for me."

We can conclude with a brief reference to his reappearance before an English crowd which has grown to look upon him with reverence and respect as the embodiment of the finest ideals of an upright Englishman.

The 16th of May, 1929, marked a great occasion in the life of His Royal Highness. On that day he emerged from retirement, and, as the senior Colonel of the Brigade of Guards and senior Field-Marshal in the Army, rode slowly on to the Horse Guards Parade to inspect the Regiment of Grenadier Guards, of which he has been the Colonel for a quarter of a century. Wearing, as is usual on such occasions, the undress uniform of the regiment of which he is the chief, and riding on a fine charger, he received an ovation from the crowds and from the windows of the Admiralty, the Horse Guards, the Foreign and Colonial Offices, the other Government buildings, and the garden of No. 10 Downing Street, the historic residence of Prime Ministers, from which a view of those well-known acres of flat gravel can be obtained. Of the ceremony itself it is only necessary to write that the troops inspected were Grenadier Guardsmen. Before and after the ceremonial the eyes of those present looked beyond the parade to the still figures of the Guardsmen in effigy on the Memorial to those of the Brigade who fell in the Great War. Beyond them stretched the waters of St James's Park lake to the white marble monument to the Great Queen and to Buckingham Palace beyond, reminding the Victorians present of the old days when the Duke of Connaught, in all the panoply of his rank and Royal state, had taken a leading part in similar ceremonial observances on the same parade. There must have been thoughts, too, of the Victorian Jubilees, when, instead of the great new Admiralty buildings, the trees of the old Admiralty garden formed a background to the scene; of the two parades in June 1902, when the Duke, in command of the troops, received Queen Alexandra and our present King, acting as deputy for King Edward, who lay on a bed of sickness in the Palace and sent a kind message to his soldiers and to the people, "having heard the cheering with satisfaction in his sick-room"; of those fateful days in 1914 when the "first hundred thousand" flocked to great marquees on the Horse Guards Parade to join the colours; and of the long years of war when the temporary buildings of mushroom Ministries covered the grass of the Park, and the lake was drained dry for fear that the gleam of water should form a guide for Zeppelins dropping destruction from the sky. Many spectators recalled the events of three reigns and the Sovereigns to whom the Duke of Connaught in his homage swore in the old Abbey the oath of allegiance, "I do become your liege man of life and limb and of earthly worship and faith and truth. I will bear unto you, to live and die, against all manner of folks. So help me God," and knew the devotion with which that promise had been fulfilled by the soldierly figure riding slowly, in his eightieth year, down those rigid ranks of Grenadiers.

We may leave the Royal soldier Duke as we watch him deputizing on the Horse Guards Parade for his nephew. His Majesty King George, by the mercy of Providence convalescent after grave illness, on the occasion of the trooping of the Colour by the Brigade of Guards.

And we conclude with the hope that there will be "many happy returns" of next May Day, when the people of many climates and diverse nationalities whom His Royal Highness has served for so long will celebrate, with acclamation, the eightieth anniversary of his birth.

L'ENVOI

We have now come, most reluctantly, to the end of our self-imposed task. We have tried, it may be inadequately, to draw a picture of the veteran Field-Marshal, eldest member but one of the Royal House of Windsor. Royal by birth, he has regarded Royalty as an impetus to perpetual public service, never as an excuse for self-indulgence or luxurious living. By his descent he was set upon a pinnacle, observed of all, unable to shelter either his public or even his intimate private life from public observation. From babyhood to childhood, from childhood to adolescence and manhood, from maturity to old age, his life has stood that severe test of public scrutiny, and in our description of his character we have been compelled to draw a portrait lacking in artistic merit for need of shadow. We are consoled by the belief that we have limned a true picture, and by the knowledge that we have indicated, even by a mere catalogue of activities and achievements, a feature of life in England little understood abroad, the service freely rendered to the community by 'men of leisure' whose time and energies are not wholly absorbed in the struggle for a livelihood. Among such we include the councils and committees of charitable and other organizations, members of municipal bodies and of County and Rural District Councils, Justices of the Peace, and innumerable other similar examples of unpaid public service, and, too, the members of the Territorial Army and of the various Naval Reserves who spend their leisure time in training themselves to defend the fabric of Empire and all for which it stands.

In all this freely rendered service the members of the Royal Family are outstanding figures, taking as their text the Prince of Wales's heraldic motto:

Ich Dien
I Serve

Other reprints available in this series

Life of Alexander II, F.E. Grahame
Alexander III, Tsar of Russia, Charles Lowe
The Intimate Life of the Last Tsarina, Princess Catherine Radziwill
My mission to Russia and other diplomatic memories, Sir George
   Buchanan
The reign of Rasputin: An empire's collapse, M.V. Rodzianko
*Collected Works: Once a Grand Duke, Always a Grand Duke,
   Twilight of Royalty*, Alexander, Grand Duke of Russia
Memories of Russia 1916-1919, Princess Paley

Frederick, Crown Prince and Emperor, Rennell Rodd
Letters of the Empress Frederick, edited by Sir Frederick Ponsonby
*Between two Emperors: The Willy-Nicky Telegrams and Letters,
   1894-1914*
Potsdam Princes, Ethel Howard

Emperor Francis Joseph of Austria, Joseph Redlich
The Story of my Life (Vols. I-III in one volume), Marie, Queen of
   Roumania
*A Royal Tragedy: Being the Story of the Assassination of King
   Alexander and Queen Draga of Servia*, Chedomille Mijatovich
My Past, Marie Larisch

The Witchery of Jane Shore, C.J.S. Thompson
Richard III, Sir Clements Markham

*The Complete Works: The Journal of a Disappointed Man,
   A Last Diary, Enjoying Life and other Literary Remains*, W.N.P.
   Barbellion

For further details please see *amazon.co.uk/amazon.com*

More titles are in preparation

Printed in Great Britain
by Amazon